Auguste Rodin
Drawings and Watercolors

Auguste Rodin
Drawings and Watercolors

Ernst-Gerhard Güse

RIZZOLI
NEW YORK

Translated from the German
Auguste Rodin: Zeichnungen und Aquarelle
by John Gabriel
and Michael Taylor (text by Claudie Judrin)

First published in the United States of America in 1985 by
RIZZOLI INTERNATIONAL PUBLICATIONS, INC.
597 Fifth Avenue, New York, NY 10017

Copyright © 1984 Landschaftsverband Westfalen-Lippe
Westfälisches Landesmuseum für Kunst und Kulturgeschichte Münster
and the authors

Library of Congress Cataloging in Publication Data

Rodin, Auguste, 1840–1917.
  Auguste Rodin, drawings and watercolors.

  Translation of: Auguste Rodin, Zeichnungen und Aquarelle.
  Bibliography: p.
  Includes index.
  1. Rodin, Auguste, 1840–1917—Catalogs. I. Güse, Ernst-Gerhard. II. Title.
N6853.R63A4 1985   741.944   85-42873
ISBN 0-8478-0625-1

Printed and bound in the German Federal Republic

CONTENTS

In memory of Hertha and Norbert Kricke

THE IDEA BEHIND MY WORKS

Auguste Rodin

What is the idea behind my works and what appeals to people about them? It is the pivot on which all art turns—equilibrium, a counterbalancing of masses which gives rise to movement. That is the crux of art, whether those who conceive art as something different from "crass reality" like it or not. Art is like love. For many people it is a dream, an event of the soul, a palace, a sweet odor, a jewel. But none of these are the real thing. What is essential in love is union. Everything else is detail—delightful, thrilling maybe, but detail. The same is true of art. If someone comes and praises my symbolism, my power of expression, still I know that the only important thing are the surfaces. Respect the surfaces, depict them correctly from every side, and movement will come; shift the masses, and create a new equilibrium. The human body can be compared to a striding temple; and like a temple, it has a center of gravity around which the volumes of the body are distributed and ordered. Once you have realized this, you know everything. It is simple, but you have to see it. Academic artists don't want to see it. Instead of realizing that this is the key to my method, people call me a poet... They say my sculpture is the sculpture of an enthusiast. I do not deny that it contains much of a violent nature, but this overwrought quality does not come out of me, it is part of nature itself and its motion. The works of God are by their very nature exaggerated; I am only true to them. Nor is my temperament overexcited; it is tranquil. Nor am I a dreamer, but a mathematician, and if my work is good, then it is because it's geometric...

When you follow nature, you find everything... It is not a matter of creating "The New"; the words "creating" and "inventing" are superfluous words. Revelation comes only to those who perceive with their eyes and minds. Everything is contained in what surrounds us. Everything is given in nature, which is imbued with eternal, uninterrupted movement. A woman's body, a mountain, a horse are one and the same thing in terms of conception, and they all are built according to the same principles.

The Early Years

Auguste Rodin, about 1862

RODIN'S DRAWINGS · 1854–1880

J. Kirk T. Varnedoe

Rodin's habits as a draftsman are both the delight and the despair of scholars. A delight, because he was not only a prolific draftsman but also a scrupulous curator of his own work, amassing an archive of several thousand drawings that is now one of the great treasures of the Musée Rodin in Paris. But the same rich resource may provoke despair; for while Rodin drew abundantly and conserved stingily, he did so to serve his art rather than his biographers, and left his collection in appropriately complex disorder. There are almost no dated drawings, and the few dates he did inscribe most often refer only to the moment of signature (for purposes of dedicating the drawing to an admirer or offering it as a gift), rather than to the time of execution. Rarely are there any drawings that can be unambiguously identified as studies for specific sculptures. Moreover, he continually returned to his drawings and reworked them, even at intervals many years apart; so that any one drawing may bear the overlay of several different sessions of work, in different years, decades, or phases of his long life. Thus the relation of this vast graphic *oeuvre* to Rodin's career as a sculptor is problematic, and not easily defined.

Despite these problems, it has generally been agreed that Rodin's work as a draftsman was dominated by two distinct styles. First, there is the most prolific and familiar mode, consisting of rapidly executed, highly summary pencil drawings of the nude, often with watercolor wash. These are known to reflect the last phase of his life, beginning at some point in the later 1890s and continuing with little change until his activity as an artist ceased. Before these late drawings from the living model, however, came a very different series of works from imagination, smaller in scale and far removed in emotion: the so-called "black" drawings, usually in ink and gouache, and frequently showing dramatically charged scenes from mythology or literature. Many of the "black" drawings refer by content and/or by inscription to Dante's *Inferno*, and the series as a whole has traditionally been associated with Rodin's work on the monumental bronze portal with scenes from Dante, *The Gates of Hell*, begun in 1880.[1]

These are the two groups of drawings for which Rodin has always been best known, in his lifetime and to the present. Yet taken together they would reflect only about thirty years of his work, while another twenty-six years — the crucial student and apprentice period in which his temperament was formed — lies in deeper shadow, despite the existence within his archive of invaluable groups of drawings which might provide illumination. The present essay will focus just on these shadowy twenty-six years, and will consider three key issues. First, I will distinguish in Rodin's earliest drawings those aspects that seem most important for his future as an artist, and in so doing redefine the nature of his apprenticeship. Secondly, I will focus on the crucial trip Rodin took to Italy in 1875, and on the encounter there with Michelangelo, which has traditionally been held to have had a decisive effect on his emergence as a mature sculptor. Finally, I will assess what Rodin learned from his early drawings, and what they add to our knowledge of the man and his art.

Rodin enrolled in 1854 at the Special Imperial School for Drawing and Mathematics, known familiarly as the Petite Ecole, or Little School, to distinguish it from the prestigious Ecole des Beaux-Arts. The Petite Ecole was a free school whose existence was connected with the gov-

ernment's desire to foster education in the applied arts, and thereby to effect a better union of art and industry. Many artists, however, saw it as a back door to a higher career; from their training here, they might launch themselves upward through a competitive examination process into the Ecole des Beaux-Arts itself. Rodin had just this in mind, for he tried three times, between 1857 and 1859, to gain admission to the grander school. He failed on all three attempts, but not on his merits as a draftsman — whatever their disagreements with his style of modelling, the examiners approved his drawings. This is a testament not so much to innate gifts as to the quality of drawing instruction at the Petite Ecole.

An extraordinary teacher, Horace Lecoq de Boisbaudran, ran the program of drawing instruction. In addition to the standard exercises, such as drawing from casts, copying from prints, and drawing from the posed model, Lecoq engaged his students in two exceptional challenges. He encouraged development of an acute visual memory, gradually training his pupils to render more and more complete images solely from recollection, without the model present. The students were also taken on special field outings, in which the models were not posed but were allowed to lounge in nature, free from the artificial strictures and cold light of the studio.[2] By these devices Lecoq sought to liberate young artists: from slavish dependence on mimicry on the one hand, and from the shackles of outworn conventions on the other hand.

Now all this sounds very promising, and we can see why Rodin would later have paid homage to Lecoq as a teacher.[3] But in fact nothing in Rodin's early drawings suggests that he profited especially from these unorthodox opportunities. We find drawings from casts of sculpture (Fig. 1) and from works of art in the Louvre (Fig. 2) that are undistinguished, and a suite of studies from the model (including ills. pp. 38–40) that are fully competent but without notable flair of individuality. Rodin seems to have run the gamut of dutiful student tasks, from studies of equine anatomy (doubtless encouraged by his study with the great *animalier* sculptor Barye, in the early 1860s) to copies after older paintings, without injecting into these exercises much personal conviction. When we study the suavely pencilled finesse of a Neo-Greek motif of the early years (Fig. 3), we find prefigured only the skilled and pleasing decorator who would later produce such winning visions as the Metropolitan Museum's *L'Age d'Or* (Fig. 4). Such works demonstrate an accomplished eclecticism that seems entirely marginal to Rodin's potent originality. If we seek the roots of the violent turbulence of the "black" drawings, or of the artist who would produce *The Gates of Hell* and then go on to redefine sculpture in his time, we must look elsewhere among the early drawings.

What we find is that Rodin learned most when instructed least. We know from his recollections that, at the very beginning of his interest in art, he went to the Louvre to draw from sculpture. Many of the drawings he preserved can only reflect these initial attempts. Crude renderings such as Figs. 5, 7, 9, and 11, with their awkwardly woven-together contours and ill-joined anatomies, must certainly record the first moments of the artist's self-education; and several such drawings, all on the same cheap, lined *papier ecolier*, can successfully be identified as being based on sculptures in the Louvre (Figs. 6, 8, 10, 12). Noteworthy in these clumsy copies are the blunt transformations Rodin imposed on his sources. Drapery is stripped to nudity, and nudity flayed to diagrammatic musculature. Space and depth are filled up or compressed, and all grace yields to brutish power.[4]

One of these drawings (Fig. 9), of an entombment scene, is especially instructive. The initial levels of rendering show an uncertain line and rudimentary command of anatomy; but the transformation of the copied model is willfully personal. In scrawling schoolboy script, Rodin identified his source: at upper right, "*mise au tombeau*", and below center "*Germain Pilon / Salle renaissance*". Yet when we juxtapose the Pilon *Mise au tombeau* from the Louvre (Fig. 10) with Rodin's copy, the differences are striking. All the tremulously agitated drapery and fluid, attenuated curvilinearity have been eliminated. Rodin's version is more square, his poses more stiffly profiled, and his gestures more clutching and compressed; the feminine, swooning Pilon has become tensely masculine. Indeed, were it not for the specific inscription and the recognizable derivation of the two embracing figures in the background, one might find the drawing almost as close in configuration to a completely different entombment scene which Rodin also drew (Figs. 7, 8).

3 Auguste Rodin, copy after an antique scene

4 Auguste Rodin, *The Golden Age*

15

5 Auguste Rodin, *Autumn*, study after a sculpture in The Louvre

6 *Bacchus, a Faun and a Genie*, contour copy of an antique sculpture in The Louvre

7 Auguste Rodin, copy after a relief in The Louvre

8 *Entombment*, Louvre, Paris

9 Auguste Rodin, *Entombment*

10 Germain Pilon, *Entombment*, Louvre, Paris

11 Auguste Rodin, group of figures around a reclining man

12 *Lamentation Ceremony*, Louvre, Paris

These acts of transformation and reduction on the part of the juvenile draftsman are at least as striking in a parallel instance, a drawing after a *Conclamation* relief in the Louvre (then thought to be antique but now regarded as a Renaissance pastiche; Figs. 11, 12). Again, Rodin strips away all drapery, transforms several poses, and brutally compresses the airy space of the original composition. What had been a still scene of mourning now becomes an unspecified narrative, in which the more agressively striding entrance of the figure to the left provokes the recoil in fright of the small child at lower right.

These copies establish for the beginning artist a distinctly personal style, separate from those seen in his diverse student exercises. It is this private manner, rather than any skill acquired in schooling, which was to prove enduring and central to Rodin's development. Most obviously, the flayed style of rendering heroically muscled male figures, dominant in the drawings associated with *The Gates of Hell*, has its origins here. Moreover, it is this group of early conceptions which eventually form the direct foundation for the more mature "black" drawings, and for Rodin's initial conception of the bas-reliefs of *The Gates*.[5]

When we look at the wash overlay on the right side of the copy after Pilon (Fig. 9), or at a group of "second-generation" reworkings of compositions originally copied in the Louvre (Figs. 13, 14), the process becomes clear. Despite their awkwardness, Rodin obviously cherished the pencil records of his earliest confrontations with the traditions of sculpture. Far from merely "correcting" their "deficiencies", he steadily sought to reinforce their willful idiosyncrasies. Adding simplifying washes of tenebrist drama to the original copies, or reconceiving them in new versions, he made these scenes still more compressed and monumentally severe, and he readjusted them to suit the demands of new iconographies, especially those of Dante. Thus the scene of Ugolino chewing on the head of the Pisan archbishop, taken from Dante's encounter with Ugolino's shade in the frozen lake in the *Inferno* (Fig. 17), came to be visualized in terms directly evolved from the much earlier copies after entombments (e.g., Fig. 7).

Such evidence suggests strongly that the ultimate origins of *The Gates of Hell* — at least in the form Rodin conceived for it in the first program of work, around 1880 — lie in the artist's earliest work. And that supposition in turn calls for a reassessment of the seemingly miraculous transformation that took place in Rodin's career in the late 1870s and early 1880s. It would seem on superficial examination that, after a lengthy and inconsequential period of frustration as an anonymous apprentice, Rodin suddenly began to find himself in the later 1870s; and that his true personality as an artist only then began to assert itself, in works like the *St. John the Baptist* of 1878, and especially in the vast outpouring of sculptures for *The Gates*. However, the corpus of early drawings — many of them now physically absorbed beneath the gouache-and-ink reworkings which produced the "black" images — shows that these years of anonymity were spent in defining, through drawing, a highly personal style of sculptural imagery. By the time opportunity came to him, Rodin had filled his albums and his imagination to the bursting point with a repertoire of scenes and figures partially copied, long contemplated, and relentlessly reshaped into a highly individual idiom. Much of the prodigious energy of the 1880s taps this pent-up store of invention.

The style of these early drawings is remarkably consistent from their first stumbling beginnings to confident maturity. While we can recognize, on two sides of the same sheet, an early and a late pole of proficiency in the rendering of the *écorché* form (compare Figs. 15 and 16), we have no reliable way to date intermediary steps in the development of this vision. The exhibition of Carpeaux's Michelangelesque sculpture of *Ugolino* in Paris in 1863 no doubt provoked Rodin's deeper engagement with the world of the *Inferno*, and we know that in the mid-1870s

13 Auguste Rodin,
Table de la foi

14 Auguste Rodin,
Table de la foi,
reproduced after a
woodcut by
Leveillé

he made his own sculpture of Ugolino (of which only a fragment now survives). Thus specifically Dantesque iconographies were almost certainly imposed on many of the drawings long before 1880. It seems logical that the transformation of the early linear pencil drawings into more fully realized gouache-and-ink visions of tenebrist relief was also well under way in the 1870s, if not before. The division between the "black" drawings and the earliest student copies is not a clear or firm one. These two types of work need to be studied together, as aspects of a more seamless continuum of personal development. Often this entails a kind of archaeology, identifying the various layers of work in a single image, that may speak of broadly separate stages in Rodin's rethinking of a given motif.

The twenty-six years between the entrance into the Petite Ecole and the commission for *The Gates of Hell* thus seem to have included a long, gradual process of self-definition, and imaginative transformation of sources in earlier sculpture, worked out in private drawings. The major stylistic character of these drawings is as consistent and idiosyncratic as their chronology is

15 Auguste Rodin,
*Three Figures with
Book*, c. 1882

16 Auguste Rodin,
*Three Nude Male
Figures with Tam-
bourine*, c. 1882

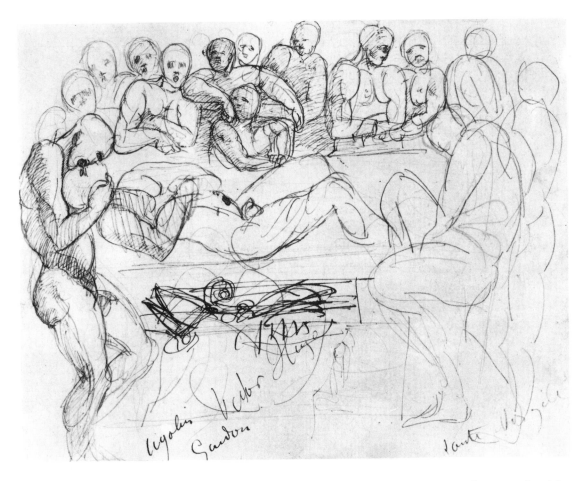

17 Auguste Rodin,
*Ugolino Devouring the
Head of Archbishop
Ruggieri*

obscure and problematic. The uncertainties surrounding these long years of apprenticeship are relieved, however, by one specific event whose date is known and whose import seems crucial: Rodin's journey to Italy in 1875. Having established the general pattern of the early development of Rodin's personal style in his drawings, and the origins of his ideas for sculpture in his early copies, we should now examine closely this specific encounter with Italian art. The small body of drawings that can be directly associated with the Italian journey provide evidence for Rodin's tastes and ways of working at a crucial juncture, when his years of preparation were drawing to a close, and the mature period of his most energetic production was about to begin.

Rodin's trip to Italy might rightly be seen as one of the seminal events in modern art. When he left Brussels in the winter of 1875 he was an obscure, albeit talented, thirty-five-year-old journeyman. When he returned, he went on to his first Salon success with the 1877 *Age of Bronze*, and then to domination of European sculpture in the 1880s and for the rest of his life. By his own testimony, Michelangelo was the agent of this change. Rodin later said that "in looking at the Medici tombs [in Florence, during the 1875 trip] I was more profoundly impressed than with anything I have ever seen";[6] and he specified further that "my liberation from academicism was via Michelangelo... He is the bridge by which I passed from one circle to another. He is the powerful Geryon that carried me."[7]

Our view of the Italian trip has traditionally centered on such recollections, and on one letter, mailed from Italy to Rose Beuret, his mistress. However Rodin's later memory was highly selective; and the letter to Rose, written when he was already half-way through the journey, dwells only on the experience of Florence. Hence we have had a misleadingly narrow picture

18 Auguste Rodin, *Reclining Figure before a Grave*

19 Vincenzo Rossi, *Tomb of Angelo Cesi*, Santa Maria della Pace, Rome

of an itinerary that went on to include Rome, Naples, Siena, Padua, and Venice. The best evidence for a full assessment of that itinerary exists in the form of scores of drawings, assembled in montage by Rodin, and now in the Musée Rodin (see for example ills. pp. 56, 57). Central among these are 38 small pages or page fragments whose common paper type, size, and binding perforations indicate that they once formed a palm-sized sketchbook.

The sketchbook pages provide our most inclusive vision of Rodin's experience of Italian art, and yet they raise as many questions as they answer. They do not, for example, record the focussed search for Michelangelo traditionally described as the motivation and substance of the journey. Instead they show that, in his whirlwind tour of Italian cities (the whole trip lasted only about three weeks), Rodin's taste in art was quite eclectic.

Two Renaissance motifs allow us to fix the portion of the trip covered by the sketchbook: one reclining figure is drawn from the tomb of Angelo Cesi, by Vincenzo di Rossi, in the church of Sta. Maria della Pace in Rome (Figs. 18, 19), and a related study (see ill. p. 56, D. 163) records the companion tomb of Cesi's mother, in the same chapel. If these fix the little book in Rome, another sketch, of Verrocchio's *Colleoni* equestrian monument (ill. p. 57, D. 188), show that the album was still in use when Rodin reached Venice.

Each of these locales yield other sources as well: a loose sketch after a Luna and Endymion scene (Fig. 20, ill. p. 57, D. 184) seems to have been based on a sarcophagus in Rome's Capitoline Museum (Fig. 21), and an unusual standing *Leda* (Fig. 22, ill. p. 57, D. 187) appears to have been copied from a marble statue in Venice's Museo San Marco (Fig. 23). In contrast to Rome and Venice, Rodin never mentioned stopping in Padua; but the sketchbook clearly documents such a visit, with multiple studies after Donatello's "Gattamelata" monument, drawn from various points in the plaza outside the church of San Antonio (ill. p. 56, D. 164, 165, 168, 173, 174). This proof of a visit to Padua in turn helps us to confirm the source of a slight sketch done inside the church, after the Donatello bronze relief of *The Miracle of the Ass* (Figs. 24, 25).

20 Auguste Rodin, sketchbook sheet

21 Roman sarcophagus, Capitoline Museum, Rome

The extreme simplicity of this latter notation raises questions that apply as well to numerous other records of Rodin's copying on this trip. How were these drawings done, and why did he save them? Several biographers reported that Rodin drew principally from memory during the Italian trip, and this might help to explain some discrepancies we find between copies and their source models. No doubt Rodin often drew from memory in order to force himself — as Lecoq de Boisbaudran's memory exercises had forced him before — to absorb more thoroughly the basic structure of the things he saw. In any event, a study like that of *The Miracle of the Ass* makes it clear that for Rodin in 1875 drawing after works of art did not mean merely copying, in the sense of being faithful to the model. Instead, just as in his earliest student copies, drawing was synonomous with interpretation, and "copying" was a process of analysis and alteration. Only those particular elements of the source model that Rodin found useful were to be preserved; and these were often noted in a private language of abstracted ciphers that are not representations in a normal sense — indeed are often not even legible to us — but which act as coded keys to a selective personal understanding of the work in question.

Consider, for example, the degree of abstraction inherent in two studies from the Vatican museum, on one of the sketchbook pages (Fig. 26). The quick pencil doodle at lower right, inverted, is based on a Roman double portrait bust (Fig. 27), and the main ink sketch is a memory of Raphael's fresco of the encounter between Attila and Leo the Great (Fig. 28). The relationship is confirmed by Rodin's scrawled inscription: "atilla, bas relief de raphaelle"; whereas the only note accompanying the sketch of the Roman busts is "Michelangesque". These notes are as revealing as the drawings are abstract. The words reminded Rodin that the Raphael was conceived in terms suitable for a relief sculpture (which helps explain his changing the fresco's arched format into a rectangle); and that the Roman work prefigured something of Michelangelo. The latter note recalls Rodin's comment that "During my journey to

Rome, Naples, Siena, and Venice, I continued drawing, in the hopes of discovering the principles on which the compositions of Michelangelo's figures were founded. I was at the same time struck with the idea that these prinicples were not original with him, but the result of discoveries made by those who preceded him."[8]

The Roman bust was seen, then, as an adjunct of his study of the central, powerful experience of Michelangelo. But just as Rodin's copies after Italian art in general show surprising omissions (there are for example no drawings after Ghiberti or Bernini), so his response to Michelangelo seems to have been curiously limited. Michelangelo's presence in the sketchbook is limited to only four images: one slight sketch of a *Leda* based on the figure of *Notte* from the Medici Tombs (ill. p. 57, D. 180), and three studies from the *Moses* ensemble in S. Pietro in Vincoli in Rome (ills. pp. 56 and 57, D. 160 and D. 192). Indeed, Rodin seems to have paid scant attention to many of the Michelangelo works available to him. There are two perfunctory sketches (not part of the sketchbook) based on the figures in the Bargello, the *David/ Apollo* and the *Victory*, and another scrap with poses loosely related to those of the Boboli figures in the Accademia (ill. p. 56, D. 161). But neither the great *David* nor the Duomo *Pieta* appear among the preserved drawings from Florence.

The works that were most impressive to Rodin were those in the Medici tombs, and yet these too are only sparsely recorded. In his letters, Rodin spoke only of drawings done *after* seeing these sculptures, not copies but "scaffoldings, systems that I fabricate in my imagination in order to understand him [Michelangelo]".[9] There are only three drawings, not on paper from the main sketchbook, that were indisputably done from these figures *in situ*. All depict the tomb of Lorenzo de Medici, from the "profile and three-quarters views" that Rodin described in a letter as being especially revealing to him (for example, Fig. 29). Surprisingly, there is no preserved drawing of either of the seated figures of the Dukes, even though Rodin's *Thinker* of 1880 would seem to be a direct descendant of the *Penseroso* figure of Lorenzo.

Indeed, if we consider all the major figure sculptures Rodin made in the years following the Italian trip, including those seemingly most directly derived from Michelangelo, we find that not one of them is prefigured in any of these Italian drawings. *The Age of Bronze* of 1876 bears a relationship to Michelangelo's *Dying Slave*; but the latter is in the Louvre, not in Italy, and there are no known Rodin drawings after it. The *Adam* of 1878–80 is a composite of gestures from the Sistine Ceiling, of which again there are no drawings, and the Duomo *Pieta*, also absent from the records. The *Thinker* is preceded neither by a sketch after *Lorenzo de'Medici* nor by any after the similarly contemplative Sistine prophet Jeremiah, despite the clear evidence that Rodin passed before both these figures with pencil and paper in hand.

These anomalies do not seem to be the result of missing drawings. Instead, it seems clear that there never was a simple, direct line of study and derivation from Michelangelo through Rodin's drawings. Instead, the connection demands to be understood in terms of a fundamentally different mode of response. When Rodin spoke of his reaction to the Medici-tomb sculp-

24 Auguste Rodin, *Scene under Three Arcades*

25 Donatello, *The Miracle of the Ass*, San Antonio, Padua

26 Auguste Rodin, sketchbook page

27 Roman double portrait bust, Vatican, Rome

28 Raphael, *Meeting of Attila and Leo the Great*, Vatican, Rome

tures, he recalled: "After looking at these figures long and well, I returned to my room at the hotel and began making sketches, to test the depth of my own capacity of composition and of the impressions I had received".[10] Rodin seems to have acted in the same way with regard to the entire experience of the Italian trip, waiting until he returned to Brussels to work it out in his own terms. A deeply felt experience called not for immediate mimicry, but for digestion, concentration, and analysis at a distance. All the *in situ* drawings after Michelangelo are therefore only preludes to the major assimilation.

The second and most decisive phase of this assimilation took place immediately after the return to Brussels, in the form of a series of drawings that Rodin described to his biographers, done from the live model posed to replicate the gestures of Michelangelo's figures. Two pages of drawings in the Musée Rodin archive seem to document this latter study (for example, Fig. 30), and they demonstrate an agressive exploration of several Michelangelo poses that — like the *David* — were ignored on the trip itself, and others — like the Louvre *Slaves* — that were not available there.

Furthermore, when Rodin returned to Paris in 1877, he continued this study, by drawing from the casts of Michelangelo's figures in the collection of the Ecole des Beaux-Arts. The large chalk studies in the Musée Rodin collection (ills. pp. 34–37, D. 5116–5119) have sometimes been attributed to the Italian trip. Their unusually large size argues against this and supports the alternative view that such drawings were done from the casts in Paris.[11] Moreover, another drawing in this series, Fig. 31, identical to the four Medici-tomb drawings in technique and format, would seem to guarantee that the series was not drawn in Florence. This latter, never mentioned in the literature on Rodin and Michelangelo, is a study after the restored version of a figure now in the Victoria and Albert Museum (Fig. 32 — shown here with the restorer's additions now removed). The figure is now thought to be a reworking by the sculptor Cilio of an antique *Narcissus*; but in the 1870s it was universally admired as "Michelangelo's Cupid". It was discovered in Florence in 1854, and sold to the Victoria and Albert as a Michelangelo in 1866. Rodin could only have drawn it, therefore, from a reproduction.

Like the other four chalk studies, this chalk rendering of the "Cupid" documents Rodin's continued study of Michelangelesque gesture in the later 1870s. Alas, however, all but one of the Medici-tomb studies in this series have been terribly disfigured by incompetent attempts at restoration. When we compare earlier photographs of the drawings (Fig. 33) with their present state, we can see that the current crude sense of light and dark, and the clumsy contours, bear little relationship to the original subtleties of Rodin's chalk studies. Of all the series, only the image of the Medici *Madonna*, in poor condition but mercifully spared the restorer's reworkings, can still tell us something of Rodin's feeling for these works of the Italian master.

30 Auguste Rodin,
sketches after
Michelangelo

Up to this point, the influence of Michelangelo on Rodin could still seem relatively unproblematic: admiration for the older master led, albeit at a remove in time and space, and through surrogates, to copying. But copying, we should remember from our previous analyses, did not have a simple role in Rodin's practice — it was always connected with a search for more personal assimilation of the source. Characteristically, Rodin found himself troubled by a disjunction he felt, a gap between his understanding of Michelangelo's formal devices, gained through the drawings, and his intuition of Michelangelo's deeper spiritual energy, which he could not satisfy himself that he had yet captured. His biographer Judith Cladel reported his recollection that "he searched the *why* of the grandeur of the sculptor of the tombs; he believed that he had found that it resided in movement, and returning to Belgium, he executed quantities of drawings imposing Michelangelesque poses on his models. But he did not capture the power and mystery of Michelangelo, he had not yet understood in what elements they resided."[12] Cladel goes on to say that this dissatisfaction lasted six months. Other accounts suggest the frustration endured as long as three years. All accounts concur, though, that Rodin felt it was only when he abandoned his attempts at direct copying of poses that his discontent ended, and that he succeeded to his satisfaction in capturing the power he had admired in Michelangelo. The two foci of his fascination, he later recalled, had been *mouvement*, the dynamic of the figure's gesture; and *caractere*, the specific expressive physiognomy of the body type. He gave up trying to copy these aspects, he said, when he realized that only by observing the natural, free movements of his models could he find the power he admired in the tomb figures.

Rodin's dissatisfaction with his copies after Michelangelo thus pushed him — as did his later dissatisfaction with the drawings for the initial stages of *The Gates of Hell* — to open himself up to the study of the unposed movements of his models. This new approach radically changed the "body language" of his sculpture in the 1880s, and gave rise, eventually in the later 1890s, to the well-known pencil-and-watercolor drawings from the moving model. Just as the first stumbling but powerful expressions of his temperament, in the student drawings of the 1850s,

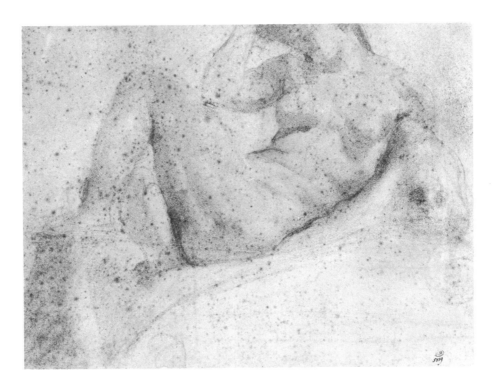

33 Auguste Rodin, study after *Night* by Michelangelo, unrestored

finally bore fruit in the "black" imagery and plans for *The Gates* in the early 1880s, so the lessons of the Italian trip waited almost twenty years to realize their full impact on Rodin's graphic work, in the transformation of method and style that brought forth his late drawing manner.

Rodin explained: "Michelangelo gave me some invaluable perceptions, and I copied him in my spirit, in certain of my works, before understanding him. Once I understood, I saw that this movement existed in nature, and that I had only to avoid losing that in my models...that this movement was something natural, not something I could impose artificially; from that point originated my drawings, which came a long time afterwards, however, and in which one will find Michelangelo again, in such a natural form that one will not suspect it".[13]

Since this changed attitude led Rodin to derive his sculptures more from direct observation and less from drawing preparations, very few of the early drawings can be directly associated with his major sculptural figures. The importance of the early drawings lies in less obvious aspects, as for example in the way their practices prefigure strategies that would become central to Rodin's sculptural method. The careful conservation and reworking of cherished motifs, the audacious collage-ing together of disparate figures, the readjustment of core gestures to differing meanings — all of these devices which contributed to the originality of Rodin's practice as a sculptor are prefigured in the individual drawings and in the mounted assemblages of the early period.

Moreover, Rodin's early drawings show us the foundations of his development as an artist, in ways that help us to understand him not only as an original creator, but as a man of his time. The transformation from the violent severity of these early personal images, with their characteristic visions of severely compressed relief, into the expressive liberty of his later work, suggests for example a parallel with Cézanne. In similar fashion, the great painter of Aix succeeded in transcending youthful imaginings of violence, by dedication to the observation of nature; and this allowed him to create from direct observation an art that he felt subsumed the great principles he admired in the art of the past.

All of Rodin's drawings document a life-long search for expressive gesture. The conflicted, compressed poses of mourning, violence, and grief that dominate the early drawings reflect Rodin's distillation, from numerous sources in the sculpture of the past, of the gestures that he found most telling in their condensation of the deep drama of human existence. His revelation, through his contact with Michelangelo, was the realization that the most telling access to the wellsprings of human expression lay not in such dedicated mining of tradition, but instead in the close observation of the natural, transitory movements of unposed models. This is a transformation that echoes not only the development of other artists such as Cézanne, but also some of the most profound currents of change in the culture of the epoch. Rodin learned that one never equals the past by imitating it, and that the essential forces found in the great traditions can be rediscovered in the present, when convention is stripped away. Freud's contemporaneous understanding of the significance of the apparently arbitrary, and his belief that the inherited representations of myth and religion are only reflections of basic human experiences recoverable from the unconscious lives of the people of the present, is perhaps the most telling parallel discovery. Not only Rodin's education, but more importantly his willful self-formation, is documented by the early drawings. And not only the foundations of his own art, but also an important element in the broad cultural upheaval of the late nineteenth century, are here revealed.

Notes

1 For an overview of previous writing on Rodin's drawings, and a discussion of their general chronology, see my essay "Rodin as a Draftsman: A Chronological Perspective", in Albert Elsen and J. Kirk T. Varnedoe eds., *The Drawings of Rodin*, 1971. The material in the present essay is largely a synthesis of observations previously published in *The Drawings of Rodin* and in two other articles: "Early Drawings by Auguste Rodin", *Burlington Magazine*, April, 1974; and "Rodin's Drawings" in Albert Elsen, ed. *Rodin Rediscovered*, National Gallery of Art, Washington, D.C., 1981.

2 See the discussion of Lecoq de Boisbaudran and his influence on Rodin in Albert Elsen, *Rodin*, 1963, pp. 160–162.

3 Rodin added a preface of homage to a later edition of Lecoq's manual *L'Education de la mémoire pittoresque*.

4 See "Early Drawings by Auguste Rodin", *op. cit.*

5 In "Early Drawings by Auguste Rodin", I published studies after bas-reliefs by Riccio in the Louvre, and discussed the Percier door in the Salle des Caryatides (which contained the Riccio reliefs until they were dismounted sometime after 1852) as a source for Rodin's initial conception of the architectural ensemble of *The Gates of Hell*.

6 Rodin quoted by T. H. Bartlett, in Albert Elsen, *Auguste Rodin, Readings on His Life and Work*, 1965, p. 31.

7 Rodin in a letter to Antoine Bourdelle, cited by Elisabeth Chase Geissbuhler, *Rodin, Later Drawings*, 1963, p. 20.

8 Rodin quoted by T. H. Bartlett, in Elsen, *Auguste Rodin, Readings on His Life and Work*, p. 31.

9 Rodin in a letter to Rose Beuret, cited by Judith Cladel, *Rodin, sa vie glorieuse et inconnue*, 1950, p. 111–112.

10 Rodin quoted by T. H. Bartlett, *op. cit.*, p. 31.

11 For a condensed history of scholarly indecision on the dating of these drawings, see footnote 59, p. 109 of *The Drawings of Rodin*.

12 Judith Cladel, *Auguste Rodin pris sur la vie*, 1903, p. 76.

13 Rodin in a letter to Antoine Bourdelle, cited by E. C. Geissbuhler, *Rodin, Later Drawings*, p. 20.

Plates marked with an * are reproduced actual size

1* Portrait of a Man with Cap; D.119

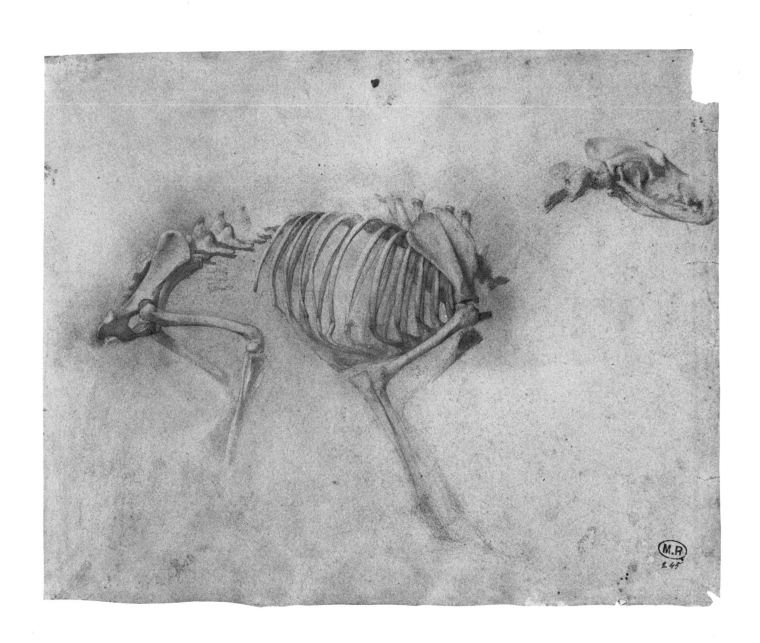

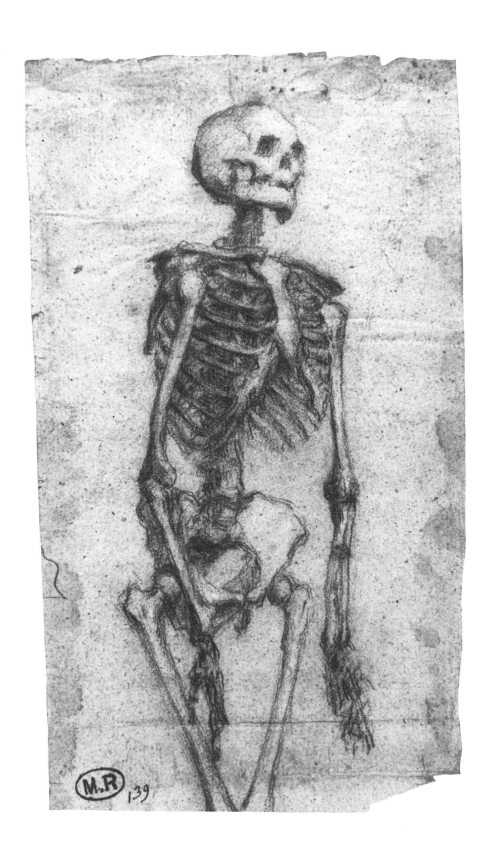

3* Human Skeleton; D.139

4 *Study after "Madonna and Child" by Michelangelo; D.5116*

5 Study after "Morning" by Michelangelo; D.5117

6 *Study after "Day" by Michelangelo; D.5118*

7 Study after "Night" by Michelangelo; D.5119

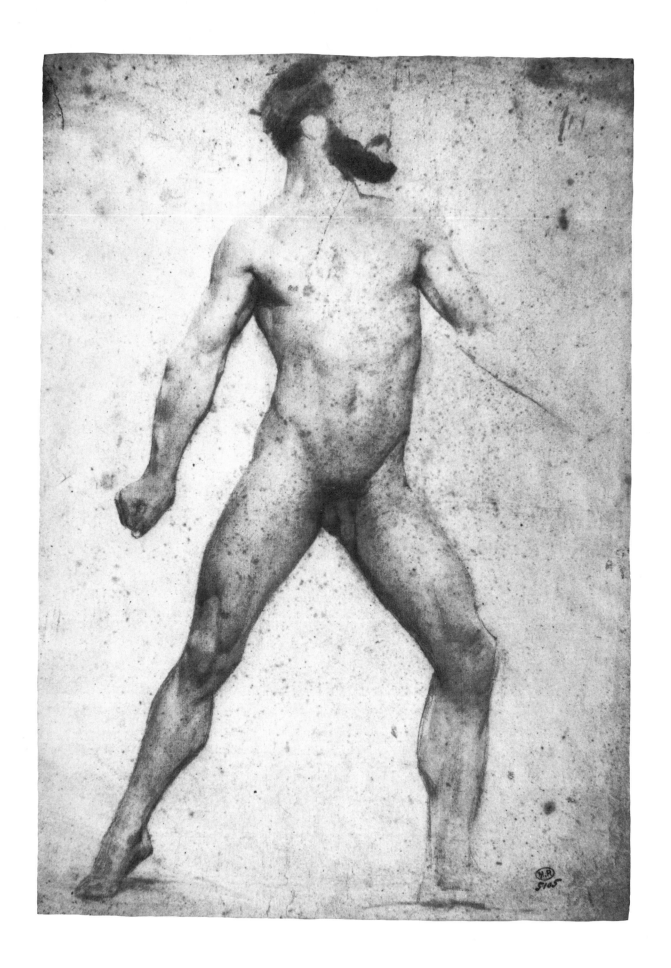

8 *Life Study of a Bearded Man; D.5105*

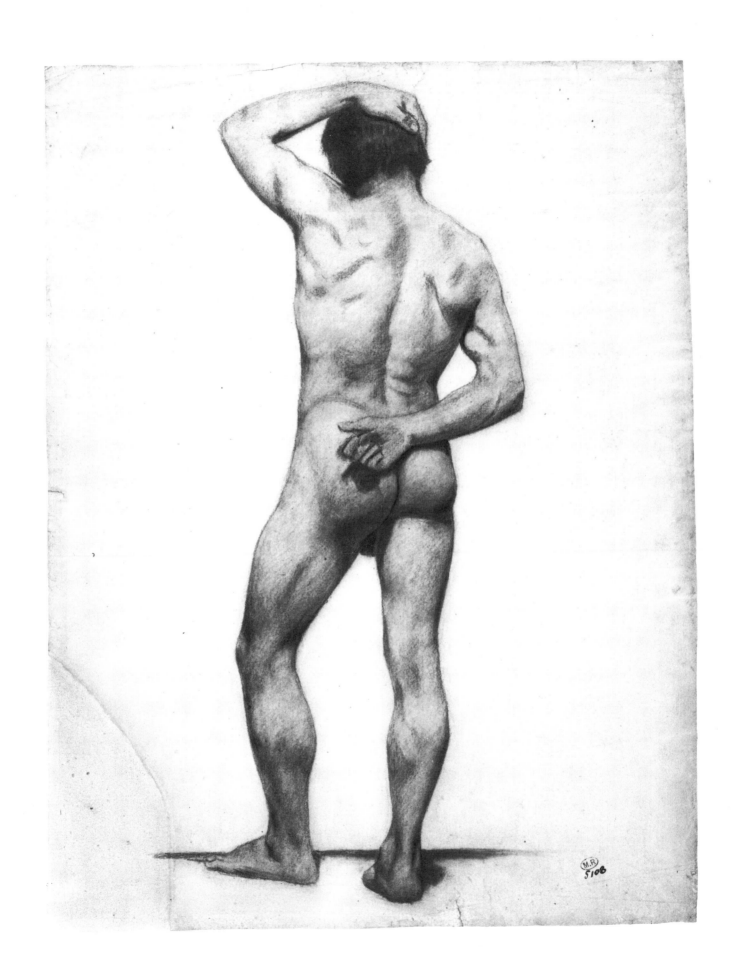

9 *Male Nude from the Back, a Hand on his Head; D.5108*

10 *Female Nude Seated on a Pedestal; D.5101*

11 *Antique Scene. Goddess of Victory Crowning an Athlete; D.109*

12 *Girls Bearing Offerings. Copy after a Parthenon Frieze; D.87*

13 *Procession. Copy after a Parthenon Frieze; D.88*

14* *Girls Bearing Offerings. Copy after a Parthenon Frieze; D.52*

44

15 *Procession. Copy after a Parthenon Frieze; D.61*

16 *Landscape; D.46*

17 *Landscape; D.195*

18 *Landscape; D.60*

19 *Head of a Young Woman; D.147*

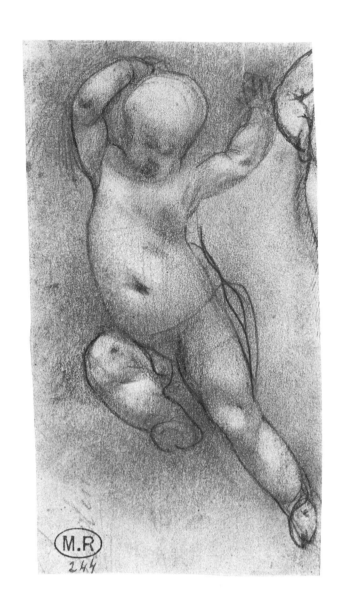

20* Nude Infant with Raised Arms; D.244

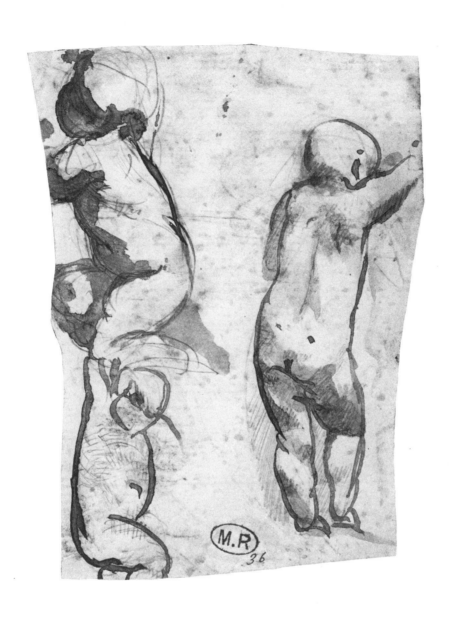

21* *Three Nude Infants; D.36*

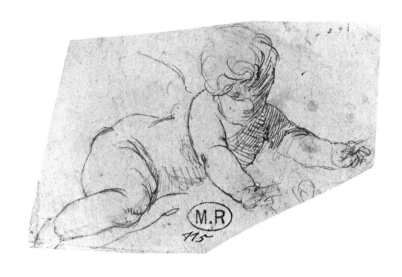

22* Semi-reclining Nude Infant; D.115

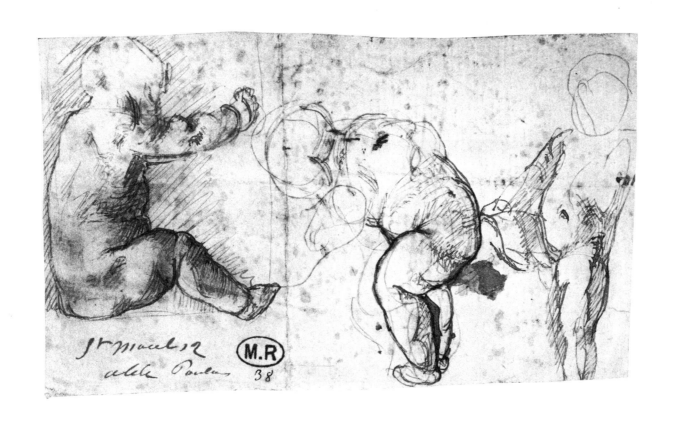

23* *Three Nude Infants; D.38*

24* *Elevation of the Cross with Three Figures; D.143*

25 *Assemblage of Drawings; D.80–86*

26 *Assemblage of Drawings; D.160–175*

27 *Assemblage of Drawings; D.180–194*

28* *Oriental Landscape; D.224*

29* *Oriental Scene in a Landscape Not Far from a City; D.63*

30* *Oriental Scene; D. 222*

The Gates of Hell Period

Auguste Rodin, about 1885

THE GATES OF HELL

Claudie Judrin

The public is generally inclined to view Rodin's drawings as preliminary sketches for his sculptures. Unfortunately this is too obvious a procedure to be generally true; and though one does encounter instances of it in the sculptor's *oeuvre*, they are rare. However, the drawings related to the *Gates of Hell* are, precisely, an exception to this rule. The drawings in which the portal's structure is worked out are obviously exploratory sketches for the project (or rather, as we will see, the different projects), whereas those inspired by Dante's cantos clearly allowed the sculptor to immerse himself in the poem's themes without actually having to transpose his ideas from paper to clay.

The impression we form when we attempt to follow Rodin's creative processes is that we are being privileged with an intimate glimpse of a rich, sometimes groping mind caught in the vicissitudes of creation. Rodin's practice of letting a quickly conceived idea lie dormant and later returning to it shows that he understood perfectly that no work of art can come into existence unless it has matured. The historian alone feels troubled by a logic that pays no heed to the inflexible chronological order. We must bear in mind that, with a few exceptions, none of Rodin's 8000 drawings is dated. Errors are easily made and surely caution is a rule no art historian should neglect. But how is a fact to be established without taking risks?

I. The Gates

Let us try to follow the order of the drawings relating to the erection of the portal designed for the Musée des Arts Décoratifs.[1]

Toward October 1880 Rodin wrote[2] to Undersecretary of State Edmond Turquet that in accordance with the latter's letter of July 17 informing him that he had agreed to commission a decorative door comprising a set of bas reliefs derived from Dante's *Divine Comedy*, for a fee of 8000 francs, he assured him that he had lost no time in starting to work on the project. He had already executed a good number of drawings and sketches in clay and was prepared to submit these to the Undersecretary for approval. He requested an advance of one-fourth the agreed sum to cover the initial expenses incurred in building an armature for the model. (The sum was paid to him in October.)

Rodin made a small sketch in wax (S.1170, $9 \times 5\frac{7}{8} \times \frac{3}{4}''$) which contains ten panels and shows the influence of his memories of Ghiberti's *Gates of Paradise* at the Baptistery in Florence. The succeeding drawings comprise only eight panels, however. On D.1963 Rodin, like Ghiberti before him, uses human figures to give a rhythmical movement to the sides of the door; the horizontal divisions are adorned with ornamental foliage. This is replaced by tangles of briars running along the base of the *Three Shades*. The notes written at the bottom of the sheet indicate that the project is still in its initial stages. The artist has added two sketches and jotted down, "Panel divided like this instead of full panel." Three figures have been sketched in a brown wash: one stands in the middle of the center upright and the other two are placed level with the lintel. In D.1970 only one figure remains at the top of the door, almost on the spot

1 First maquette for *Gates of Hell*, 9 × 5⅞ × ¾″, S.1170

2 Design for *Gates of Hell* with separate relief fields, D.1963, cf. fig. p.85

3 Design for *Gates of Hell* with separate relief fields, D.1970

where Dante the Thinker will be placed later. Charcoal drawing D.1969 is more elaborate in scale (21⅝ × 17¼″) and quite different in intention. At first glance, the uprights seem to be missing, but on closer scrutiny they are visible on the right side of the door. The sculptor's interest is focused on the bas-reliefs. The upper corners contain with seated slaves.

Next come four random drawings in a notebook which can be dated 1881. One page contains drawings of the portal of the Abbaye de St. Pierre at Auxerre, where Rodin spent that year (D.6951, 6952). We know that he was a guest of the sculptor Adrien Gaudez (1845–1902) at Montigny-sur-Loing in June (see Rodin's correspondance in the Musée Rodin archives). Did he visit Auxerre on this occasion? The portal as he now conceives it is flanked by statues of Adam and Eve. He mentions them for the first time on October 20 to the Undersecretary of State for Fine Arts. At this juncture the door's appearance has changed significantly. *The Thinker's* proper place has been found, but unfortunately some of the threads holding the pages in the notebook have been loosened and the order of the pages has been altered; some leaves have even been removed. D.6940 shows a greater number of panels, but the uprights are left bare. On the right-hand sketch on D.6948 the lower half of the door is modified, perhaps with a view to reducing the dimensions of the bas-relief panels. In D.6956 the panels have been reduced in scale and their internal composition has been altered. After examining the

4 Design for *Gates of Hell* with separate relief fields, D.1969

5, 6 Portal of St. Pierre Abbey in Auxerre, D.6951, 6952

7 *The Gates of Hell,*
1880–1917

65

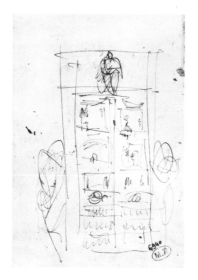

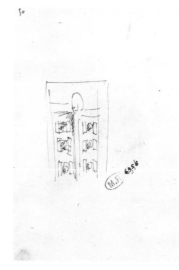

notebook and the nature of the changes in the drawings, I feel confident in placing D.6937 after the other leaves. With this drawing we seem to be approaching the plaster model referred to as the third architectural maquette (S.1189, $43\frac{5}{8} \times 29\frac{1}{8} \times 11\frac{3}{4}''$). The lintel behind *The Thinker* is still unadorned but three distinct areas can now be discerned on each leaf of the double door. This arrangement is repeated in D.7197 and in D.1966, where the uprights are treated anecdotally, as in the plaster model. The appearance of a multitude of human figures above the arms of the cross on the lintel may well have come after the stages I have described thus far. If so, the upper part of the portal in what is called the second architectural sketch (S.1169, $64\frac{7}{8} \times 53\frac{1}{8} \times 10\frac{1}{4}''$) corresponds to D.3719. The note "*mettre une barre*" (place a horizontal bar) can be interpreted to mean that the lintel was to be reinforced.

It is not my purpose here to examine the portal's genesis—it has been abundantly analysed by Albert Elsen—but to refer to it as a way of shedding light on the drawings. When the English poet William Ernest Henley writes in a letter dated April 24, 1882, that he would have liked to see the drawings for the portal and that the engraver Alphonse Legros had told him such wonderful things about it that he was very disappointed to learn that Rodin could not let him have them, we wonder whether he is referring to the architectural drawings or to the imaginative drawings derived from the *Divine Comedy*. Rodin, who was busy with a large number of

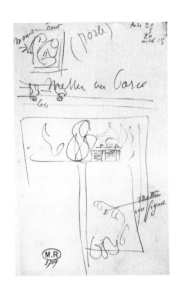

14 *Reclining Woman Embracing a Child*, and sketch for *Gates of Hell*, D. 1966, cf. fig. p. 84

15 Second maquette for *Gates of Hell*, 64⅞×53⅛×10¼", S. 1169

16 Design for *Gates of Hell*, D. 3719

projects including the *Burghers of Calais*, temporarily abandoned work on his portal and avoided callers who asked to see it, like Goncourt on February 9, 1886 (see Rodin's correspondence in the Musée Rodin archives), or who wished to photograph it, like Arsène Alexandre in 1889. The sculptor was later to comment on the difficulties created by showing a work before it was permanently installed in its intended (Musée Rodin archives, Rodin's letter to the notary O. Meunier, 1910). Rodin hoped to exhibit his door in 1889, probably at the Georges Petit Gallery with Claude Monet (Musée Rodin archives, Inv. L. 61). As early as August 1886, he stated to Mme Dewavrin, the wife of the mayor of Calais, that he was journeying back down to hell to shoulder his stone again (Musée Rodin archives, L. 132). On December 30, 1887, he wrote that he had to complete the portal he had abandoned. On October 7, 1888, he replied to M. Noirot, who had asked him to do a bust of him, that he was working feverishly on the gates (Musée Rodin archives, L. 61). On May 19, 1887, Gustave Geffroy reported in the newspaper *La Justice* that the portal, which was being sculpted in advance for an as yet non-existent monument, one that would require a great architect, was almost finished. Then, each time a new location for the gates is discussed, we see the sculptor resume work on them. He talks over the latest developments with friends who are concerned about the project's outcome. The Normand poet Charles Frémine, who was on the staff of the newspaper *Le Rappel*, wrote to him on May 26, 1896: "After having spoken about your Portal, I had the following thought: there is talk about building a Fine-Arts palace for [the Exposition Universelle of] 1900; now every palace must have its portal—might this not be an opportunity for placing your Gates? If this were agreable to you, I would gladly mount a campaign in *Le Rappel* to have the State acquire your work... but I will not mention this matter unless I have your consent. perhaps you have other plans?"

Rodin may have had the 1900 exhibition in mind as early as 1897 when he executed a curious series of drawings while visiting Maurice Fenaille at the Château de Montrozier in the Aveyron. Fenaille, a great patron of the arts, had commissioned the famous album of drawings published by Goupil, Boussod, Manzi, and Joyant in August. He had invited Rodin to spend several days in September at his castle. There, 1950 feet above sea level, as the sculptor noted with delight in a letter to his friend Hélène Porgès, he "tried to get some rest" (Musée Rodin archives, Inv. L. 682). A number of photographs and sketches executed in the margins of architectural drawings indicate that the local villagers did a peasant dance in his honor. On some ten leaves, the portal is placed on a perron over two arches reached by a double flight of

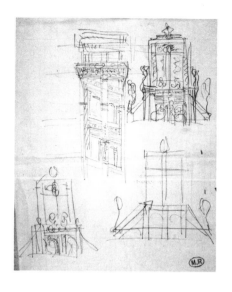

17 Design of stairs
and setting of *Gates
of Hell*, D. 3495
verso

18 *Woman Moving
in Dance* and two
sketches for *Gates of
Hell*, D. 3498, cf.
fig. p. 88

stairs shaped like an open horseshoe with convex sides. Four large sculptures, almost certainly including *Adam* and *Eve* rhythm, give to this astonishing project topped by the *Three Shades* (D. 3495 verso, 3498, 3502, 3505 recto and verso, 3518 verso). On a discarded envelope (D. 1961) Rodin jotted down the date September 1897 and the address of the review *Le Monde moderne*, 5 rue Saint-Benoît. These ambitious designs for an unknown location never led to anything. On May 28, 1898, *L'Illustration* reported that Rodin had no intention of showing his great door before 1900 and had declared that he would unveil it at the Exposition Universelle. One year later, on June 11, 1899, the local newspaper of Amélie-les-Bains (Jean Bernard in *Amélie-Journal*) announced that Rodin and the authorities were dickering over the site where the sculptor's incomparable masterpiece was to be exhibited the following year.

But the complications delaying the completion of the *Gates of Hell* were far from over, even though Rodin did exhibit his great door, lacking some of its decorations, beween June 1 and the end of November at the Pavillon de l'Alma. On May 10, 1901, the newspapers reported that the Musée des Arts Décoratifs, which had been conceded to the Union des Arts Décoratifs in a bill dated November 17, 1897, was to be housed in the Pavillon de Marsan at the Louvre. Rodin was questioned about this site. "I don't know," he replied with a gentle smile. "A few months ago M. Georges Berger asked me to got to the Pavillon de Marsan to study an appropriate location for my Door, but I'm afraid that the official architects aren't very enthusiastic about this project. And when the officials say no, there is nothing one can do. It is a *camorra* (an

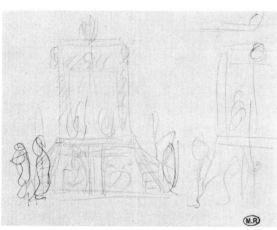

19 Design for set-
ting of *Gates of Hell*,
D. 3502

20 Design for set-
ting of *Gates of Hell*,
D. 3505 verso

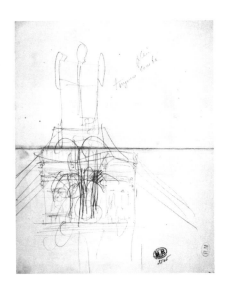

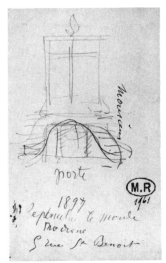

21 Design for setting of *Gates of Hell*, D.3505 recto

22 Sketch of *Gates of Hell*, D.1961, cf. fig. p.89

intrigue) like the one that killed Carpeaux. As far as I am concerned, it makes no difference whether the Door is here or there. All I am interested in is interpreting bas reliefs in a new way, creating a work in which the decorative setting is fully integrated into the whole and diversifies, through the interplay of light and shadow, the sculptural motifs. I hope to succeed. And that is all I am interested in... The Administration that commissioned the Door and paid for it will take delivery of it in Meudon, where it is currently located, and will install it where it pleases" (Le Nain Jaune in *L'Echo de Paris*, May 10, 1901).

A certain note of weariness began to creep into Rodin's statements. On May 27, 1905, the Musée des Arts Décoratifs was inaugurated—without the portal. Two years later yet a new project was discussed. The new Sulpician seminary on the rue Bonaparte, which had been built in 1820 and closed down in 1906 after the law on the separation of Church and State had been voted, was to house the Musée Luxembourg. Rodin was asked to decorate one of the rooms (Pipelet in *L'Action,* November 9, 1907). In October 1907 Dujardin-Beaumetz, the new Undersecretary of State for Fine Arts, opened an exhibition of drawings at the Galérie Bernheim and, in front of Rodin's watercolors of Cambodian dancers, commissioned the sculptor to paint a fresco—perhaps because he had noticed the word "fresques" in Rodin's handwriting in the margin of several drawings (Inv. D.4443 and 4445, *Rodin et l'Extrême Orient* cata-

23 Palace Facades with *Gates of Hell*, D.3518 verso

24 *The Gates of Hell* in marble and bronze, D.7637

25 Sketch for *Gates of Hell*, D.5478, cf. fig. p.87

26 *The Gates of Hell* framed with a fresco, D.6128

27 Sketch for *Gates of Hell*, D.5497

logue, Musèe Rodin, 1979, p.69). Extremely interested in this proposal, Rodin gave free rein to his imagination. He pictured himself designing a second Sistine Chapel in the choir of the seminary chapel, with the *Gates of Hell* framed by a fresco representing paradise. He dashed off a sketch and made an estimate of costs (D.7637), indicating that the uprights on either side of the door, the tympanum, and the *Three Shades* group were to be in marble, while the door itself was to be cast in bronze. This is confirmed beyond a shadow of doubt by an article by the Conservateur of the Musée du Luxembourg, Léonce Bénédite (*Les Arts au Musée Rodin*, 1918, Nr.168). Contrary to Mr.Elsen I place this project at the Sulpician seminary between 1908 and 1910 at the latest and not at the Musée Rodin chapel in 1917 or 1918. A photograph even shows the sculptor studying the choir with an architects's eye and calculating the dimensions of the space his door was to occupy. Several drawings show the creation of the earth with the planets in motion (D.5478, 6128, 5497). On December 2, 1910, a contract was signed, granting Rodin 10,000 francs for executing part of the fresco. The sculptor intended to paint directly on the wall rather than on a primed canvas. He was anxious to take a crack at an art which he felt was closer to sculpture than to painting (*Paris Journal*, September 29, 1911 or 1912). He questioned a number of artists, including Jeanne Bardey, Charles Henri Charlier, and Marie Cazin, on technical matters. All these developments were reported in the press between 1907 and 1912. There was even some talk about installing a Rodin museum in the seminary (*Le*

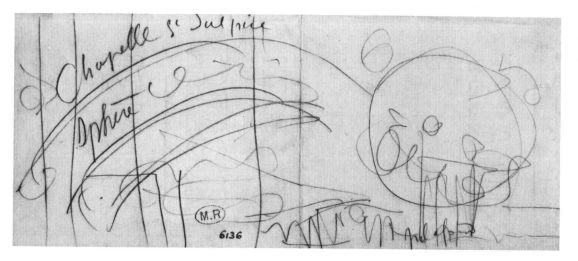

28 Fresco design for setting of *Gates of Hell*, D.6136

Temps, January 10, 1912), awaiting more suitable premises. (The Hôtel Biron became the Musée Rodin in 1916 only a few month before the sculptor's death.) It was only in 1937—some twenty years later—that the *Gates of Hell* was cast and installed at the Musée Rodin.

It is not overstating matters to speak of the *Gates'* hell. The career of this work and its various metamorphoses forms an extraordinary story, one that occupied 40 years in the life of a man who carried on his work with the same dogged dedication with which he clung to a glorious and difficult prospect.

II. Hell

Rodin's drawings for the *Gates of Hell* are much more closely related to the actual text of Dante's poem than are the sculptures of the portal itself.

Except for a few groups which Rodin identifies, such as *Ugolino* and *Paolo and Francesca*, most of the figures named by the poet are anonymous shades under the sculptor's hand.

Between 1880 and 1883[3] (the years when most of his exploratory work on the *Inferno* was carried out) Rodin's close reading of the poem did not prevent him from interpreting it as a draftsman with an astonishing degree of inventiveness. The repeated references to Dante's lines in the margins of the drawings are a scrupulous record of his reading; far from hampering his imagination, they seem to have stimulated it to soar on ever more daring flights. What we are confronted with, in fact, is an extraordinary inversion. Whereas in Rodin's mature period—the period we are examining here—the sculptor's inspiration was as "black" as the media he used (pen and ink, gray washes, gouaches), his last creations rarely departed from the physical presence of female models; but then, on the other hand, the comments he jotted down in the margins recoiled, so to speak, from the sheer physical nature of the representation to seek refuge in symbolic or fanciful titles—as if Rodin had always felt obliged to temper the truth of an impression with an imaginative reinterpretation. At times he was the servant, at other times the ethereal master of the works which he executed in the apparent diversity of two styles.

Given the fact that Rodin's "black" drawings can be considered to include the works inspired by Victor Hugo and Baudelaire as well as those marked by the sculptor's experience at the Sevres Manufactory, it is difficult to evaluate their number, but at a rough guess the drawings included here represent about one tenth of his output as a draftsman during this period.

Seldom exhibited during his lifetime, they were (or about a third of them was) reproduced in facsimile in 1897 by the firm of Goupil and published by Boussod, Manzi, and Joyant in an edition limited to 125 copies. In his preface Octave Mirbeau rejoiced in the fact—so different were the times!—that the album was a unique example of an art book that was neither a commercial venture nor a "popular vulgarization," but the perfect and durable expression of an admiration. The drawings, it seemed to the writer, were like a sharing of the artist's secret thoughts—or a confession; and in his opinion they were sufficient to establish Rodin's reputation.

Hell is a more powerful source of inspiration than heaven, as we all know. This was certainly the case with Rodin. Like many of the artists and writers of the nineteenth century, the sculptor derived a certain fascinated pleasure from plumbing the lower depths of man's nature. He read Dante with the same studious absorption and the same exacting standards of truthful-

29 *Dante and Bea-trice*, D.5598, cf. fig. p.90

30 *Charon's Boat*, D.2057, cf. fig. p.91

31 *Shade*, D.5613, cf. fig. p.93

ness that characterized his quest for Balzac in Touraine and for Hugo on the island of Guernsey; the same standards that had led him to study the nude figures of the *Burghers of Calais* before clothing them. He clung to the poem's authenticity in order to steep himself more thoroughly in it. Let us journey down, following in his footsteps, to his Hell—which is also Dante's Hell and no doubt our own as well.

But the underworld's trials cannot be surmounted without the guidance of a tutelary spirit and an inspiring muse. At Beatrice's behest, Virgil agrees in Canto II to guide Dante past the perils of Hell, up the slopes of Mount Purgatory to the gates of Paradise. Rodin felt that Beatrice did not belong on his door among the naked figures of the damned (*Chicago Times Herald*, October 1, 1893). The drawing (D.5598) published in the Goupil album under the title *Dante et Béatrice* also contains an allusion to Musset's *Nuit de Mai*.

The drawing in the same album which Rodin entitled, perhaps in 1897, *La barque de Caron*[4] is deeply ambiguous (D.2057). At first glance it looks like a mother-and-child; in fact it represents the Ferryman of Hell who steers Dante and Virgil across the black waters of the Acheron in Canto III.

The setting of Canto IV is Limbo.[5] Rodin jots down this word above a bowed, muscular male figure shown in profile (D.5613). It has the power of a Michelangelo figure; and of course it reminds us as well of *The Thinker;* Rodin himself used this drawing in 1887 to illustrate the

32 *Minos*, D.5593, cf. fig. p.94

33 *Minos on his Throne*, fig. 46 in Goupil Album

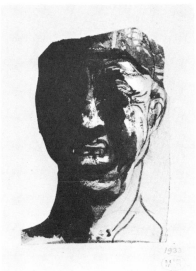

poem "*Réversibilité*" in *Les Fleurs du Mal*. Now we know that Baudelaire originally planned to give his book the title *Les Limbes*—a coincidence that is surely noteworthy.

In Canto V the two poets enter the second circle where Minos sits in judgement surrounded by lesser judges (D.5593; Goupil, *Minos*, pl. 46; D.1965). This scene fascinated Rodin; he placed several human figures around a table and showed the damned, overcome by their sentence, crouching in the shadows in the foreground. Rodin undoubtedly planned to include bas reliefs of this type in his project of a multiple-panel door (D.1969). As early as 1883, the critic Dargenty published in *l'Art*, on the occasion of the Salon National, two heads of damned souls: one is now in the National Galerie in Berlin under the title *Une des furies* (one of the Furies), the other is reproduced here, see p. 73 top left (D.1933). In the Goupil album (1897) Rodin calls it *Masque de Minos* (the mask of Minos). These tragic faces, executed in thick layers of dark tints highlighted with flashes of gouache, are cut out and glued to a neutral ground which gives them a spectral appearance.

The first soul to address Dante is Francesca da Rimini; the poet is so moved by her words that he swoons. Among the multiple embracing couples derived from this scene, it is sometimes

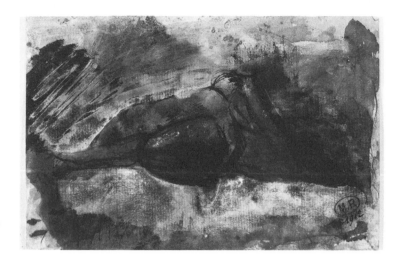

39 *Reclining Couple,
Embracing*, D.1912,
cf. fig. p.96

40 *Rain, Circle of
Vexation*, D.7605,
cf. fig. p.101

difficult to distinguish Dante and Virgil from Paolo and Francesca (D.5630, D.3760, D.3763). On some drawings (e.g. D.5630) Rodin wrote down references to both pairs; he also added the word *Contemplations* as a tribute to Victor Hugo and an inexactly quoted line from Baudelaire's *"La Mort des amants"*. Drawn time and time again to the theme of the couple damned for carnal lust, Rodin sculpted *The Kiss* but did not assign it a place on his portal, feeling that the happiness it expressed did not belong in the regions of perdition. Instead he created two beings eternally clutching each other in despair rather than ecstasy. In a departure from the sculptor's usual practice, D.1912 appears to be a preliminary sketch for this group. It is interesting to note in passing that the sex of the human figures in the "black" period is ill defined.

Recovering from his swoon, Dante encounters Cerberus, the menacing three-headed Hound of Hell, and the Gluttons assailed by "an inexhaustible torrent of Hell's sooty, frozen rain" (Canto VI, D.7605). A drawing formerly in the collection of Octave Mirbeau shows four sinuous silhouettes staggering under gray washes of India ink.

Canto VII brings us to the circle of Hoarders and Wasters, represented by a male figure vainly trying to grasp a hoard of spilling pieces of gold (D.2071). Rodin combines this figure with Luxury in a sculpture of the gates. In D.1936 Plutus, the god of wealth, rendered helpless by his symbolic fatness, is carried by two henchmen. After embarking with Phlegyas, the Boat-

41 *Shade of an
Avaricious Man*,
D.2071, cf. fig.
p.102

42 *Pluto (?)*,
D.1936, cf. fig.
p.103

43 *Dante and Virgil
in a Boat*, D.5373

44 *The Styx*, illustrated on p. 41 of the Goupil Album

45 *Medusa*, D. 1996, cf. fig. p. 104

46 *If Medusa saw you, you would have ceased to live*, D. 3781, cf. fig. p. 105

man of the river Styx, who ferries them across to Lower Hell (D. 5373 and Goupil album, p. 41)—a scene immortalized by Delacroix—the poet is threatened by three infernal furies, symbols of eternal remorse. Medusa, who turns to stone all those who look at her, appears next (D. 1996); in a related drawing (D. 3781) Virgil shields Dante from this danger and warns him, *"Si Méduse te voyait, tu aurais cessé de vivre"* (if Medusa should see you, you would be dead). Rodin made no drawings in response to Cantos X and XI. On the other hand, the theme of the Violent and the Centaurs in Canto XII inspired a significant series, which has been examined in a publication of the Musée Rodin (*Dossier* No. 1, 1981). The drawing entitled *Fête de centaure* in the Goupil album (D. 5429) is typical of this series.

In the 1897 album Rodin entitled a drawing (D. 3772) of souls clinging together like grapes in a bunch: *Blasphème* (Blasphemy). This is inspired by Canto XIV: "…Some were stretched supine upon the ground, / some squatted with their arms about themselves, / and others without pause roamed round and round."[6]

In order to descend to the circle of the Fraudulent, Dante mounts Geryon in front of Virgil, who protects him from the monster's lashing tail (Canto XVII, D. 3769). According to medieval tradition this fantastic steed was a mythical king of Spain who killed and robbed strangers whom he lured into his realm with a smile. The allusion to the hero Perseus who rode on Pegasus does not seem to have been derived from Dante. Swept into the air by the monster,

47 *Centaur Embracing Two Women*, D. 5429, cf. fig. p. 107

48 *Blasphemy*, D. 3772, cf. fig. p. 106

49 *Dante and Virgil on a Ghostly Horse*, D. 3769, cf. fig. p. 109

50 *Icarus and Phaeton*, D. 3759, cf. fig. p. 108

Dante compares his own fear to that of Phaeton when he lost control of the Chariot of the Sun, and to that of Icarus when his wax wings melted and he plunged to earth while his father Daedalus looked on helplessly. Rodin may be confusing the two myths in D. 3759, where he shows a father and son embracing.

In Canto XVIII Dante visits the Seducers and sees Jason who beguiled Medea. In D. 2056 the princess is seen embracing her two sons. Rodin inclined to have the same view of the two myths gave scenes of this type either the title *Médée* or *Niobé*. He inscribed the words "*au feu*" (fire!) on the completed drawing, imagining a mother gathering up her children to save them from flames.

In the *bolgia* of the Panderers and Seducers (D. 7616), Dante recognizes Alessio Interminelli da Lucca sunk in filth. "...And I saw long lines / of people in a river of excrement / that seemed the overflow of the world's latrines./ I saw among the felons of that pit / one wraith who might or might not have been tonsured— / one could not tell, he was so smeared with shit." Rodin executed several versions of this scene: a sketch owned by Octave Mirbeau (auction sale of February 24, 1919, No. 42a) which was published in facsimile in the Goupil album (pl. 69); a figure in the collection of Mrs. Katherine Graham (*Rodin Rediscovered* catalogue, Washington, No. 249); and a man crouching in a ditch formerly in the possession of Maurice

51 *Medea*, D. 2056, cf. fig. p. 110

52 *Dans la m...*, D. 7616, cf. fig. p. 111

Fenaille and now in the Musée Rodin collecion. These drawings show us the sculptor "concocting" his art, gluing a drawing of restricted dimensions onto a leaf in an accounting book which he then inserts into a larger scene treated with washes of gouache and red and purple ink. The sewage-filled ditch in which the shade is seated is contained on a raised rectangle of paper.

In Canto XXII Dante and Virgil reach the *bolgia* of the Grafters, who are immersed in boiling pitch (D. 5594). Dante describes one of the demons who prey on these sinners as having two tusks; in Rodin's interpretation this becomes two horns. The sculptor as usual seems to find it difficult to make up his mind about which title he wants: he considers using *Ecce Homo* and *Prometheus* before finally opting for *Demons montrant une ombre tombée dans la poix* (Goupil album, 1897, Demon pointing to a shade who has fallen into pitch).

In the sixth *bolgia,* the Hypocrites (D. 5086) walk slowly round weighted down by great leaden cloaks with enormous hoods. "The outside is all dazzle, golden and fair; / the inside, lead…" The jovial Bolognese Friar Catalano speaks to Dante.

In Cantos XXIV and XXV, the thieves of Florence are assailed by monstrous reptiles. Buoso, whom Rodin calls *Boso*, is condemned to the "horrible combination" (D. 2069) of a double metamorphosis from serpent to man and from man to serpent (D. 1932 and D. 7617). Drawn

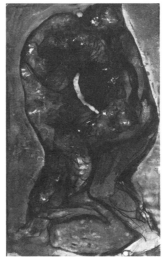

several times to this frightening passage in Dante's poem, Rodin envisaged including a bas-relief of it in his first project for the portal; the serpents are incidentally present on the left-hand leaf of the door as it now stands.[7]

Deeply impressed by the tragic story of Count Guido da Montefeltro in Canto XXVII, Rodin executed no fewer than ten drawings on the theme of the brave warrior who lived and fought by cunning and in old age repented and became a Franciscan monk—to no avail, for after his death his soul was snatched by a demon from the hands of Saint Francis (D. 5617, 1928, 5591, 3767, 5590, 3762, 6903). The victim lies stretched out, helpless to influence the outcome of the struggle between the demon and the saint; Rodin made a number of experiments with horizontal and vertical compositions, intending to include the scene in a bas-relief at the base of the portal (D. 1928). Guido's soul seldom participates in the struggle (D. 6903)—not even when it is stretched out on the "dissecting table" exposed to a mob of furies quarreling over his remains (D. 5591). The notation *Oreste* suggests that the story of Guido has fused with the myth of Orestes in Dante's mind.

In Canto XXVIII the Sowers of Discord are punished. Dante notices one soul "split from his chin to the mouth with which man farts. / Between his legs all of his red guts hung (D. 5633) / with the heart, the lungs, the liver, the gall bladder, / and the shrivelled sac that passes shit to the bung." Catching sight of Dante, the shade opens his own breast with both his hands and cries: "...See how I rip myself! / See how Mahomet's mangled and split open!" This theme is treated in a drawing now in the collection of Mrs. Katherine Graham (*Rodin Rediscovered*, No. 243).

After visiting the Alchemists, the Counterfeiters, the False Witnesses, and Falsifiers of every kind, Dante reaches the bottom of hell's pit and witnesses the supreme punishment: Count Ugolino della Gherardesca gnawing on the skull of the Archbishop of Pisa, Ruggieri degli Ubaldini, who accused him of betrayal. The poet who had served as soldier with one of Ugolino's grandsons, Nino, is profoundly moved by the Count's harrowing tale. Some thirty Rodin drawings are derived from this episode; I have already analysed them in a Musée Rodin publication (*Dossier* No. 2, 1982). Condemned for having intrigued and borne arms against a rival branch of the Pisan Guelphs (the Papal party opposed to the Ghibellines, who supported the Holy Roman emperor), Ugolino was imprisoned with his two sons Gaddo and Uguiccione and two grandsons, Brigata and Anselmuccio. They were left to starve to death in February 1289 in a tower near Pisa which came to be known as the Tower of Hunger. Rodin pictured the different stages of this ordeal, which is said to have lasted a week. The hitherto unpublished

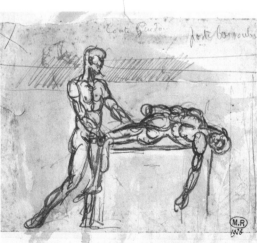

58 *Damned Souls around Count Guido*, D. 5617, cf. fig. p. 117

59 *Count Guido*, D. 1928, cf. fig. p. 119

60 *Count Guido
between Satan and
St. Francis*, D. 3767,
cf. fig. p. 120

61 *Shade of Count
Guido*, D. 3762, cf.
fig. p. 116

62 *Demon Carrying
Off his Prize (Count
Guido)*, D. 6903

63 *Mohammed with
Dangling Intestines*,
D. 5633, cf. fig.
p. 122

64 *Ugolino*,
D. 7627, cf. fig.
p. 123

65 *Satan and
St. Francis Fighting
over Count Guido*,
D. 5591, cf. fig.
p. 118

66 *Count Guido*,
D. 5590, cf. fig.
p. 121

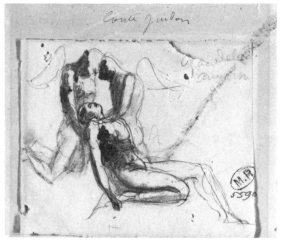

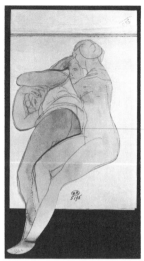

67 *Demon in Space*, D. 5665, cf. fig. p. 130

68 *Three Embracing Women*, D. 5196, cf. fig. p. 261

drawing D. 7627 reproduced here illustrates (as does Carpeaux's sculpture) the second day, when Ugolino bites his hands in helpless grief. His sons and grandsons, thinking he is chewing on his own flesh out of hunger, say to him, "Father, it would give us much less pain / if you ate us…" We know that Rodin finally choose the moment when Ugolino, crawing on all fours, is about to devour the flesh of his dead sons.

This episode (Canto XXXIII) is followed by Dante's encounter with Lucifer at the center of the earth and his first glimpse of light dawning on the slopes of Mount Purgatory. With a few exceptions, the regions where hope reigns did not inspire Rodin. The nine drawings that conclude the series of works discussed in these pages undoubtedly belong to the infernal cycle, but neither Rodin's annotations nor the titles that were given to those published in the sculptor's lifetime, make it clear which specific cantos, if any, they are derived from. There is no question about their quality. The appearance of a cut-out (D. 5665) as early as the 1880s—and it is not an isolated example—is an eloquent testimony to the remarkable inventiveness of the sculptor and draftsman. We know what advantage the artist himself (not to mention several early twentieth century artists) was soon to draw from the technique of *papiers-collés* (D. 5196). Observant viewers will not fail to notice the astonishing technical and imaginative richness displayed by Rodin the draftsman, and they will note how closely imagination and technique are interwoven in his drawings. The cut-out process with its multiple layers and degrees of collage—a small scene inserted into a larger one, thus at times giving it a new meaning, a new topography—is not unrelated to Rodin's method of constructing his sculptures. Throughout his life Rodin approached his sculptures and drawings in much the same spirit; nevertheless it would be vain to try and establish perfect parallels between a specific drawing and a specific sculpture.

Notes

1 The Musée des Arts Décoratifs was to be built on the site of the Gare d'Orsay—which will soon house the Paris Museum of Nineteenth-Century Art.

2 Archives Nationales, F. 2109.

3 *In Dante et Virgile aux enfers* (*Dossier* No. 3), published by the Musée Rodin in 1983, I have commented extensively on a letter (May 11, 1883) from Rodin to the art critic Léon Gauchez, which says: "At the moment, my drawings are rather an illustration of Dante from a sculptural point of view; they are quite numerous. It seems to me that the poet's expression is always simple and concretely visual." (Haus-, Hof- und Staatsarchiv, Vienna).

4 In *The American Architect and Building News* of May 11, 1889, T. H. Bartlett describes the lintel of the *Gates of Hell*. On the right, he saw the arrival of the souls awaiting Charon's boat, on the left the Judgement.

5 *Ibid.* In his article of May 25, 1889, Bartlett saw the souls in Limbo on the right pilaster of the portal.

6 This and following quotations from the *Divine Comedy* are from John Ciardi's translation of *The Inferno*, 1954. Léonce Bénédite, the Curator of the Musée Rodin from 1917 to 1925, writes that Rodin read Artaud de Montor's translation of Dante's poem (*Dante et Rodin, mélange de critique et d'éruditions française*, Paris 1921, p. 211).

7 This drawing from the Museum der Bildenden Künste in Leipzig (study with a group of human figures, see catalogue No. 48a) may be a commentary on Canto XXVI, where Virgil questions Ulysses's shade.

31 *Self-portrait; D.7102*

32* *Reclining Woman Embracing a Child, and Sketch of Gates of Hell; D.1966*

84

33* *Design for The Gates of Hell; D.1963*

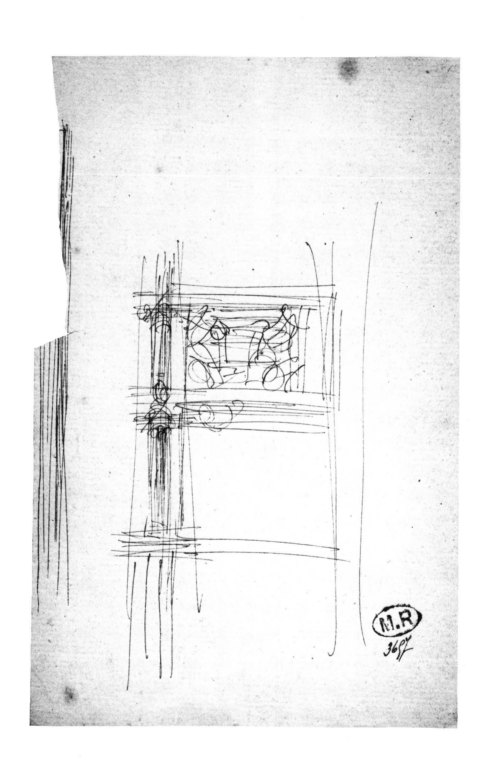

34* *Relief Panel for The Gates of Hell; D.3657*

35* *Sketch for The Gates of Hell; D.5478*

36 *Woman Moving in a Dance, and Two Sketches for The Gates of Hell; D.3498*

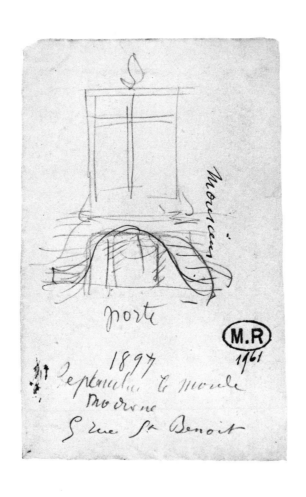

37* *Sketch for The Gates of Hell; D.1961*

38* *Dante and Beatrice; D.5598*

39* Charon's Boat; D.2057

40* *Study for The Gates of Hell*

41* *Shade; D.5613*

42* *Minos; D.5593*

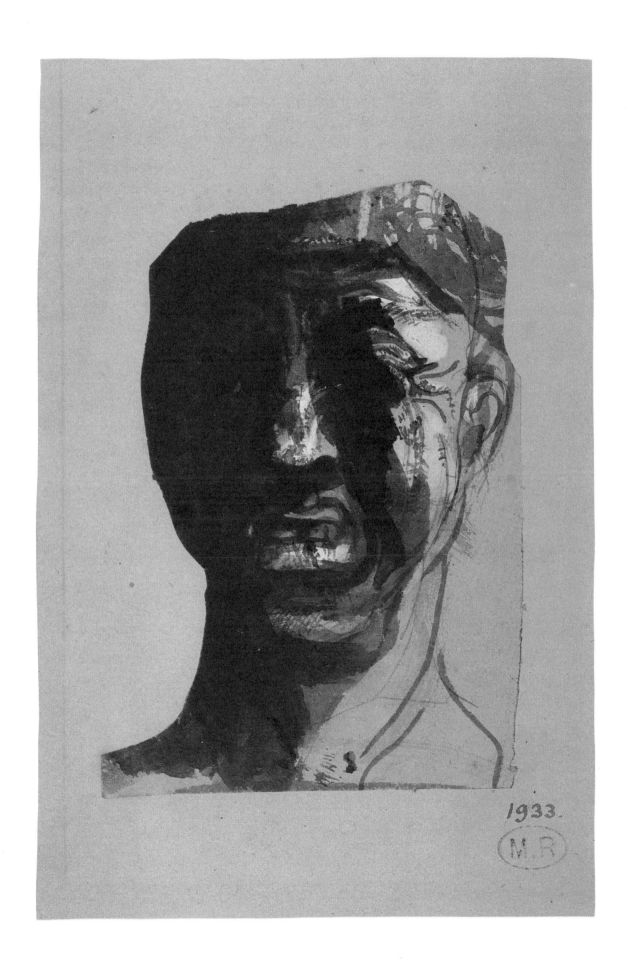

1933.

43* *Mask of Minos; D. 1933*

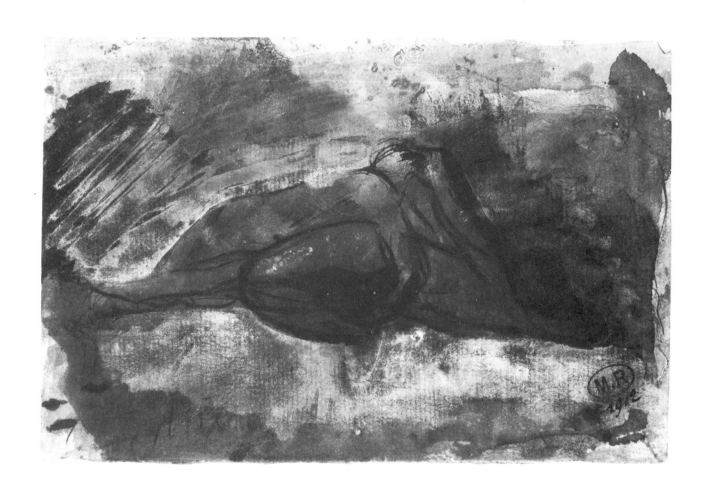

44* *Reclining Couple, Embracing; D.1912*

45* *Embracing Couple; D.5630*

47* *Paolo and Francesca da Rimini; D.3763*

48* *Deposition*

49* *Rain, Circle of Vexation; D. 7605*

50* *Shade of an Avaricious Man; D. 2071*

51* Pluto (?); D.1936

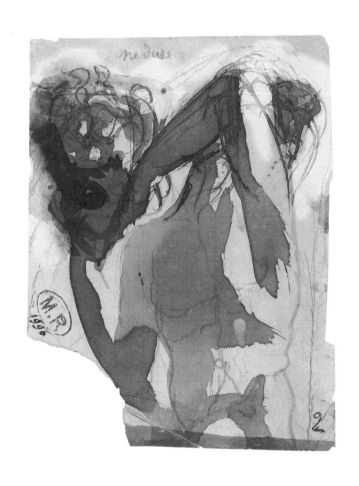

53 *If Medusa saw you, you would have ceased to live; D.3781*

54* *Blasphemy; D.3772*

55 *Centaur Embracing Two Women; D.5429*

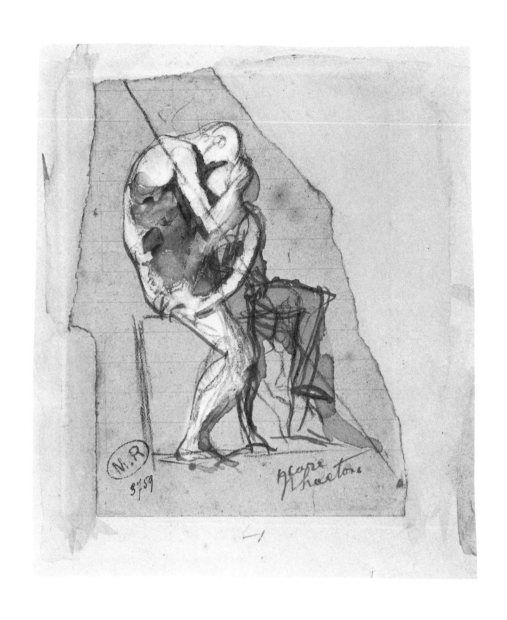

56* *Icarus and Phaeton; D.3759*

Dante et Virgile . le cheval plus Chimérique
(Pégase

57* *Dante and Virgil on a Ghostly Horse; D.3769*

58* *Medea; D.2056*

59* *Dans la m…; D.7616*

60* *Demon Holding Up a Shade Who Has Fallen in Tar; D.5594*

61* *Cloak of Lead; D.5086*

l'horrible Melange

63* *Boso and the Snake; D.1932*

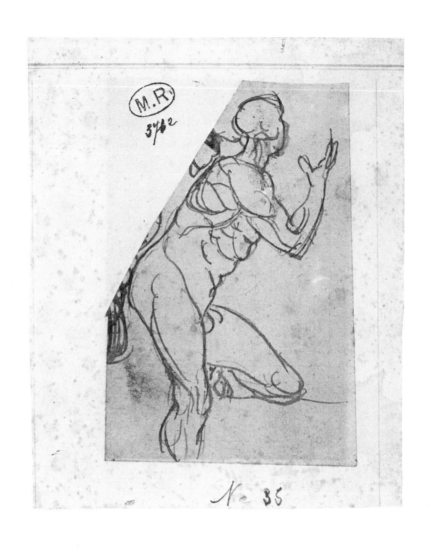

64* *Shade of Count Guido; D.3762*

65* *Damned Souls around Count Guido; D.5617*

66* *Satan and St. Francis Fighting over Count Guido; D.5591* 118

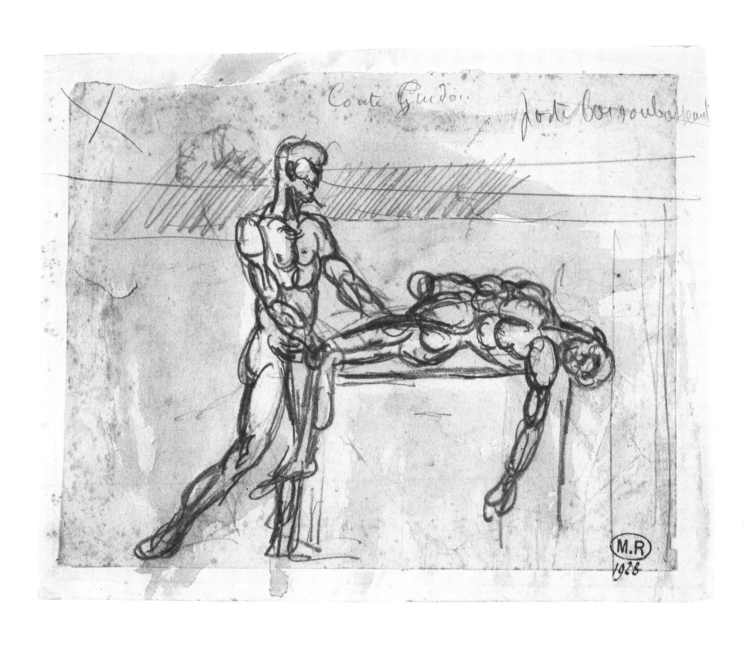

67 *Count Guido; D.1928*

68* *Count Guido between Satan and St. Francis; D.3767*

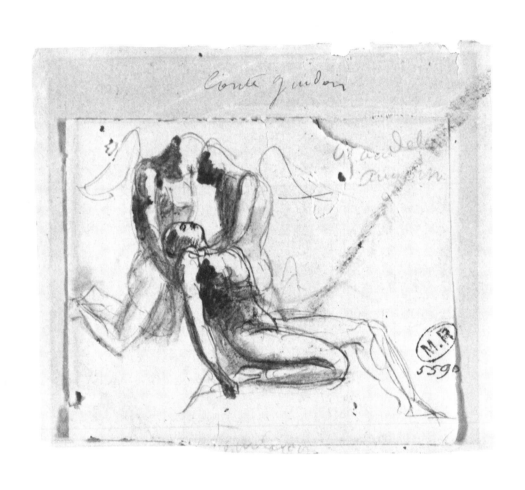

69* Count Guido; D.5590

70* *Mohammed with Dangling Intestines; D.5633*

71* *Ugolino; D.7627*

72* *Depiction of an Entombment; D.7629*

73* Entombment; D.7614

74* *Mephisto; D.5609*

C. XXXI

75* *Embrace; D.1904*

76* *Group with Three Figures; D.1930*

77* *Head of a Woman; D.2049*

78* *Demon in Space; D.5665*

Architectural Drawings

Auguste Rodin, about 1906

RODIN'S DRAWINGS OF ARCHITECTURE

Elisabeth Chase Geissbuhler

Here are the latest of Rodin's graphic works to come before the public and which it is the honor of this exhibition to present for the first time outside the Paris Rodin Museum. The drawings are seen here as they came from the sculptor's hand without the least editing, just as he set them down, first in pencil in the open air and in the presence of the great stone monuments that he admired. The old churches and cathedrals that were his models became his "Muses" and their authors became his masters.

But we know this realisation developed slowly for he wrote: "It is little by little that I have come to our old Cathedrals, that I have been able to penetrate the secret of their life as it is constantly renewed beneath a changing sky."[1]

Not until 1914, his seventy-fifth year, when the epoch, like his fame, approached the point of temporary eclipse, when the first edition of his book dedicated to the Cathedrals of France was published with one hundred and fifty-eight large pages, $9\frac{1}{2} \times 11$ inches, of written notes, and one hundred of the same that are devoted to his drawings of architecture. Only then did these drawings become available to the public. Seen there of course in facsimile, which the publishers affirm "were made under Rodin's close supervision,"[2] they lack something more important than an even closer rendering of the original drawings could give. They lack the written words Rodin often added to his drawings of architecture. For example, across his drawing of the Church of Notre Dame at Tonnerre (Figs. 1, 2), he has written: "Ma porte · contrefort cassé flanqué de tours ronde · épaisseur · pilastre inclus · portail console tête d'ange · écusson blond." The first words: "My portal," tell that Rodin was thinking of his *Gates of Hell*. This drawing was therefore made after 1880 and the broken buttresses that flank the bays of the double doors at Tonnerre were to be remembered for the frame of his *Gates*, as were the decorative subjects that he also named. The words which are eliminated from the drawings reproduced in his book are keys to an understanding of Rodin's intention. They are important because in his book no drawing is keyed to the text.

Unfavorable though the year of its publication was for every art work, Rodin's book was ordered by museum and university libraries throughout most of the world, where it is hoped many copies still exist, for the book has never been reissued in its original form with its full number of drawings.[3]

Following that brief and incomplete appearance the drawings of architecture disappeared until 1966 when eight unpublished drawings and written notes from the Philadelphia Rodin Museum were reproduced and discussed in an article entitled *Rodin's Abstractions*. Five years later, in the catalogue published by Praeger for the exhibition *The Drawings of Rodin*, by Albert Elsen and Kirk Varnedoe, a few drawings of architecture from the Musée Rodin in Paris were discussed and illustrated. But loan of the original architectural drawings for exhibition was denied by the former direction of that Museum. So again it was the reproductions that Rodin approved, with four original, unpublished drawings from the Philadelphia Rodin Museum, that were shown. This account of their brief history is to affirm from the view point of the art world, that the present exhibition is indeed the true debut of Rodin's drawings of architecture.

I

Rodin had been drawing from as far back as he could remember until drawing became his means for responding to all that interested him in nature, in life, and in art. In this sense drawing was his first language, it was also his way of studying. What seems not to have been noticed is that the art to which he first responded was the subject matter of these drawings. It was the art of *architecture*, the religious architecture of Medieval France that awakened Rodin's sense of wonder and his need to understand a particular masterpiece of that art.

This happened first at Beauvais, 79 kilometers north of Rodin's home in Paris, where for the first time he lived in the country and experienced a great cathedral, the Cathedral of Saint Pierre (Fig. 3) where the neighboring oak forest of Compiegne is recreated in stone. In Paris, before coming to Beauvais, he had certainly visited the Cathedral of Notre Dame with his devout parents and sister, but he only experienced that Cathedral later, for when questioned concerning his childhood remembrance of Notre Dame, he answered, "I remarked its great size and that was all."[4]

It was at Beauvais from age nine and a half through thirteen, while attending his uncle's school that the pain of homesickness, endured for three years, sharpened his perceptions of the forest, of the Cathedral, and of the kinship between them. There it was natural, as later he often remarked, to be reminded of the forest in the Cathedral and the Cathedral in the forest (Fig. 4).[5]

From a certain distance, the whole south facade of the Cathedral at Beauvais appears corrugated like the bark of an old oak tree. The vertical ridges and grooves that mount from the foundations to the top of the towers, increase the momentum and unity of this Cathedral that might have been planned and carried out by a single generation, so consistent it is, rather than by several generations. This is partly the effect of the empty, scooped-out niches (Fig. 5), empty since the Revolution of 1793, of the myriad figures whose presence could only have weighed the building down and impeded the ascent of the whole.

Impressions of this facade entered Rodin's visual memory in boyhood and were deepened as he returned to study at Beauvais in manhood. He first returned in the fall of 1877, and following that, year after year. How do we know the continued importance of this Cathedral for Rodin although architecturally it is far from the one he most admired? We know because the style he named "sixteenth-century Gothic," was more his own, though less admired than earlier Gothic, and because more than at any other to which we followed him, resemblances exist between the Cathedral at Beauvais and the longest and most ambitious of his works of sculpture.

1 Portal of Notre Dame Church in Tonnerre

2 Auguste Rodin, *Church Portal in Tonnerre*

 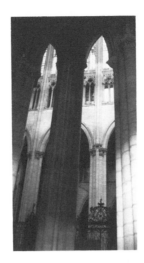  

3–6 St. Pierre
Cathedral in
Beauvais

3 South facade
4 The stone forest
5 Empty niches
6 Stone branches,
leaves and acorns

For the same reason we believe Rodin as a boy observed the oak leaves, twigs, and acorns that are carved in the grooves between the prismatic moldings of the Cathedral portal and made them his own by drawing them (Fig. 6). This we believe, not because such a drawing exists from his early years at Beauvais, but because such a written note exists: "The rib or vein that holds this leaf as it climbs vigorously, is the sap that transmits life. It boils, it does violence to the leaf that is molded beneath its effort. Who made this masterpiece? An anonymous Gothic artist formed those beautiful openings, those cast or projected shadows! Does anyone understand how much grandeur there is in the lumps and holes by which the simple portrait of a plant is made? There is indeed so much grandeur that these holes and lumps are on a par with the highest thoughts. In other words, Nature is there in her fullness, sensitive nature, outcome of all the forces that work in secret."[6] Of this quotation we notice first that it is not the thought of a boy or a young man, it belongs with the meditations of Rodin's later years. Yet it reflects the earliest observation of his boyhood: of the forest in the cathedral, and the cathedral in the forest, or Nature as the source of art. If this later quotation says more, that is because it followed a lifetime of belief in Nature and practice in studying her laws.

Not that the particular landscape loved by Corot, or the transcendant grandeur of the Cathedral whose columns and arches Rodin saw "moving in chorus toward the choir," could cure his homesickness. They could, however, nourish his need for beauty, increase his sense of depth, and initiate his taste for mists, for northern forests and "deep Gothic shadows."

Nothing appears to have been lost of Rodin's life at Beauvais, as forty years after his sojourn there we hear, in a few words he exchanged with the poet Anna de Noailles, the heritage of wisdom that survived his early sorrow: "'You will soon be back in Meudon Monsieur Rodin?' 'No, because for a while I'm going to watch the mist.' I spoke with him of sorrow. The story of Nelly who leaves the little one. 'For me,' he said, 'sorrow adds modeling to the world.'"[7] The outcome of his experience at Beauvais is also heard in his frequent remark: "A superior beauty resides in the effects of depth."

II

In his thirteenth year, when Rodin was allowed to return to Paris, he probably banished from conscious thought all memory of Beauvais. Entering the Special Free School for Drawing and Mathematics, a short walk from his home on the rue Fosées St. Jacques, in the year 1854, meant that he missed by four years the course entitled *Historical Styles in Ornament* taught by the already renowned architect-restorer Eugène Viollet-le-Duc. Viollet had been teaching there for sixteen years, until 1850, when chosen to assist the architect Jean-Baptist Lassus in restoring the Cathedral of Notre Dame. Following Lassus's sudden death in 1857, Viollet-le-Duc completed that work alone.

Because he needed hundreds of just such workmen as were being trained at the school where he had taught, his influence must still have been felt there. Yet Rodin never expressed a word of regret for having lost the opportunity of Viollet-le-Duc's classes in which he would at least have heard Medieval French architecture described and celebrated.

Rodin chose the freehand drawing course where his teacher, Horace Lecoq de Boisbaudran, never spoke of the leading art of France. Philosophically Lecoq taught Nature as the source of art. Of the truth of this teaching Rodin had been convinced by instinct and experience at Beauvais. Lecoq was the author of three manuals for art teachers where his principles are written. He said that observation of nature is the only way to true originality, and that each student's sensibility is his genius, which must always be protected. His lessons in line drawing followed the standard for all primary art schools of his day, only he administrated them with more compassion than others. For example, he suggested first studying shapes and distances by a line of light touches in order, second, to be able to set down a clear, uninterrupted statement at a single stroke. One sees right away how this practice would serve the development of Rodin's later life-drawings.[8]

Kirk Varnedoe has shown that Rodin used Lecoq's preliminary strategy to explore a three-quarter profile of Victor Hugo's skull in one of his drypoint etchings made in 1884.[9] Our Fig. 9 shows a different use of the same tool in a later work where it served the less usual purpose of verifying the wavelike forms of an architectural fragment. In this drawing Rodin has made many vertical lines to depict the forms of an upright molding revealed by light and shade as he must have seen it out-of-doors on a bright day. Next he studied the same subject laterally, as by a single tortuous, horizontal line of small touches (Fig. 8) laid on top of his myriad, vertical lines he demonstrated what he could not actually see, but understood as a cross-section of those vertically flowing forms. This second, lateral study tells what a blind person might "see" by running a hand crosswise over the rise and fall of such a molding. Rodin's purpose was

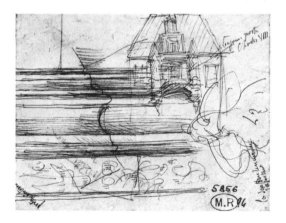

7 Auguste Rodin, *Moldings and Door in Charles VIII Style*

8 Auguste Rodin, architectural drawing. The dashed line which Lecoq de Boisbaudran taught in his drawing course can be seen here

9 Auguste Rodin,
architectural draw-
ing

10 Auguste Rodin,
architectural draw-
ing

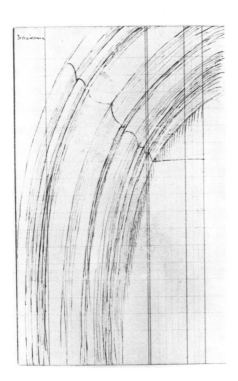 

obviously to verify his first statement by altering the direction for his second, as one may check an addition by subtraction.[10]

From this sort of humble yet passionate study, made for the sole purpose of understanding, and which Rodin devoted to countless Gothic and Rennaissance doorways or window frames, there resulted many serenely beautiful drawings. These drawings frequently transcend Rodin's purpose in making them by suggesting other subjects than were intended, especially where he has drawn several moldings on a single page (Fig. 7). They may be enjoyed for themselves, for the subjects they suggest, and to illustrate Rodin's personal use of Lecoq's first drawing lessons, or to contrast with his later life-drawings that were made around the same time.

Certain drawings of moldings are unique among all Rodin's drawings of whatever subject by being conceived and rendered solely by their shadows. They are line drawings only to the extent that Rodin has drawn the shapes and the intensity of the shadows that the moldings project by the finest of parallel lines (Fig. 8.) The lines begin and end with the shadows, they have no arbitrary boundaries. All other drawings by Rodin are without exception outlined, including those whose outlines have disappeared through being deliberately rubbed (Fig. 10), covered by cross hatching, or dark gouache paint (Figs. 12, 13).

These particular drawings of moldings are more numerous in Rodin's book than drawings of any other subject and are shown there last. So are they written about last in the text of that book. By placing these drawings last, Rodin seems to say "here is the culmination of my special study," as if we were expected to see in these drawings Rodin's understanding of the art of the Gothic masters summarized.[11] We have described them out of sequence to show that none of Lecoq's teaching was lost, even his simple, precautionary line of light touches, offered to his first-year students, was remembered and used by Rodin after fifty years (Fig. 8).

While at Drawing School Rodin's attraction for the old architecture of France must have been willfully forgotten, and not only because of his teacher's disinterest. He told Judith Cladel: "In my youth I believed like the others that Gothic art was bad."[12] "The others" were his class-

mates who laughed at Gothic works that later Rodin most admired. Presumably those young students of "artistic anatomy" ridiculed the column figures, not the architecture, to which their attention was not directed. At Beauvais, except on the double oaken doors of the south portal, no human figures are visible from ground level. There it was indeed the architecture that had awakened Rodin's wonder and admiration.[13]

Only several years after drawing school, while working as an art-mason for a sculptor named Bièze, one among many who were engaged under Viollet-le-Duc in "restoring" Notre Dame Cathedral, only then, Rodin said he was able to rid himself of the influence of his school environment and see the beauty of Gothic Art with his own eyes.[14]

It is not known how long Rodin worked for Bièze or what work he did, but it was long enough and near enough to Notre Dame for him to experience that Cathedral as six or seven years earlier he had experienced the Cathedral at Beauvais. It was long enough also for him to turn against all restoring and restorers, especially against Viollet-le-Duc, for the rest of his life. Then as he acquired more assurance, but only at about the age of twenty-five, he said he began his "special study of Gothic Art," meaning these drawings we are thinking about and to which, gradually, the written notes that became the text of his book, were added.

III

No one's neglect can be blamed for the general unawareness of Rodin's drawings of architecture before 1914. His friends knew of his study trips because he never resisted speaking of their objectives, the old monuments which alone could account for his periodic absence from his studio. They knew drawing was his way of studying and therefore that many drawings of architecture must exist. But not even Antoine Bourdelle, the younger sculptor who had carved for Rodin since 1893, who shared his taste for the old works and with whom, in 1905, Rodin exchanged written notes, had seen his drawings of architecture.[15] This was not because Rodin wanted to hide them, they were simply not what mattered. Five years later he withheld his signature from the one hundred drawings of architecture that he lent to the firm of Armand Colin for publication in his book, while he placed his initials on each one of the reproductions that he approved. Those initialed reproductions are now at the Rodin Museum in Philadelphia.

Rodin had a particular reason for thinking of the sketches that were his means for studying architecture as *notes*. This may also explain why few or none of the earliest have survived. His evaluation should be remembered because anyone coming to these almost unknown studies after admiring his imaginative, dark gouache drawings or his later life-drawings, and expecting to find a similar subjective interest, is sure to be disappointed. His intention in making his drawings of architecture was so different that comparison with his later life-drawings would be senseless, were it not that to say his drawings of the living model supremely are, is to say what these drawings of buildings cannot be, and *why*.

So we evoke the vibrant response to life of his later life-drawings believing them his most lyrical expression; believing it was life in the sculptor responding to life in his model that made the magic of the later life-drawings. Magic of that kind was just what Rodin would not consciously express in his drawings of architecture. No one was more responsive than he to the different magic in the cathedrals and no one rejoiced as he did in those triumphs of human genius, but here, in his drawings of architecture, he was determined to suppress his imagination, his intuition, and every faculty of consciousness except observation, first in order not to veil his perception of what was before him, and second, not to betray one of his principles: that in art each work is unique and restorations prove it. "All restorations are copies, this is why

14 Notre Dame in Mantes

15 Auguste Rodin, *Church Facade in Mantes* (Notre Dame, main and right side portals)

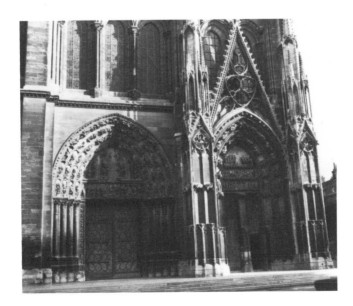

they are condemned in advance, for one must not copy with a passion for fidelity anything other than nature herself; the copying of works of art is forbidden by the very principle of art."[16]

Rodin studied Gothic masterpieces in which such a "magic conjuration," as he said he often experienced in copying all the profiles of his model for a portrait bust, had been accomplished, but accomplished centuries ago, and could never be repeated. Therefore in drawing ancient monuments, Rodin strove to understand and to admire ever more fully, but never to duplicate or to make works of his own that might look in the least as if they could be from "the Antique" or the Middle Ages.

It follows that Rodin refused to be "creative" in these studies. He would not dramatize Gothic forms by attempting to increase the deep Gothic shadows that he admired, or to dissolve them in light. Also he was mindful, in making these drawings, of his safeguard: to consider and to analyze the old monuments from the viewpoint of their execution, in order not to be borne away by the feelings they inspire.

Except those that represent moldings, which are exceptions in being expressed solely by shadow, there are few shadows in Rodin's drawings of architecture in the Paris or the Philadelphia Rodin Museums where the two largest collections are found. Yet his will to understand deep, Gothic shadows and the more shallow golden shadows of the "Second Renaissance" and to apply that understanding to his own works was one of the major purposes of his study of architecture. Another equally important purpose and need was to understand the Gothic masters' balance of masses, to learn how their greater and lesser forms are held in harmonious equilibrium. These two concerns are one insofar as it is by the oblique planes of the bell-shaped voussoirs and porches that the beautiful masses of shadow and of light are directed (Figs. 14, 15).

Rodin knew that true shadows in architecture as in sculpture are born of forms knowingly controlled for their sakes, whether the small forms of a portrait bust or the vast forms of a cathedral. He knew that the Gothic masters' science of form, learned from their study of Nature, was the heart of the matter he needed to understand. Therefore he was content simply to write on many of his line drawings where no shadows appear: "noir," "plus noir," or "blond," words which we know refer to the shadows he was studying but would not stop to draw (Fig. 17).

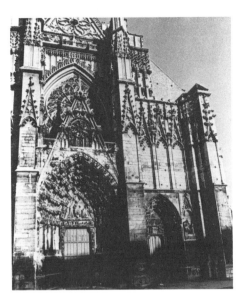 

We have seen shadows in some, but not in all the illustrations that Rodin was prevailed upon, sometime after 1910, to have published in his book: *Les Cathédrales de France*.[17] For example, Figs. 11–13 show the porch of the south portal at the Abbey Church of Saint Pierre at Auxerre, whose shadows Rodin has expressed in dark gouache, while to the Cathedral of Saint Etienne, also in Auxerre, he has added light brown, transparent watercolor for the same purpose (Figs. 18, 19). These are also Rodin's studies. For us, however, they are less interesting than the line drawings from which we learn not only what he admired, but the progressive steps of his study, and often what he was seeking as well as what he found, because of the written notes that he added simultaneously.

Some line drawings that became illustrations are just as Rodin made them for himself, without thought of publication. One such is Fig. 21, Planche LXXV in his book. This drawing shows one of the flying buttresses that brace the wall between two apse windows at the back of the church at Caen (Fig. 20) which Rodin knew as "le vieux Saint-Etienne." What most in- terested him in this subject, this flying buttress whose pinnacle is like a small rectangular temple with a projecting roof, with slender inset columns at the corners and François Premier

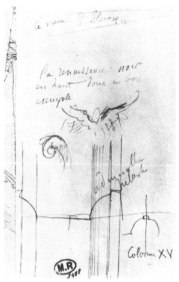

22 Renaissance pilaster, St. Etienne Church in Caen

23 Auguste Rodin, architectural drawing: *"Le vieux St. Etienne"*. The angel's head and other ornamental details are clearly visible on the right capital and the pilaster

decorations, diamonds and circles, on the side walls, was the dark stroke under the roof: "noir en haut," and the sharp line of shadow behind the right small inset column. Both of these, the roof and the column, Rodin emphasized in ink.

While making this drawing, he evidently noticed the "admirable Renaissance pilastre" or rather the two pilasters with a round column between them that support the flying buttress and form the angle of the wall at roof level of one of the chapels (Fig. 22). So he made a second, this time unpublished pencil drawing on another page in order to study the separate parts of the pilasters, in whose capitals are angels' heads with wings, one which he drew separately (Fig. 23). The round column between the pilasters has a dome-shaped head; this Rodin also drew separately, judging it to be from the fifteenth century. So we learn of other thoughts and stages of study that were no doubt written on these drawings but which have been eliminated from the illustrations, to our loss. In writing on this unpublished sketch "noir en hout, doux en bas," Rodin was repeating what he had found to be true of thirteenth- to sixteenth-century Gothic forms generally, and in writing "example" he was saying: "here again is the principle of gothic opposition and contrast that I admire." The models for both of these drawings made at Caen, are at an elevation of about 24 feet, thus they also tell something of the degree to which Rodin's myopia was corrected by study.

IV

At this point we would like to be able to say which drawings of architecture were made earlier than the others. But this will be possible only if we find a different principle for measuring than has been valid for the chronology of Rodin's other drawings. No chronological perspective has been proposed for these drawings, partly because with one exception, Rodin developed no distinctive and consistent technique for making them. The single exception is of course his series of drawings of moldings that are drawn by their shadows alone and have no arbitrary outlines.

Rodin was already in possession of his repertory of drawing techniques by the mid-1860s when he began his special study of architecture. If we consider his pencilled outline minus shadows, over which he spread a wash of transparent watercolor, as one of his techniques, then his drawing of the Church of Notre Dame at Tonnerre (Fig. 2) may be judged contemporary with the last of his later life-drawings, known as "les aquarelles." Which leaves their great differences, due to Rodin's attitude toward their subjects, intact.

All the techniques described in Varnedoe's *Chronological Perspective* appear also among Rodin's drawings of architecture but they appear irregularly, meaning such a drawing as for example the south portal to the Abbey Church of Saint Pierre at Auxerre (Fig. 13) was not surely made in the 1880s or '90s, at the time of his imaginative drawings because of the dark gouache. Nor was his drawing of an unidentified niche for sculpture, from the Mastbaum Collection of the Philadelphia Rodin Museum, surely from the 1900s because the pencilled lines are rubbed like some of the later life-drawings (Fig. 10).

We see Rodin's drawing techniques used in making his drawings of architecture as tools which once mastered may be laid down and taken up again, not consistently within a certain fixed period of time, but at *any* time, depending upon his state of mind and the subject he wished to record. This is why his architectural drawings have not yet been arranged chronologically according to technique.

We can say of his two drawings made of "le vieux Saint-Etienne" at Caen (Figs. 21 and 23) that they are *not* among his earliest, not from the mid-1860s when he had only limited time for his study trips because Caen in Normandy is too far from Paris to be visited on a Sunday afternoon. For a proper chronology we would need to find not only the names of the places that Rodin visited, of which we do know more than one hundred cities and towns whose names he did sometimes write on the drawings themselves, and also the names of the particular buildings that he drew, usually several at each place, whose names he rarely wrote, as well as the dates of his visits, which with the exception of a notebook filled at Melun, he *never* wrote. At times the subject of one of his drawings is easily recognized from the drawing itself. More frequently he studied fragments rather than whole buildings, as inside Saint Martin's Church at Champeaux (Figs. 24, 25) or above the altar in the Church of Saint Jacques and Saint Christophe at Houdan (Figs. 16, 17).

In his drawings of fragments, whether of moldings, cornices, or window frames, Rodin could always recognize or remember by their character the whole works from which he had drawn them. However we could not. So, in following him we simply photographed all that we had

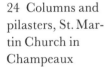

24 Columns and pilasters, St. Martin Church in Champeaux

25 Auguste Rodin, *Columns of the Church in Champeaux*

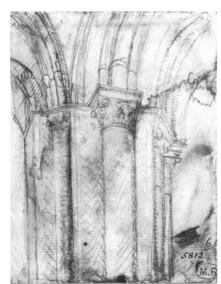

26 Buttresses and capitals of Palace Chapel in Ussé

27 Auguste Rodin, *Ussé*

learned of his taste, all therefore that he might have liked, at each one of the places where we knew he had studied, and later, when we were lucky, we found drawings to match our photographs.

Rodin's drawings made at places too far to visit on a Sunday afternoon, as far from Paris as Ussé (Figs. 26, 27), and Auxerre (Figs. 28, 29) were surely made as late or later than 1875. That year, in which because of his letter to Rose written on his way to Italy, we know he visited Reims Cathedral for the first time. Nor can it be said that his drawings of such nearby buildings as the Church of Notre Dame at Mantes, (Figs. 14, 15) of Saint Jacques and Saint Christophe at Houdan, (Figs. 30, 31) or Saint Pierre Church at Montfort Lamaury (Figs. 32, 33) are surely among the early ones. We know Rodin continued to visit those nearby churches frequently, probably each year, and nothing in his manner of drawing them tells which drawings were earlier or later.

So, while we can read in his drawings and written notes of architecture his wish to understand the Gothic artists' expression of depth by their oblique planes that control the light of day and of the two twilights, we cannot always tell when he made this or that drawing.

28 Portal to courtyard of St. Pierre Abbey and Church in Auxerre

29 Auguste Rodin, *Portal of St. Pierre Abbey in Auxerre*

30 Facade of
St. Jacques and
St. Christophe
Church in Houdan

31 Auguste Rodin,
*Facade of the
St. Jacques et
St. Christophe Church
in Houdan*

If for him his graphic studies of architecture were only copies, and if all copies except of nature "are forbidden by the very principle of art," it is understandable that he took less care of these drawings of architecture and expected less attention for them than for his drawings made from life. It is therefore reasonable that some of the earlier ones have been lost.

We have said that Rodin's own evaluation of his architectural drawings should be remembered, not that we should accept it, but that it may be taken into account while seeing them all as he recommended, "with one's own eyes." For us his 338 small notebook pages, plus four drawings of larger size and four original illustrations at the Philadelphia Rodin Museum, as well as his more than 800 drawings on loose leaves of various sizes at the Paris Rodin Museum, are *not copies*. For how can any two-dimensional drawings of three-dimensional works aspire to be copies in the literal sense of replicas? We know and agree with Rodin's thoughts about such literal copies as modern stone carvings made to replace lost Gothic statuary. But his ban on copying really included all copies not made from nature or life; he refused the status of art to copies of man-made objects of every kind, including his own.

For us Rodin's drawings of buildings and any parts thereof, are more than copies; they are at

32 Buttresses and
waterspouts,
St. Pierre Church,
Montfort Lamaury

33 Auguste Rodin,
Buttresses of a Church

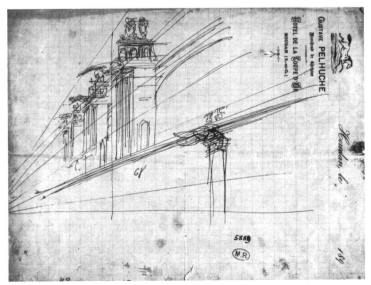

least translations, and at most new two-dimensional works which we are free to see as works of art according to the way they affect us. Although for him they may have been merely transitive means for understanding, merely documents or records and not works of art in themselves, they allowed him to analyze and so in a way to participate in the art that he admired. We revere these least assuming of Rodin's works, of which he never spoke, although he spoke endlessly of their subjects, and which he never signed, sold, or gave away. We revere them because he said they accompanied his happiest hours: "These moments of study, when I immerse myself in nature and the works of great centuries, when I try to bring what I learn into my own works, are my moments of perfect joy. I am the ever more docile pupil of the masters of those epochs."[18]

Notes

1 "C'est peu à peu que je suis venu à nos vieilles Cathédrales, que j'ai pu pénétrer le secret de leur vie sans cesse renouvelée sous le ciel changeant." *Les Cathédrales de France*, Armand Colin, Paris, 1914, pp. 16–17.

2 In the three-page announcement that was sent before publication of Rodin's book.

3 Republication of the original edition was discouraged by loss of the expensive plates for the drawings. The drawings themselves were returned to Rodin in 1914 when he had approved of their reproductions.

In 1921 the identical text of the 1914 edition was published without illustrations by the same publisher in a small book of 225 pages plus a four-page introduction by Léonce Bénédite, first director of the Musée Rodin. This unillustrated edition was kept in print until the mid-1950s. The original French of our quotations from Rodin's book are given in these notes from that small-size 1921 edition.

We know of two German-language editions of Rodin's book, one published by Kurt Wolf Verlag, Leipzig, undated, no translator named, in which 32 drawings by Rodin are reproduced in pen and sepia ink. The other published by F. Bruckmann K.G., Munich, 1964, translated by Max Brod, with five drawings by Rodin reproduced in black and white and with 32 photographs of French cathedrals.

4 Auguste Rodin, *Gothic in the Churches and Cathedrals of France*, an essay by Rodin published in *The North American Review*, Feb. 1905, p. 220. This was taken down by a French stenographer as Rodin spoke and was translated by Frederick Lawton. The original French has not been found.

5 "Autant que les vieilles pierres dont l'amoncellement constitue les Cathédrales, j'aime les arbres puissantes, entre celles-ci et ceux-là je perçois une parenté." *Les Cathédrales de France, op. cit.*, p. 45. There are many other such comparisons between the forests and the cathedrals in Rodin's book, and not there only. In his *North American Review* article, on page 227 we read, "You enter a Cathedral, you find it full of the mysterious life of the forest; the reason is that it reproduces that life by artistic compression, the rock, the tree, Nature is there; an epitome of Nature."

With Louis Gillet, a writer of l'Academie Française, Rodin spoke of the country surrounding Beauvais, of the neighboring forest, of what these and the Cathedral of that city meant to him in his boyhood. Their conversations must have taken place before May, 1910, before Rodin and Charles Morice signed the contract with Armand Colin, because Rodin had suggested that Louis Gillet might edit his book. This was reported by Gillet in a clipping at the Paris Library of Art and Archaeology, Fond Doucet.

6 "Cette nervure qui tend cette feuille en rampant vigoureusement, c'est la sève qui porte la vie. Elle bouillonne, elle violente la feuille qui se modèle sous l'effort. Qui a fait ce chef d'œuvre? Un Gothique sans nom. Ces ombres portées ou projétées! Comprend-on qu'il y ait tant de grandeur dans les bosses et les trous au moyen desquels on a fait le simple portrait d'une plante? Et il y a, en effet, tant de grandeur qu'avec ces trous et ce bosses le plus hautes pensées vont de pair. C'est que la Nature est là, dans sa plénitude, la Nature sensible, l'effet de toutes les forces qui travaillent en secret." *Les Cathédrales de France, op. cit.*, p. 69.

7 "'Vous serez vite rentré à Meudon, Monsieur Rodin?' 'Non, parceque je vais un peu regarder le brouillard.' Je lui parle de la douleur. L'histoire de Nelly qui quitte le petit – il dit: 'Moi, la douleur, celà met du modelé sur le monde.'" Maurice Barres, *Mes Cahiers*, Tome Quatrième, 1904–1906, Madame de Noailles et Rodin, p. 127.

8 Rodin remained grateful for Lecoq's teaching of nature as the source of art, and for his training of the visual memory which Lecoq considered his pioneer achievement, although Viollet-le-Duc said the Greeks had both practiced and taught that discipline. Study of Lecoq's third manual: *Letters to a Young Professor*, Vve. A Morel et Cie, Paris 1876, shows that when it came to drawing figures from life, Lecoq believed in neo-classical idealization of nature as much as any good academician, which of course Rodin would never admit. With that exception all Lecoq's teaching was justified and surpassed in Rodin's achievement long after he left drawing school. At school Lecoq discovered Rodin's near-sightedness but not his genius.

9 Albert E. Elsen and J. Kirk T. Varnedoe, *The Drawings of Rodin*, New York, Praeger, 1971, p. 63, Fig. 47.

10 In our photographs the line of light touches appears to merge, but in the drawings they are clearly separated.

11 As on the last page of his book Rodin has written that moldings depict the essence of the master-builder's spirit and thought: "La moulure, dans son esprit, dans son essence, représente, signifie toute la pensée de maître d'œuvre."

12 Judith Cladel, *Rodin, Sa vie glorieuse, sa vie inconnue*, definitive edition, Paris, Grasset, 1950.

13 Rodin's *North American Review* article, *op. cit.*, p. 220.

14 "Only when I was in full possession of myself at the age of about twenty-five did I begin to make a special study of Gothic Art, which was generally decried. To some extent indeed before I was twenty my eyes had been opened while I was working for a sculptor named Bièze who had a lot to do with the 'restoring' of Notre Dame." *Ibid.*, p. 227.

15 Antoine Bourdelle, *La Sculpture et Rodin*, Paris, Emile-Paul, 1937, pp. 201–207.

16 "Toutes les restorations sont des copies, c'est pourquoi elles sont d'avance condamneés, car il ne faut copier, laissez-moi le répéter, avec la passion de la fidélité, que la nature: la copie des œuvres d'art est interdite par le principe même de l'art." *Les Cathédrales de France, op. cit.*, p. 131.

17 *Les Cathédrales de France, op. cit.*, 1914 edition.

18 "Ce sont pour moi des moments d'étude d'une joie parfaite; je m'imprègne de tout, nature et œuvres des grands siècles et j'essaye de le transporter dans mes œuvres à moi, qui suis l'élève toujours plus docile des maîtres de ces époques." Judith Cladel, *Revue Hebdomadaire Rodin et l'Art Gothique*, November 7, 1908, p. 92.

79* *Church Portal in Nantes; D.5764*

80* *Church Facade in Mantes; D.5806*

81* *Facade of the St. Jacques et St. Christophe Church in Houdan; D. 5828*

82 *Facade of the St. Jacques et St. Christophe Church in Houdan; D.5778*

83* *Moldings and Door in Charles VIII Style; D.5856*

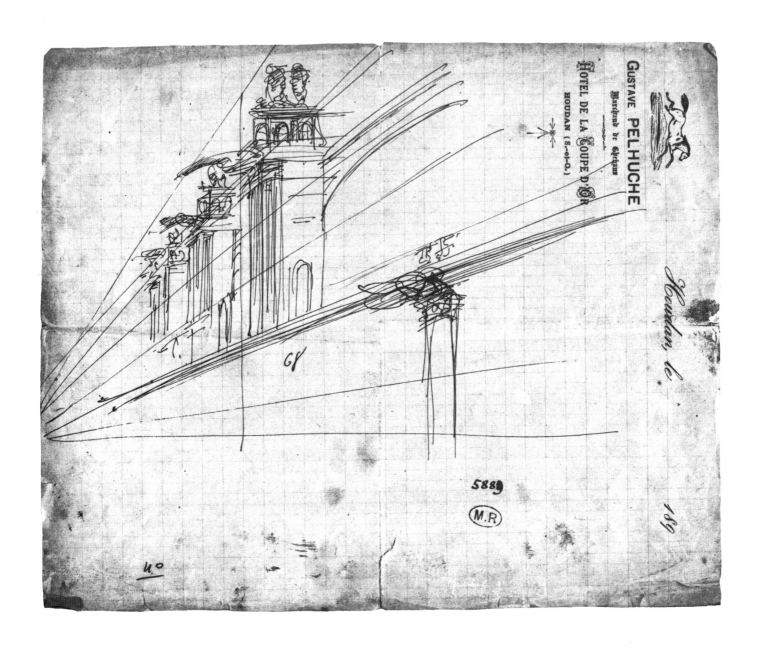

84 *Buttresses of a Church; D.5889*

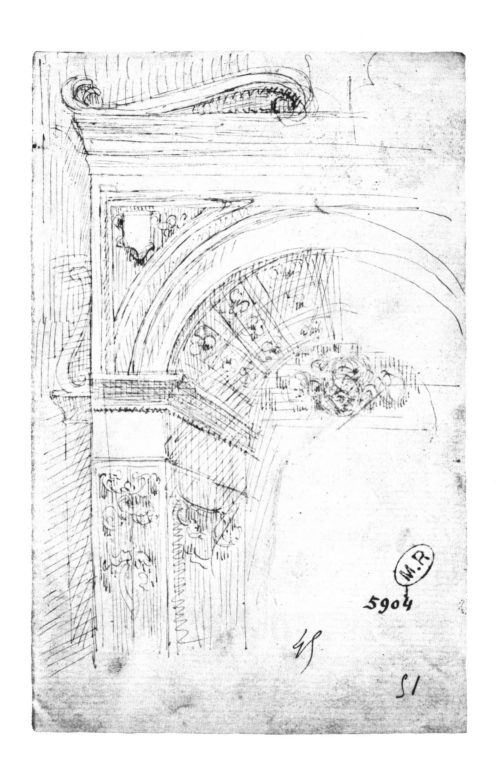

85* *Vestibule in Toulouse; D.5904*

86* *Church Portal in Tonnerre; D.5942*

87* *Portal in Toulouse; D.5902*

88* *Facade in Toulouse (?); D.5920*

89* *Facade with Portal in Auxerre; D.5916, 5918*

90 *Portal of St. Pierre Abbey in Auxerre; D.5925*

91* *Two Studies of Niche for Henley Bust; D.5877*

92 *Sculpture before a Portal; D.5921*

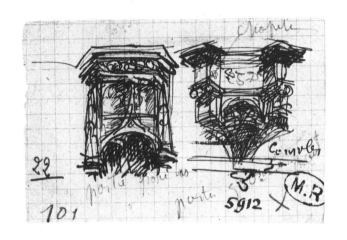

94* *Corbel in Quimperlé (?); D.5879*

27

60

5884

95* *Renaissance Cornice; D.5884*

96 *Cornice in Chambord (?); D.5887*

97* *Columns of the Church in Champeaux; D.5812*

167
          98 *Ussé; D.5818*

The Transition Period

Auguste Rodin, about 1895

RODIN'S DRAWINGS OF THE NINETIES
THE TRANSITION PERIOD

Ernst-Gerhard Güse

The 1890s involved Rodin particularly in work on important commissions which took a great deal of his time and energy. Indeed his projects for monumental sculptures during this decade might even be called the culmination of his life's work. There was his *Balzac* monument, which placed demands on him for years, indeed almost the entire decade, and which intensely concerned him. Almost equal claims on Rodin's time and energy were made by the casting of his *Burghers of Calais* and its erection, which touched off heated controversy. He was also involved in creating a monument for the Argentine president, Domingo Faustino Sarmiento. In all of these projects Rodin was hindered by poor health—he suffered from depression and his capacity to work began to falter. In 1898, finally, his long and troubled, even tormenting relationship to Camille Claudel came to an end.

All in all, the claims made on his time by personal affairs, and especially by his work as a sculptor, apparently prevented Rodin from doing much drawing during these years. As Haavard Rostrup has written, in an essay of 1938 which has proved so significant in defining Rodin's periods and a preliminary order for his drawings, "From about 1890 Rodin was occupied so deeply by his many and gigantic sculptural works that he had no time to devote himself as before to drawing."[1] For Rostrup, the dark, dramatic gouaches of the 1870s and 1880s, the "Période dantesque," as its link with Dante's *Divine Comedy* led him to term it, seemed a thing apart from the brilliant freedom of the *Cambodian Dancers*, that group of drawings done in 1906 which, in Rostrup's eyes, marked the beginning of the second significant period in Rodin's drawing style. "These drawings of male and especially female dancers from Cambodia," he remarked, "were to introduce a second great culmination in Rodin's draftsmanship, a period which—in contrast to the gouache-drawings of about 1880—can be termed a period of drawings with watercolor."[2] In the decade between these two great complexes, however, Rodin the draftsman simply ceased to exist for Rostrup.

It was Kirk Varnedoe who contradicted the notion that the 1880s drawings and those which can be dated around 1900 were unrelated, and who isolated a group of drawings which can be seen as a link between the two great periods.[3] These drawings, which Varnedoe dated from about 1891 to 1896, both contain elements of the immediately preceding period and anticipate certain features of the later contour drawings with watercolor wash. The question of the beginning of Rodin's late style, and with it the end of the transition period, is treated in detail here by J. A. Schmoll gen. Eisenwerth, in his essay "Rodin's Late Drawings and Watercolors" (p. 211 ff.).

For the period in question, and indeed for the corpus of Rodin's drawings as a whole, hardly any dated works exist which would ease orientation and help us determine the chronology of his drawings with any accuracy. An exception are the illustrations to Baudelaire's *Les Fleurs du Mal*, which the publisher Paul Gallimard commissioned from Rodin in 1887. From then until 1888, Rodin executed twenty-five illustrations, six of them graphic translations of his sculptures. In stylistic terms these illustrations, done just before the onset of the 1890s, are closely related to Rodin's etchings. Varnedoe points especially to their link with his *Portrait of Henri Becque* of 1885 (Fig. 1) and to their looser style of hatching.[4] Among the Baudelaire illustrations

are several which no longer evince the strict crosshatching used to model musculature which still characterized the pen-and-ink drawings after sculptures done just a few years before (Figs. 2, 3). These illustrations continue the development seen in the *Henri Becque* etching—a flowing hatching suggestive of atmosphere and descriptive of an actual situation. Particularly *Le Guignon* and *La Beauté* (Figs. 5, 6) show increasingly autonomous networks of hatching which integrate the surrounding space in the design. The chiaroscuro of these drawings relates them to the gouaches of the Dante period; the treatment and dark color scheme of *De profundis clamavi* (Fig. 7) comes particularly close to the "painterly" character of the 1880s gouaches.

This series of designs for *Les Fleurs du Mal* includes pure contour drawings as well, such as the frontispiece (Fig. 4), a drawing that was both anticipated by such gouaches as *Group of Figures (Le Temps)* (Fig. 9) and that itself points forward to the drawings of the 1890s. Rodin's illustration to *La Mort des Pauvres* (Fig. 8) also deserves mention here, a sheet about whose content Rilke remarked, "The pen-and-ink drawing accompanying the poem 'La Mort des Pauvres' reaches beyond these great verses with a gesture of such simple, continually growing grandeur that one feels it contains the world from beginning to end."[5]

The Baudelaire illustrations introduced a period in which new accents began to determine Rodin's drawing style. Over the following years he gradually abandoned the drama and fantasy of the Dante gouaches to develop the lyrical, light-infused style of his late period. Approaches existing side by side in the *Les Fleurs du Mal* illustrations are even more clearly evident in drawings done subsequently. These justify discussing the first half of the 1890s separately as a phase of transition.

Among them are such sheets as D. 4349 and D. 4363 (plates on pp. 194, 195), studies of dancing girls that are not only stylistically closely related but whose sequential movement suggests

2, 3 *John the Baptist,*
1880

a single figure seen once *en face* and again in profile. Yet dance has been captured in these drawings not only as a certain sequence of movement; the obvious rapidity with which they were rendered contributes greatly to the effect of whirling motion. The outlines of the body are given by a brief contour and the extremities are merely suggested. But it is above all the motor activity of the artist's hand that finds expression in the interwoven hatching, giving an impression of hectic movement that robs the figures of all solidity and statuesqueness. Both drawings are the result of a number of superimposed, interwoven, correcting and improving phases of work that are difficult to disentangle. In the case of D.4349, Rodin first applied a light-grey ground, followed by a contour drawing rich in *pentimenti*, which together with linear suggestions of gown and hair gives rise to a chaos of line which obscures the structure of the body and prevents it from taking on corporeality. The hatching around the figure serves to clarify it and, like the dark-grey passages in the figure, to emphasize its lineaments and separate it from the ground. In a later phase of work, Rodin roughly retraced and simplified the curve of the head with a broad brushed line, and applied broad strokes over the torso and legs that have no direct relation to the organic facts. While the pen-and-ink drawings done after sculptures in the 1880s evince carefully modulated hatching that lends the figures volume, the hatching in D.4349 and D.4363, part of a system of correcting and superimposed line, seems to disembody the figures and actually to flatten them on the plane. This type of hatching has an autonomous graphic value, independent of descriptive anatomy.

In these two drawings, Rodin concentrated less on plasticity and voluminosity than on the phenomenon of movement, which indeed fascinated him throughout his life's work. "Depiction of absolute calm is very rare with me," he once said in conversation with Paul Gsell. "I have always tried to express the life of the soul through the mobility of the muscles... The illusion of life, in my art, is achieved through good modelling and movement. These two

4 Frontispiece to Charles Baudelaire, *Les Fleurs du Mal*, 1888

5 *Le Guignon*, illustration for *Les Fleurs du Mal*

6 *La Beauté*, illustration for *Les Fleurs du Mal*

features are, so to speak, the lifeblood and breath of all good art."[6] Then Rodin added, "Every painter or sculptor who lends his figures movement... represents the transition from one pose to another, explores how one merges imperceptibly into the next. In their work you can still recognize something of what just was, and also something of what is just coming into being."[7]

The transitory moment, evoked in D.4349 particularly by the corrections of the left leg, which appear almost Futurist in approach, remained essential for Rodin in these drawings as well. Drawing D.4379 (plate 105, p.192) is also stylistically related to the drawings just mentioned. It shows two female figures in silhouette, their arms raised to their shoulders and their bodies concealed by gowns rendered in vertical strokes. The figures are linked together by a wide, flowing contour line. Only in the left figure has a suggestion of the volumes of the body and its striding motion been added later, by correcting strokes drawn over the garment.

The color scheme of the drawings named, their broad contour lines, their painterly elements, and finally the extreme intensity of their execution, relate them to the Dante period. On the other hand, some of the finest drawings of the post-1900 group are anticipated, particularly by the dance motif in D.4349 and D.4363. Within the chronology of the 1890s drawings, these certainly still retain much of the character of the gouaches, and hence may have been executed around 1890.

Another sheet that belongs in this context is D.4266 (plate 114, p.201), since it shows the same spontaneous attempt to fix a transitory movement. The contour, rich in *pentimenti* which

7 *De profundis clamavi*, illustration for *Les Fleurs du Mal*

8 *La Mort des Pauvres*, illustration for *Les Fleurs du Mal*

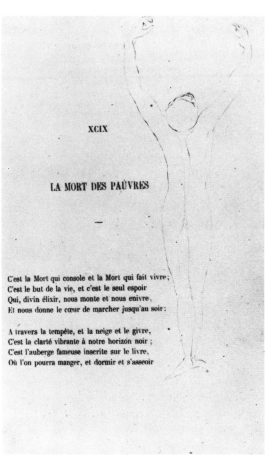

make it almost impossible to say which is the definitive outline, and the tentative, interlaced, and contradictory lines, bear no comparison to the carefully executed networks of crosshatching which characterize the renderings after sculptures Rodin did during the 1880s. Color as a means of dramatic emphasis is missing here, and indeed compared with the examples given above, the drawing does not contain all of the procedures and phases of work which were available to Rodin at this period.

Here as in the other drawings mentioned, he has done without the literary allusions characteristic of the gouaches to spontaneously sketch what by comparison are everyday unposed movements. During the 1890s, drawings inspired by literature were superseded by sketches based on direct observation. In 1902, Rilke said of Rodin the draftsman (inadvertently explaining the female figure bending to the side in this drawing): "Yet finally there emerged all those strange documents of the momentary, the imperceptibly fleeting. Rodin supposed that the insignificant movements which the model made when she thought herself unobserved, if rapidly recorded, might contain a force of expression which we cannot imagine because we are not accustomed to follow such movements with close, active attention."[8]

10 *Ames du Pur-gatoire*, frontispiece to Gustave Geffroy, *La Vie Artistique*, 1893

No linear and logical development seems to link the Dante gouaches with the late contour drawings of around 1900. Nor did any single type of drawing predominate during this period. In the transition period of the early 1890s, contour drawings of the kind found among the illustrations to *Les Fleurs du Mal* exist side by side with drawings containing elements of the gouaches. Sheets with tentative, repeatedly corrected lines alternate with drawings characterized by smooth, tranquil contour, until finally contour drawings with watercolor wash begin to predominate, which are frequently not sketches from the model but clean renderings done after such sketches. The etching *Ames du Purgatoire* (Fig. 10), published in 1893 as the frontispiece to Gustave Geffroy's *La Vie Artistique*, provides a reference point for the dating of these drawings. To cite Rilke again, whose description of the etchings applies just as well to the delicate contour drawings of the early 1890s: "And the same is true of the drypoint etchings, in which the trace of incredibly delicate lines resembles the extreme outside contour of some beautiful crystalline thing which, fixed precisely at every moment, flows over into the essence of a reality."[9] A drawing like D. 4282 (plate 103, p. 190) can be placed in temporal proximity to the thin-lined pen-and-ink drawings of slender nude figures which Rodin made during the

11 *Woman from the
Front, Putting On a
Garment*, D.4311

12 *Woman from the
Front, Putting On a
Garment*, D.4294

early 1890s. It shows a female nude bending slightly forward, holding her falling garment with both hands. Less agitated than D.4266 (plate 114, p.201), it contains few corrections, and already begins to approach that closed, thin pen-and-ink contour line seen in such sheets as D.4304 (p.188) and even more clearly in D.4283 (p.189). It would seem that direct observation provided the inspiration for this pose captured in a moment of transition, but that other drawings—possibly made from memory—followed in which the original pose was further simplified. Heads were reduced to ovals, faces to points and strokes without individual characterization, and upper and lower arms pulled together into a single flowing form regardless of anatomical description (Figs.11, 12). The subsequent watercolor wash pulls together the unclothed parts of the figure—head, torso, arms (Figs.13, 14)—and contributes to further simplification. "Average taste understands nothing about daring condensation that rapidly passes over unnecessary details, cleaving only to the truth of the overall impression. Nor does it understand anything about serious observation which despises theatrical poses and attends only to the very simple physical attitudes of real life, which appeal far more to honest feeling," remarked Rodin about his drawings to Paul Gsell.[10] Variations of this approach are found in countless drawings. By a certain point in time, Rodin had apparently made it part of his repertoire, hardly needing to rediscover it every time he faced a new model.

Looking at a drawing like D.4282 (p.190), it becomes apparent how the contouring pen-line developed, gradually tracing the figures' outlines in a single sweep, almost without interruption. The standing figure in D.4276 (p.191), gathering her dress together at her midriff, represents a further step toward that lucidity and directness of line which to Rilke seemed like "the extreme outside contour of some crystalline thing" and which Rodin brought to perfec-

13 *Woman Bent Slightly Forward, Putting On a Garment*, D.4302

14 *Woman Bent Forward, Putting On a Garment*, D.4321

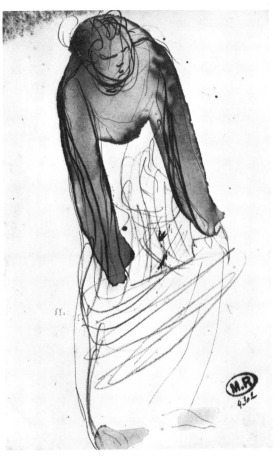

tion in drawings like D.4304 and D.4283 (pp.188 and 189). Here his various techniques —pen-and-ink, pencil, watercolor—were not used to correct first impressions but to create a compelling, harmonious whole.

Mythological themes became gradually less frequent during the course of the 1890s, as Rodin increasingly began to observe his models in such mundane activities as combing their hair or dressing. Yet even here, mythological allusion was not excluded, as can be seen from D.4283 (p.189), where the attribute of a shell characterizes the nude as an Anadyomene, an Aphrodite born of the sea-foam. Watercolor wash, employed to accentuate the figure itself in the drawings discussed above, is now used to create a contrast between the light-colored body and its immediate surroundings, the shell, and the figure's flowing hair. While D.4277 (Fig.15) appears to be a rapid sketch from the model later finished with watercolor, D.4283 represents a fair rendering and translation into mythological terms of this or some similar drawing.

Rodin's drawing procedure becomes particularly evident in such sheets as D.4275 and D.4278 (pp.202 and 203). Both pen-and-ink drawings are based on a rapid pencil sketch made directly from the model, which was then worked over in ink without slavishly adhering to the pencil lines, setting down the basic configurations in a few flowing strokes. In D.4278, not the figures are accented in color—as they were to be in drawings of the late period—but the background. Though drawn with a broader nib, the slender bodies and their simplified contour lines which take no account of anatomical details, speak for a dating in the first half of the 1890s, in temporal proximity to the other contour drawings of these years. While D.4275 obviously describes a mother-and-child situation, D.4278 represents an embracing female couple, a theme that Rodin treated repeatedly in both sculpture and drawing (Fig.18). The

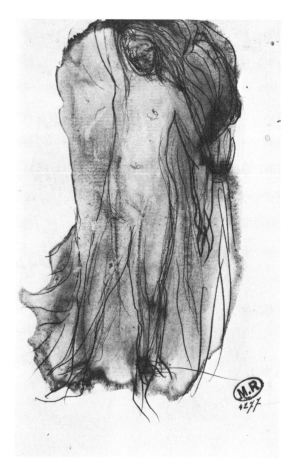

sheet bears the inscription "le crépuscule," twilight. Rodin frequently gave his depictions of nudes allegorical titles, and their inscriptions are rife with cosmic, mythological, religious, and also literary allusions.

The drawings D.4261 and D.4370 (pp. 204 and 205) each show a female figure standing erect, and before her a second nude, bent far over with her face averted from the viewer. This composition, illustrating the contrast of vertical and horizontal, can hardly have arisen by chance; it was probably consciously worked out in the sketching stage. The pure contour drawing is supplemented with watercolor, which flows beyond the contour in many places and adds a new quality to it. As here, red, yellow, orange and violet tones predominate in most of the drawings of the 1890s.

A comparatively large group of drawings are devoted to female nudes with billowing veils behind them (Figs. 15, 16), depictions in intense colors which emphasize the contrast between the light-hued body and a darker ground, and whose liveliness and movement contrast with the tranquil contour drawings Rodin made almost simultaneously. The increasing emphasis on volume in these drawings likewise anticipates later compositions, although the special significance of color in them, which instead of merely accentuating figure or garment flows across them like a concealing veil, is more reminiscent of the 1880s gouaches.

Also to the second half of the 1890s belong those watercolors based on a pencil sketch of the model in motion. These were made by setting down the contours of the figure in tentative lines without looking at the sheet, then adding watercolor to increase the effect of volume and modelling (D.4340, p.207; and Fig.17). These drawings immediately precede Rodin's late style, the onset of which can be dated about 1897. The inception of comparable drawings has

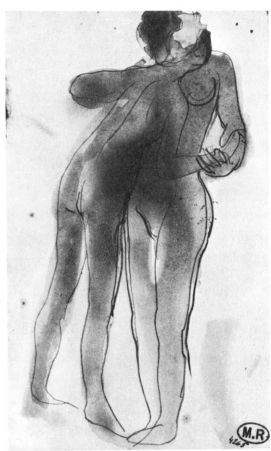

been frequently described: "These graphic snapshots were traced with a pencil stroke on the loose sheet while the artist kept his eye fixed on the model—split-second sketches that suffered neither reworking nor correction, reflex actions of the hand, as it were, triggered by the sight of a significant gesture. Rodin heightened the drawings with extremely thinned paint applied in broad swaths, sometimes relying on thinned, sienna-brown ink alone."[11]

Yet what most characterizes Rodin's work of the 1890s was his involvement with the *Balzac Monument*, which was commissioned in 1891 by the Société des Gens de Lettres and occupied him until 1898. Only a very few sketches exist for the Balzac figure and monument, two of which, probably the first and last, are reproduced on pp.186 and 187. Rodin began this project by undertaking extensive research, initially with respect to his portrait of Balzac. He travelled through Touraine, Balzac's home province, tracked down the existing portraits and descriptions of the writer, consulted Balzac's tailor to get some idea of his outward appearance, and finally began modelling portrait studies and eventually full-length figures. In 1892 Rodin was able to present a conception of the monument to the Société des Gens de Lettres —Balzac in the monk's habit he was accustomed to wear when working, his arms crossed over his chest. Rodin's clients were satisfied with this design and awaited its execution in marble. The sculptor, however, by no means himself satisfied, began his studies of head and figure anew. Now he modelled Balzac nude, standing with his legs spread wide (Fig.23). It was apparently during this phase of work that Rodin made the first sketch, which includes four small pen-and-ink figures of the nude Balzac in front of a chair, and also a sketch of the facade of the Saint-Jacques et Saint-Christophe church in Houdan (p.186). Claudie Judrin dates this sheet circa 1895. The surviving sketches of the Balzac figure do not reveal any systematic

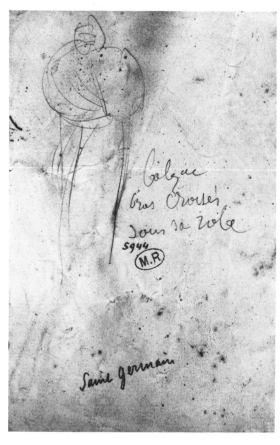

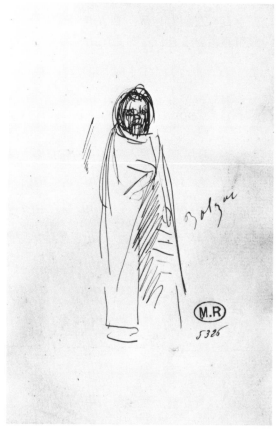

19 *Balzac with Arms Crossed under his Cloak*, D.5944

20 *Study for Balzac*, D.5326

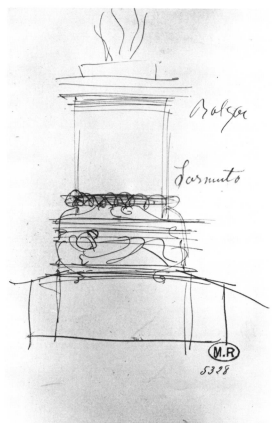

21 *Study for Balzac in Dressing Gown*, D.1780

22 *Pedestal Design for Balzac and Sarmiento Monument*, D.5328

23 *The Nude Balzac,*
1892

24 *Page of Sketches*
(sketches for *Balzac*
at left), D. 5320

development of the work towards a definitive conception; rather, they are isolated sketches done at various phases of the project (Figs. 19–22, 24). What can be concluded from these sketches, however, is that after he had conceived Balzac as a nude figure, Rodin began to depict him with his dressing gown thrown over his shoulders. Repeated requests of the Société des Gens de Lettres to hold to their agreement and finish the monument went unheeded as Rodin continued to make change after change, until finally, in 1898, he completed his *Balzac* and exhibited the 118 inches high sculpture at the Salon. It drew violent criticism on opening day, setting off a scandal and embittered, protracted controversy. The Société des Gens de Lettres refused the statue. Rodin finally took it to his Meudon studio in disgust. Never cast during his lifetime, the *Balzac* had to wait until 1939 for its erection in Paris. The Musée Rodin drawing D. 5329 (p. 187) gives the final figure with all its details, as it was exhibited in 1898. The drawing was possibly not made until after Rodin had completed the statue.

According to Varnedoe, Rodin's transition period lasted no longer than five years. On the quality of the drawings that formed a link between the so different groups of the gouaches and the drawings with watercolor, Varnedoe writes that "Seemingly the least complex or ambitious drawings Rodin ever executed, these transitional works are also (perhaps for that reason) among his lightest and most charming."[12]

Notes

1 Haavard Rostrup, "Dessins de Rodin." In: *Bulletin de la Glyptothèque Ny Carlsberg*, vol. 2, Copenhagen, 1938, p. 4: "Aux environs de 1890, Rodin était à un tel point absorbé par ses nombreux et gigantesques travaux sculpturaux, qu'il n'avait pas le temps de s'adonner au dessin comme jusqu'alors."

2 *Ibid.*, p. 4: "Ces dessins d'après les danseurs, et surtout les danseuses, du Cambodge viennent à former le commencement d'une seconde grande période d'apogée dans les dessins de Rodin, la période qui par opposition à celle des 'dessins gouachée' de 1880 environ—peut se nommer 'Période des dessins aquarellés.'"

3 J. Kirk T. Varnedoe, "Rodin's Drawings." In: Albert E. Elsen (ed.), *Rodin Rediscovered*. Exhibition catalogue, National Gallery of Art, Washington, 1981–82, p. 175; and also J. Kirk T. Varnedoe, "Rodin as a Draftsman – A Chronological Perspective." In: Albert Elsen and J. Kirk T. Varnedoe, *The Drawings of Rodin*. Exhibition catalogue, Washington and New York, 1971–72, pp. 69–87.

4 *Ibid.*, p. 68.

5 Rainer Maria Rilke, *Auguste Rodin*. Leipzig, 1922, p. 47.

6 *Auguste Rodin. Die Kunst.* Conversations with the master collected by Paul Gsell, Munich, 1925, p. 43.

7 Rilke, *op. cit.*, pp. 45–46.

8 *Ibid.*, pp. 47–48.

9 *Ibid.*, p. 47.

10 *Auguste Rodin. Die Kunst, op. cit.*, p. 64.

11 Bernard Champigneulle, *Rodin*. Gütersloh, n. d., p. 123.

12 J. Kirk T. Varnedoe, "Rodin's Drawings," *op. cit.*

99* *Four Sketches for the Nude Balzac and a Church Facade; D. 5324, 5325*

100 Balzac Study; D.5329

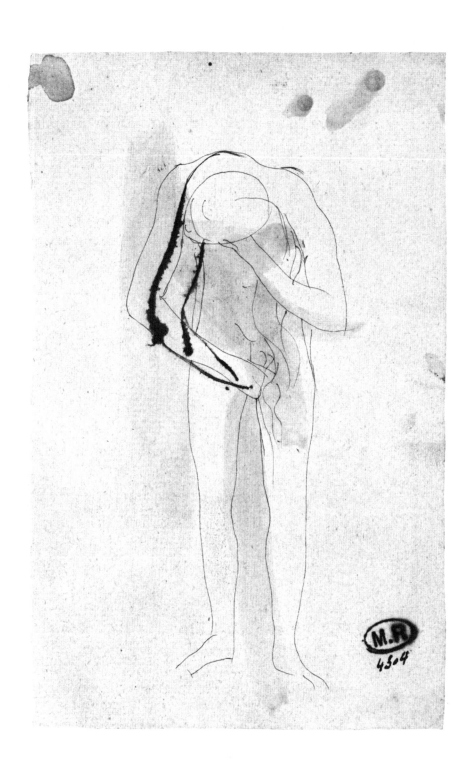

101* *Standing Nude Woman with Head Bent Forward and Hands in her Hair; D.4304*

102* *Nude Woman with Long Veil, a Shell at her Feet; D.4283*

103* *Woman Putting On a Garment; D.4282*

104* *Clothed Woman, her Hands in the Folds of her Garment; D.4276*

105* *Two Clothed Women; D. 4379*

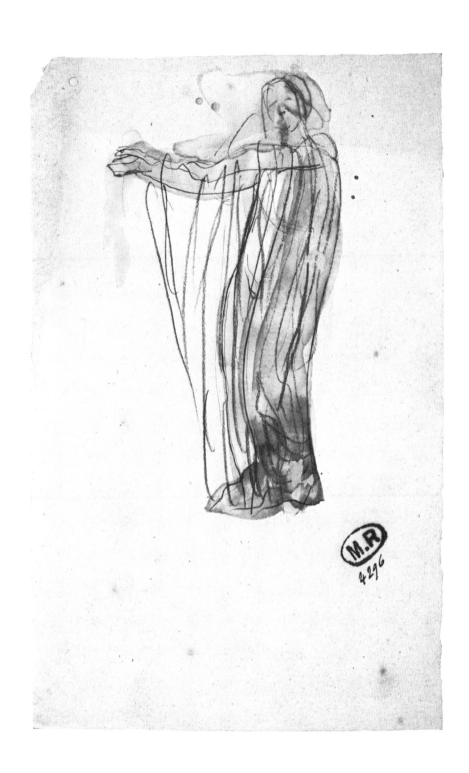

106* *Clothed Woman with Outstretched Arm; D. 4296*

107* *Woman Seen from the Side, in a Dancing Pose; D. 4363*

108* *Woman Dancing with Veils; D. 4349*

110* *Standing Female Nude with Veils*

111* *Naked Woman with Open Garment; D.4305*

112* *Standing Woman with Garment Lifted to her Hips; D.4373*

113* *Nude Woman Swirling her Veils; D.4309*

114* *Semi-nude Woman Bending to the Side; D.4266*

115* *Sapphic Couple in an Embrace; D.4275*

116* *Twilight; D. 4278*

117* *Nude Woman Bending Forward in Front of a Standing Woman with Open Hair; D.4261*

118* *Nude Woman Bending Forward in Front of a Standing Woman; D. 4370*

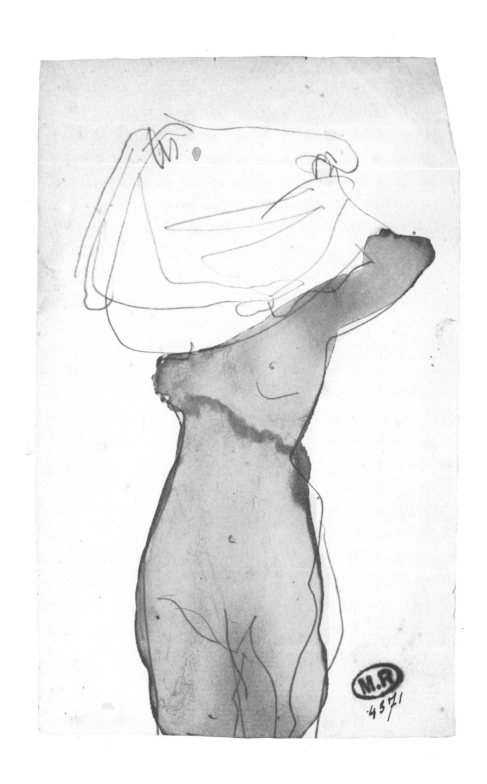

119* *Standing Woman (Torso), Pulling on a Garment; D. 4371*

120* *Standing Nude Woman from the Side, a Garment in her Hand; D. 4340*

Around 1900

Auguste Rodin, about 1900

RODIN'S LATE DRAWINGS AND WATERCOLORS

J. A. Schmoll gen. Eisenwerth

From a personal knowledge of Rodin's last twenty-five years, Judith Cladel wrote the most exhaustive contemporary biography and her third monograph on the artist, which is still an important source today (*Auguste Rodin, sa vie inconnue et glorieuse*, Paris, 1936). In Chapter XIII, over the passage on Rodin's late drawings, she set the words "Couronnement de l'œuvre: les dessins"—His Crowning Achievement: The Drawings. By this she meant primarily his late drawings and watercolors.

Rodin drew from childhood, and accompanied his work in sculpture with a never-ending series of sketches, studies of nudes, portraits, notes both rapid and precise in pencil, pen-and-ink, and charcoal, ideas for projects, *croquis* after earlier works of art, and architectural impressions. These were known initially only to his friends and to a handful of connoisseurs. A larger if still limited public interested in art did not become aware of the abundant and unique production of Rodin the draftsman until 1897, when Goupil, Paris, published its superbly designed volume of facsimiles of 142 selected drawings (based on Maurice Fenaille's suggestions and with a preface by Octave Mirbeau). This luxury edition, however, was limited to only 125 copies, and it contained mainly the so-called "black drawings", sheets in dark grey, blue, brown, or blackish watercolor wash and occasionally opaque gouache over pencil and pen contours and hatching, which were associated with the major sculptural work Rodin began in 1880, his *Gates of Hell*. These drawings suddenly revealed a sculptor-draftsman of profound gifts, a "late-Romantic" artist plagued by dark visions and torments like those described by Dante, Victor Hugo, and Baudelaire. They revealed a master of his art who was worthy of being named with Goya, Géricault, Delacroix, and Daumier, to list only the greatest of the dynamic draftsmen of the nineteenth century—a century whose drawings and sculpture alike Rodin was known to have admired. Later observers were also put in mind of the fantastic and eerily obscure ink drawings of Victor Hugo, and of the proliferating imagination of Gustave Doré's illustrations.

Rodin, as everyone realized with surprise, was not only a very gifted modeller but also a superb draftsman of the full figure, in astonishing control of his graphic means, particularly when it came to capturing the naked human body in its ever-changing moods and movements.

In retrospect, the 1897 Goupil publication seems a summing-up, a *compte rendu* of Rodin's middle period of drawing, on the verge of his mature late style. For indeed the volume did not yet contain those drawings which Judith Cladel and many other authors later declared to be the culmination of his life's work. The hymn of praise to Rodin the draftsman did not begin until several years later, and about ten years had to pass until it swelled into a choir, inspired by the astonishing quality and number of nude drawings which Rodin managed to produce during the last twenty years of his career.

When Did Rodin's Late Style of Drawing Begin?

The specialists have never tired of asking when the new quality of expression, the mature style of this unique *sculpteur-dessinateur* actually commenced. For the art public and most art historians, the year of the Universal Exposition in Paris, 1900, has tended to mark the inception of the late phase in Rodin's masterful rendering of the nude figure in contour and frequently watercolor wash. In his private pavilion on Place d'Alma, outside the official exhibition, he had installed a selection of his sculptural œuvre (with catalogue numbers), the largest overview of his work ever presented, and accompanied it with about one hundred of his drawings "of a new kind" (not listed in the catalogue) which had never been seen so extensively in Paris before. The previous year, 1899, at a one-man exhibition in Brussels which had a certain pilot function for the Universal Exposition (and which was also on view in Amsterdam and Rotterdam), Rodin had already shown a hundred drawings or so alongside his sculptures. Though the reactions in the Paris press were not many, an anonymous author did write in *L'Echo de Paris* of May 10, 1899, under the heading "Rodin dessinateur", that a new direction had become visible in his art of drawing.

The American Rodin expert J. Kirk T. Varnedoe (New York), in his study on the chronological development of Rodin's drawing style (1972[1]), has taken a very close look at the documents which might serve as clues to determine the inception of his liberated, mature style. Varnedoe concludes that the beginnings must lie *before* 1899, the year of the exhibitions in Brussels, Amsterdam, and Rotterdam, at which large numbers of drawings in the new style were presented for the first time. He refers to the circumstance, last mentioned by Claudie Judrin in the catalogue *Rodin et les écrivains de son temps* (Paris, 1976), that even the contour-and-watercolor nudes which Rodin earmarked as illustrations to Octave Mirbeau's poem *Le Jardin des supplices* (Garden of Torments), twenty of which were included as lithographs in Vollard's luxury edition (contract of February 10, 1899), were probably executed in 1898 if not earlier, although the volume of prints did not appear until 1902. Varnedoe dates even earlier, to about 1895, the frontispiece to a previous edition of *Le Jardin des supplices,* less opulent and without other illustrations, published in 1899. He sees a stylistic resemblance between this lithographed drawing and the etching *Ames du Purgatoire* (three female nudes) of 1893.

This drypoint was in turn preceded by drawings which Victoria Thorson (1975[2]) dates to the period 1885–1892/93. Even earlier examples can indeed be found to compare to the sketch of a male model doing a handstand published by Varnedoe (Musée Rodin, D.464), which he associated with the early pencil contour drawings which date to about 1900[3]. The examples I mean are drawings made largely without a controlling glance at pencil and paper. Rodin, looking intently at the model, would allow the pencil to follow his or her movements and contours without checking the results—his hand, so to speak, mechanically tracing his visual impressions. This technique was described by several contemporary authors as a peculiarity of Rodin's when sketching rapidly from the model; among others by Clément Janin in 1903[4]. Long practice must have gone into the development of this technique, however, because signs of it are already found in some of the sketches of male models for the group of six *Burghers of Calais*. Claudie Judrin has commented on these drawings in the catalogue to the exhibition *Auguste Rodin—Le Monument des Bourgeois de Calais (1884–1895) dans les collections du Musée Rodin Paris et du Musée des Beaux-Arts de Calais* (1977; pp. 238–245). They already clearly evince Rodin's free, "uncontrolled" drawing style, with its emphasis on contours and an impression of movement that was more important to Rodin than any distortions or even deformations it might lead to. These were sketches from the model for the eldest of the *Burghers of Calais,*

Eustache de St. Pierre; they must have been rapidly recorded, as interim notes for the three-dimensional sketches he was working on between the end of 1885 and 1886 (Fig. 1). Claude Keisch, in the catalogue to the 1979 Rodin exhibition at the Nationalgalerie, East Berlin, refers in passing to this conjunction. Keisch discusses the pencil and watercolor drawing *Neptune*, possibly from the collection of Max Klinger, which shows similarities to Rodin's sketch for the figure of Eustache de St. Pierre (on loan to the Museum der bildenden Künste, Leipzig; Berlin cat. no. 94, p. 199; plate and commentary p. 200), and which is the only loan from the GDR in the present exhibition (plate on p. 258). The Musée Rodin possesses a variant of the *Neptune;* it is reproduced in Claudie Judrin, *Rodin, 100 Zeichnungen,* 1982 (plate 12).

Many authors have noted the fact that the new style in Rodin's late drawings of nudes was related to his practice of letting his models move freely around his studio. He recorded their natural, flowing movements in a kind of shorthand, in scant pencil contours. Varnedoe supposes that not until the 1890s, when his earnings had risen significantly, could Rodin afford to engage models more frequently, sometimes several at once. Before that he likely used models only for specific figure projects, having them take preconceived poses—such as the Belgian soldier, Auguste Neyt, who posed for *The Bronze Age* in Brussels in 1876, the Italian model Pignatelli for *John the Baptist* (Paris, 1878), another Italian model for *Eve* (1880), and Pignatelli and Cazin for *The Burghers of Calais* (1885 on). With his new freedom of means, both artistic and financial, Rodin began in the 1890s to study models, principally female ones, quite independently of sculptural projects, and indeed much as artists had always been accustomed to study animals, whether in their natural habitat (farm, pasture, wilderness, or wildlife preserve) or in captivity (in cages or zoos). Géricault, at the start of the century, had set an example in this regard that was avidly followed and disseminated by his pupils Delacroix and Barye. Rodin himself, at Barye's suggestion or under his direct supervision, had made animal studies at the Jardin des Plantes in Paris. It would appear that the problem of representing movement in his group of six *Burghers of Calais* had recalled him to the necessity of creating natural and vivacious, as opposed to conventionally pathetic, attitudes, by letting his models move freely after explaining the "plot" of the action to them.[5] This may truly be the clue to the beginning of a new approach, both with respect to his models and to his sketching style. Rodin obviously began to systematize this new principle during the 1890s, but its roots apparently reach back to the phase of his studies for *The Burghers of Calais*, the mid-1880s.

By the time the 1897 facsimile edition of his older "black drawings" appeared with Goupil, Rodin was already deeply involved in working out his new "late style", in which insights came to maturity that had served him well for over a decade and that must have seemed extremely promising to him. This brings us to another feature of his work as a draftsman—it was never of a "one-track" kind. Throughout his work in drawing and sculpture, he always employed a variety of different expressive, technical, and stylistic possibilities in parallel. This contributed greatly to the richness and variety of his œuvre. It is quite striking how different the flow of Rodin's pen and pencil lines often is, and how variously he employed watercolor, india ink, and gouache—in his earlier years to create dark, relieflike shadow, and later to evoke shimmering transparency. Hence it should always be kept in mind that the famous achievements of his old age, with their free-flowing and often seemingly free-floating female nudes heightened with diaphanous or brilliant watercolor washes, by no means represent the sole drawing technique available to Rodin between 1897 and 1917. He also produced pen-and-ink drawings of a completely different character, including many whose appearance misleadingly suggests an earlier date.

Points of Reference Within the Late Style

If a chronological point of departure is provided by the watercolored drawings to Octave Mirbeau's *Le Jardin des supplices*, which presumably were made between 1897 and 1899, Rodin's death in November 1917, indeed his gradual physical decline from 1916 on, set a natural limit on the period under discussion. Even narrower limits are set by the Universal Exposition of 1900 and the outbreak of war in 1914, though Rodin continued to sculpt and draw from 1914 to 1916—in 1915, after sessions in Rome, he completed the portrait head of Pope Benedict XV, and in 1916 that of his friend and designated executor of his will, the former minister Etienne Clémentel. The year 1916, however, also brought his second stroke, from which he did not recover as completely as from his first in 1912.

The drawings assembled here to represent the late phase begin, as far as reliable chronology is concerned, with a portrait study of Séverine executed in 1893 (plate on p. 235). This is one of a series of unusually expressive charcoal drawings which one would not think were contemporaneous with that tranquil drypoint etching of the same year, *Ames du Purgatoire*, which, based completely on delicate contour, manifests the other side of Rodin's late graphic style. Then come drawings associated with the free illustrations, mentioned above, to Mirbeau's *Le Jardin des supplices*.

Rodin's checkered relationship to Germany and Germany's to him has been made notorious by the gift, arranged by Count Harry Kessler, of fourteen (fifteen) watercolored drawings to the Grand Ducal Museum in Weimar, whose exhibition the following year touched off protests and intrigues against "the much too progressive" Kessler. Rodin's nudes were pilloried as profoundly immoral, and Kessler was forced to resign from his directorship of the museum. These drawings were exhibited in 1979 at the Nationalgalerie, East Berlin, in conjunction with a large Rodin exhibition, and annotated in the catalogue; unfortunately we were not able to include them in the West German exhibition, though one is illustrated here (Fig. 5).

The year 1906 also marked a special triumph for Rodin's draftmanship, however, because it brought his meeting with King Sisowath's Cambodian dance troupe. Inspired by the exotic charm and ritualistic form of the dances, by the harmony of the dancers' movements and the sinuosity of their bodies, Rodin created his famous series of richly orchestrated watercolor and gouache drawings, a high point of his art in whatever medium. He treasured these works, very rarely making a gift of one to a friend. Rilke was the fortunate owner of a *Cambodgienne*, which, however, was impounded in Paris with the rest of his possessions after the outbreak of war in 1914 and later auctioned off.

In 1907 Rodin decided to show his *Cambodgienne* drawings in Paris (at Bernheim Jeune) and later in Brussels and Vienna. They represented yet another superb facet of the artist's gigantic achievement. No less than seventeen of these drawings are presented here, one of them from the estate of Georg Kolbe, the German sculptor, who had visited Rodin, presumably in 1912 (plates on pp. 274–290).

In 1908 Rodin met Hanako, a Japanese dancer who was then making a guest appearance in Paris, and modelled a series of masks and heads that record her expressive features. (At one point the dark, pent energy of a variant of these masks even moved Rodin to consider titling it *Beethoven*!) Rodin also made many motion studies of Hanako, who like Isadora Duncan in 1911 and Vaclav Nijinski in 1912 danced for him in the nude. In the present publication Hanako is represented only by a portrait drawing (Fig. 3).

These are the points of reference for an overview of the late drawings, chronologically arranged and related to the examples presented here as well as to biographical events associated with the individual works. Many of the drawings with watercolor, however, offer no precise clues as to their date of execution or place within Rodin's œuvre. In a few cases, the dates on which they were purchased by their first owners provide a *terminus ante quem*.

Roughly speaking, it can be assumed that the late watercolored nudes were executed throughout the period from about 1897 to about 1916, though many of them initially remained in the state of pencil sketches. Rodin returned to them and reworked them again and again later. The watercolor wash was as a rule applied after the event, sometimes years later. Besides making corrections and additions, Rodin often added allusive titles, writing them in the margins of the sheet in pencil or, more rarely, in ink. As with his sculptures, he frequently changed the titles of his drawings. Many of them seem contradictory; all of them suggest only *one* aspect of a possible interpretation. Each added word gives another name, a further allusion…

Let us now turn to a phase-by-phase discussion of Rodin's late drawings, based on the chronology of reliably dated drawings just outlined.

Four Portrait Studies of Women: Séverine—Two Anonymous Models—Hanako

Our collection of the late drawings begins with the charcoal drawing *Portrait of Séverine*, 1893 (plate on p. 235). It has been repeatedly noted that this study (and a few others) of this unusual, committed, enthusiastic, and empathetic woman hold a unique place in Rodin's drawing œuvre. Rarely did the sculptor capture a face in charcoal so expressively, indeed passionately. The model must have spontaneously inspired him to this achievement. Caroline Rémy (1855–1925) wrote her books and articles, and fought for women's rights and political and social reform, under the name Séverine. After the failure of her marriage and entry into a male-dominated profession, the vicissitudes of life brought experiences that only strengthened her resolve. Also, she supported Rodin's art at critical junctures. Out of gratitude he offered to model her portrait. In 1893 Séverine was thirty-eight years old. Her expressive face with its slightly upturned lips and eloquent eyes, their gaze searching or tormented, full of pity and sometimes almost tragic, appears in a small mask (Fig. 2), and also in five known drawings (four in the Musée Rodin, Paris, and one in the Budapest Museum of Fine Arts[6]) which were apparently made in rapid succession, as if during a conversation. Rodin's portrait sketches and sculpture contrast surprisingly to the two existing paintings of Séverine—one by Renoir, executed about 1885 (Washington, National Gallery of Art), and the other by the English symbolist, Louis Welden Hawkins, 1895 (Paris, The Louvre). Both artists show us a quiet young woman, whom Hawkins has infused almost with a saintlike ecstasy. Her "damply wistful glance", as Claude Keisch called it in the catalogue to the 1979 Rodin exhibition in East Berlin, is really not so far removed from what Rodin, too, saw in Séverine's eyes. The journalist Henri Rochefort once cynically called her "Notre-Dame de la larme à l'Oeil" (Madonna of the Lachrymose Eye), as Jacques de Caso has been able to determine.[7] Rodin apparently had Séverine sit slightly above him, and looked up at her face while drawing. Two of the sheets show her in three-quarter profile; three more *en face*. The flat edge of the charcoal has often been used to model the lively shadows, an immediate preparation for work in clay which is almost unique among Rodin's preparatory drawings for sculptural portraits. Outlines and interior contours, and especially the hair and folds of the dress around the neck and shoulders, have been set down in short, sharp, curving strokes (in charcoal and perhaps chalk as well). The vehemence of this drawing (found again in the Budapest portrait) is astonishing, and it reflects not only the model's emotion but that of the artist as well, as he abandoned himself to the joy of creation. It is well to recall that this drawing was done by the master of the emerging *Balzac* statue, during a phase, that is, when his art was outgrowing naturalism to take on more and more expressive traits. Séverine's face, too, might be called that of "an element", to use the term coined by Sainte-Beuve for his contemporary Balzac, and which Rodin hoped to fill with life in his visionary monument to the great writer.

As captivating as Séverine herself is the letter which she wrote to Rodin on April 30, 1894. Speaking of her portrait, she affirmed that "…les autres firent mes traits, mais vous, vous ferez mon âme!" ("Others depict my features, but you, you reveal my soul!") Rodin hoped that this "angel of eloquence", as he called her, might someday speak a few words over his grave. She fulfilled his wish on November 24, 1917, in Meudon. At his funeral service (documented in a photograph, p. 315) Séverine held a fervent *éloge funèbre*, then took a rose in her hand, kissed it, and threw it into the open grave at the feet of *The Thinker*.[8]

In contrast to the portraits of Séverine, Rodin's pencil drawing of a young woman (plate on p. 236) is more reserved, concentrates more on the volumes of head and shoulders, the contours of which have been emphasized over and over again—particularly the profile line from nose to chin. There is no lack of hatching to model the volumes and bring out the plastic values, either in the face or in the hair, which, carelessly parted, falls to a knot at the neck. Rapid diagonal strokes, rubbed with the finger to grey halftones, are as much in evidence as eraser work to create highlights on forehead and under the right eye. All of this contributes to the three-dimensionality of the head. Another striking feature is the model's sidelong glance,

her eyes turned to the extreme left, as if staring at something. Since the line of the neck suggests extension, one has the impression that the young woman is watching some happening intently and expectantly. Neck and shoulder contours, with suggestions of a *décolleté* at the right and pleats falling to the left upper arm, evoke a sturdy body. One is put in mind of the *Femme slave* type which inspired Rodin to do a bust about 1906 (marble, Paris, Musée Rodin, cat. Grappe 1944, No. 364) and a sculpture of a woman sitting on the shore known as *Devant la Mer* (plaster, Paris, Musée Rodin, cat. Grappe, No. 365; marble, New York, Metropolitan Museum). However, the features of these two sculptures bear only a certain similarity to this portrait. (Let me note in passing that it does slightly resemble the German actress Tilla Durieux, who of course sat to many artists for her portrait, among them Renoir, Stuck and Barlach. Compare especially Stuck's portrait photographs of 1912. Miss Durieux's husband, the progressive Berlin art dealer and publisher Paul Cassirer, arranged to have Rodin's drawings included in exhibitions of the Berlin Secession and purchased many for his own gallery. Whether his wife accompanied him on his visits to Rodin, however, remains to be determined.)

The sheet contains another, spontaneous contour line, which appears to be a profile sketch drawn without looking at the paper. It is upside down, which indicates that Rodin rejected his first attempt, then turned the sheet through 180 degrees and began the drawing under discussion.[9]

Rodin's pencil sketch of an unknown model (plate on p. 237) is unusual for the veiled expression of the face. Unlike his many drawings of nudes, whose heads and faces are usually treated summarily, often with surprisingly few strokes, Rodin has concentrated here on the face of this unknown beauty, rendering it in a rapid notation that yet reveals a carefully calculated range of nuance. The model faces us frontally, her head bent slightly to the left (to the right, from our point of view). The delicate pencil strokes are visible with which the sculptor was accustomed to first tentatively determining the overall form of the face, before applying the final outlines in heavier strokes and rubbing the fine hatching in the shadows with his fingertips to produce an effect of volume. In the area of mouth, nostrils, and eyes, as well as in the hair, both delicate rubbed passages and stronger strokes to heighten the expression of the features are evident. The neck has been merely suggested; a zigzag line might have been meant for the high collar of a blouse—at any rate, this line suddenly swings around in a hairpin turn und runs out to the right edge of the paper, as if it were the final stroke in a sketch meant to concentrate on the head, and leave shoulders and bust undefined. The woman's slightly pouting mouth, stub nose, and veiled eyes turned aside, together with her puffs of blond hair, give the impression of a rather broadsshouldered, tantalizing feline woman, a mixture of dreamy innocence and maturing knowledge. Similar Parisiennes are found among the midinettes of Steinlen and in Picasso's early work (and, ravaged and fascinating, in his 1901 painting *Pierette, Hand on her Shoulder*, Barcelona, Museo Picasso).

Women of this type often modelled for Rodin's nude drawings, though we find them in only about three of those in our selection (plates on pp. 239, 241, 268). The technique of this drawing indicates a late date, after 1900, recalling pencil studies of nudes in which the graphite has been rubbed to create shaded plasticity (plates on pp. 264–267). Compared to the charcoal studies of Séverine's face, with their compelling force, this pencil portrait of a woman (p. 237) remains reserved, devoted completely to a delicate rendering of well-nigh animal calm.

A fourth female face of another kind altogether is seen in Rodin's pencil drawing of Hanako (Fig. 3). In this case we know that the undated sheet must have been executed between 1907 and 1910. (The literature generally gives 1908. For a careful dating of all the documents related to Rodin's acquaintance with the Japanese actress—photographs, postcards, letters, statements by third parties, drawings, and especially Rodin's sculptural studies of her face—see the catalogue *Rodin et l'Extrême Orient*, Paris, Musée Rodin, 1979, in which Monique Laurent and Claudie Judrin sift all the available material.)

Rodin initially saw Hanako for only a short time, during his visit to Marseille in July 1906, where he had gone to draw the Cambodian dancers (cf. p. 227ff.). The Japanese actress happened to be in Marseille at the time, where a large colonial exhibition was being held. Rodin was fascinated by Hanako's acting and especially by her mobile features. The American dancer Loïe Fuller (1862–1928), long a friend of Rodin's, sometimes worked as a manager for Hanako and other drama and dance troupes, and presumably it was she who brought Rodin and Hanako together again in Paris, in 1907. The relationship continued until 1916, interrupted only by Hanako's many tours to all the capitals of Europe (especially Vienna, Berlin, and Petersburg). There must have been countless sessions in Rodin's studios in Paris and Meudon. Sometimes Hanako posed in the nude for the sculptor-draftsman, as witnessed by about three drawings (Paris, Musée Rodin). And over the course of time emerged that superb series sof sculptural portraits with continually changing expressions, *fifty-three* all told! Hanako, born Hisako Ohta or Ota Hisa in 1868 near Nagoya, was given by her impoverished parents at a very young age to a group of itinerant provincial actors. Finally she managed to join a better troupe, which went to Europe and appeared in various countries as an oriental "curiosity". About 1904 or 1905 she was discovered by Loïe Fuller, who took her and her troupe under contract, and also gave her the Western pseudonym Hanako.

By 1907 when Rodin engaged her as a model, she had had a number of successes, particularly in the starring role of a sensational Far Eastern drama called *Revenge of the Geisha*. At that time she was already thirty-nine years old. Rodin admired her hardened body ("like a well-trained terrier"), her physical power and almost acrobatic skills, and particularly her mimicry and

force of expression. Among the masks he modelled of her there is an extreme study "in deathly fear" and one which he considered making into a mask of Beethoven, so strongly did her tragic features recall the dramatic, visionary countenance of the great composer, viewed through the period's cult of genius.

By comparison to the masks and heads in terracotta (Fig. 4), *pâte-de-verre*, plaster and bronze, the pencil *Portrait of Hanako* (Fig. 3) is a relatively delicate sketch, though it, too, does not lack for nervous agitation. The tilted oval of head and masklike countenance contains only spare indications of mouth and eyes, supplemented by the lines of arched brows and rudimentary marks to indicate the tip of the nose. Otherwise the oval remains devoid of modelling hatching or halftones, which further increases its masklike effect. The full mouth, noted with a few nervous strokes, seems about to speak; the pupils, following the tilt of the head, look to the right (from the spectator's point of view, to the left), lending the face a thoughtfully inquiring expression. With a few confident curves Rodin has suggested the actress's topknot coiffure, and also her high-collared costume. If we recall the other portrait drawings just discussed (Séverine; the unknown model with her resemblance to Tilla Durieux; and the "nude model"), it becomes obvious by comparison that Rodin adapted his method and graphic means to the personality of each sitter in a truly astonishing way. These four drawings, so different in conception and structure, document his stylistic pluralism, though in all four his touch remains inimitably his own.

The drawing just discussed is authenticated by Hanako's own signature in Japanese and English transliteration (her postcards to Rodin from all over the world were written in English).

The Late Nude Studies

Pencil Drawings

As I said at the outset, Rodin devoted himself increasingly to studies of the nude figure from the 1890s at the latest. In striking contrast to the "fantastic" or "black" drawings, such as those reproduced in the facsimile edition of 1897, which almost without exception depict nude figures or constellations of figures partially inspired by Dante and drawn from imagination, the later drawings are direct studies of models. I use the word "later", of course, in the very general sense of an approximate chronology. This does not exclude that Rodin may already have occasionally executed drawings of this type, as memoranda of poses and movements, in the late 1880s or earlier. Comparisons with his technically very different, finely crosshatched drawings after such of his own sculptures as *The Bronze Age* (The Louvre, Cabinet des Dessins; reproduced in *Gazette des Beaux-Arts*, December 1883) and *John the Baptist* (Fogg Art Museum, Harvard University, Cambridge, Mass.) say little, since these were probably done after photographs—possibly even by the then common tracing procedure—especially for reproduction in periodicals and books, the autotype printing method having yet to be invented. (Similarly, I have been able to identify Manet's drawing *Faure as Hamlet*, formerly in the Hahnloser Collection, as a "reproduction drawing" of this kind which Manet did after a photograph of his painting.[10]

A drawing like that of the kneeling woman (plate on p. 250) bears all the traits of a rapid record of a pose—kneeling, her upper body thrown far back—which the model cannot have been able to hold for long. Technically, this sheet must be distinguished from the following pencil drawings with their painterly and sculptural effects created by smearing the soft pencil dust, as well as from those heightened with watercolor. Yet we do know (from Helene von Nostitz's report, among others) that Rodin loved to take out older drawings of nudes in his leisure time and "color" them with watercolors. Hence the fact that a drawing contains watercolor wash says little about its precise date of execution—this practice, too, may well have begun in the 1890s.

All of the "free" nude studies of this mature, late phase from 1895 to 1915 are characterized by Rodin's indifference to alterations, *pentimenti*, distortions, and even deformations. In the drawing of the kneeling model just mentioned, for instance, the contour of the arm was initially much steeper, indicating that the model must have been leaning much farther back to start with. Rodin then sketched her final position and marked the contours more sharply at decisive points. His retention of the earlier lines increases the vitality of the contour, evoking motion and making the model seem almost to breathe. The shapes of head and features have been merely blocked in, with a tiny oval for the mouth, slits for eyes, and curves indicating eyebrows and nose. It is difficult to say whether the girl's other arm lies across her raised thigh as it seems to, and how her left hand gripping her left foot actually "works". Nevertheless, the whole is absolutely convincing, precisely because of the open-endedness of this "snapshot". There are many other drawings that evince a similar approach. The two of reclining nudes (plates on pp. 248, 249) appear even more spontaneous, wilder. Their nervous contours, attempted twice, three times, sometimes as many as five times, nevertheless solidly support the figure, and deviations from the "first draft" are frequent. Thighs and calves were shifted again and again until the artist, satisfied that he had found the right position, marked it with a confident, heavier stroke. Yet the tentative initial outlines still contribute, like a first comprehensive glance, to the effect of the whole, increasing the impression of the model's vital movement.

Rodin, as we know from many reports, enjoyed letting his models move completely at their ease around his studio. If he valued freedom in such attitudes as walking, kneeling, and bending over, he valued it even more in all variations of reclining position. He encouraged his models to relax, stretch, and sprawl, pull up their legs or spread them, because to him these movements were just as natural as, say, a child's kicking and playing with himself or a cat's licking itself clean. Rodin loved the natural innocence of such attitudes, and they distinguish his nudes from those, for example, of Félicien Rops (1833–1890), who was only too aware of breaking taboos and of the coquettish enticingness of his generally semi-naked women in erotically charged poses. Not a few of his drawings of nudes Rodin declined to send to exhibitions because he knew they would be misunderstood. Yet for him, they simply belonged to a comprehensive picture of the female body. A number of parallels exist to the second of the drawings just named (plate on p. 249), among those published by Georges Grappe in the early album in the Galerie d'Estampes series (Braun & Cie), 1933. These are numbers 1 (D. 2290), 10 (D. 2299), 26 (D. 2249), 27 (D. 1773), and 30 (D. 2204). Others are found in the new volume by Claudie Judrin, head of the Département des Dessins at the Musée Rodin, Paris: *Rodin, 100 Zeichnungen und Aquarelle* (1982), plate 86 (D. 5396) and especially plate 31 (D. 5402). All are pencil drawings of young models with their legs drawn up or spread such that their genitals are more or less revealed, and often with one or both hands over or near them. These poses, from the point of view of tradition and convention, are indeed ""daring", and they were often called that in the earlier literature; compared however to Far Eastern and even some modern Western erotic art they are anything but that.

Rodin also drew detailed views of the body in which breasts and pubic region are the main motifs. These drawings correspond to his bronze, terracotta, and plaster torsi without heads and sometimes without arms and feet. Examples are his renderings of nude, reclining female torsi (plates on pp. 264–266). In each case, a young woman is seen from above, her thighs slightly spread; the pubic region and the volumes of the body are emphasized by dark zones of shadow. For Rodin, the center of the body, particularly the female body, stood for the life forces, fertility, vitality. He felt no qualms whatsoever about depicting the body in such positions, since for him they symbolized the underlying organic principle of life, unveiled, free of false shame, unhampered by clothing or "drapery". More aggressive than most is his drawing (plate on p. 267) in which the model, legs spread and the soles of her feet pressed together, stretches out on the bed as if longingly, her body arched over a pillow and the backs of her hands covering her face. Inscriptions give the names "Salambo" (more correctly, "Salammbô") and "St. Antoine"—both titles of novels by Flaubert (published 1862 and 1874) which stand for the notions of desire, seduction, and "woman the temptress", as they used to say around 1900.

There are other parallels among Rodin's published drawings, for instance in one of a woman seen straight on, her thighs spread enticingly (New York, Metropolitan Museum, donation of Georgia O'Keeffe). Here, however, the sculptor has transformed his model, giving her goat's legs below the knee and this way changing her into a *Satyresse*, a symbol of natural and uninhibited sexual desire.[11] Confronted with these drawings it is well to recall that Rodin gave a few of his sculptural fragments similarly daring poses, above all his study of the flying messenger of the gods, *Iris* (c. 1890–1892), the bronze of which was branded obscene because the goddess offers herself with wide open thighs, drawing her right foot up to her body with one hand.

One might conclude that in Rodin's eyes, every physical gesture and attitude had equal value. He devoted the same attention to women crawling (plate on p. 262), propped up on one arm and seen from behind (p.263), lying quietly and completely draped (p.241), and opening their legs with dress thrown back (p.239). All of these attitudes are natural; they express warm-blooded human existence without denying the erotic stimulus.

The Nude Drawings with Watercolor

Of the drawings just discussed, the last three already had an application of watercolor wash (plates on pp.239, 241, 263). This puts them in the category of watercolors, although they are certainly not images developed solely out of the interflow of transparent color. Since his student days at the School of Arts and Crafts, Rodin was practiced in the use of ink, watercolor, and opaque paints (gouache) to tint contour renderings. For a long time, particularly between 1880 and 1895, however, he preferred washes in very dark hues, as evidenced by the "black" drawings with their predominating blue-black, frequent dark browns, and occasional nuances of other colors such as red. Not until the late 1890s did he turn to lighter tones; by 1900, he had begun cultivating delicate watercolor wash applied to pencil sketches of nudes. In an essay written for an exhibition of Rodin's drawings from the Ribemond Collection at Galerie Flechtheim, Berlin, and printed in the *Deutsche Allgemeine Zeitung* for May 16, 1930,[12] Helene von Nostitz described an evening at Meudon, summing up her meetings with the sculptor: "The sun is going down. Under the lofty vault of his museum in Meudon high above Paris, Rodin sits holding a few of his drawings in his lap. He looks lovingly at them, attempting to penetrate their secret, which apparently eludes even him. He casts a delicate watercolor tone over the figures, which muse, sleep, embrace the universe, which strive towards the light like plants. The last ray of the setting sun falls across the paper; an arm shines out here, a breast there, like ripe fruit. 'Ce donne de la douceur', says the maestro to himself, as he continues to work… Women's bodies lie stretched out there like pink blossoms, and seem to breathe gently." Scenes like this must have taken place again and again during the last two productive decades of Rodin's life—or perhaps only during the sixteen years before the outbreak of World War I. In his hours of "leisure" Rodin selected from his well-nigh inexhaustible store of nude drawings those which seemed particularly suited to heightening with watercolor, to lend them additional "sweetness" (the English word does not quite capture the tender overtones of the French *la douceur*), or better, to lend them charm and a soft glow. This may have been done many years after the pencil drawing was executed, just as many a correcting contour may have been a later addition rather than a last spontaneous stroke to finish a sketch. All of this must be kept in mind before one too rashly attempts to precisely date Rodin's hundreds and thousands of drawings.

Though his watercolor washes always complement the forms, they frequently go confidently beyond the contour lines. This treatment appeared eccentric and "modern" to Rodin's contemporaries, and it doubtless influenced many younger artists—Matisse, Léger, Laurens, Zadkine and many others. In some cases Rodin employed watercolor to interpret his pencil studies after the fact, lending them a symbolic content or evoking the mood of a certain landscape or certain time of day. As a rule he heightened the incarnadine of his nudes by yellowish, rose, or brownish ocher tones, allowing them to flow across and beyond the limbs to increase their suppleness. To create contrast he colored the figures' flowing or piled hair, the material of their garments or their beds, and often also the entire background or sections of the empty sheet in hues of blue, grey, green, or red. The paint has invariably been applied extremely wet, and has flowed, bubbled, sometimes mixed or puddled in spots or along the edges; but it is almost always transparent. In the article just quoted, Helene von Nostitz speaks of Rodin's "delicate *sfumato*" (a term that goes back to Leonardo's veiled painting), "which dips all of these apparitions as if into a mist, yet without lessening the precision of the drawing." She goes on to say, very poetically (and in the exalted language of Art Nouveau), that "...this bevy of wistful figures surrounds us, always on the verge of ultimate expression, like Beatitudes, like the Condemned of Inferno and Eden. Spring breezes caress them; or the waves of the sea wash their brilliant limbs, on which light and shadows play so vivaciously that they seem always in motion..."

The impression of mermaids and sirens cavorting in the waves, which so well suited many of the nudes, reclining yet in motion, was also one which Rodin evoked later, by applying blue and green watercolor. An example is one of the Nostitz drawings, *Néréide dans la mer*, a title which the artist wrote at the lower right, under the supplementary "attribute" of a shell. An analogous process may be traced in the following drawings, which have been grouped together to illustrate the systematic development of another of Rodin's favorite ideas. This is the metamorphosis of the female body into a vase.

The first example (plate on p. 245), shows a young woman kneeling with her arms behind her back, which forces her breasts outward. Her upper arms are just visible behind shoulders and waist. The drawing is tinted in delicate nuances of watercolor—the skin soft pink and the cap of hair brown with yellow lights, a color that runs down in places over the very schematically suggested features, covering forehead and eyes. Striations of light blue of varying intensity run across figure and paper surface, blending with the shimmering pink incarnadine beneath to produce nuances of violet. Visible under the veil of color are the pencil outlines, and also some hatching and smudged shadow, which throw the figure into slight relief.

In a second sheet (plate on p. 246) what is basically the same figure reappears—a kneeling woman with arms behind her. But her head is now bent so far back that all we see is a triangle formed by the peak of her neck and raised chin. This makes the vase-shape of her torso even clearer. Her body is tinted a diaphanous rose-orange-yellow, over which, below her hips, a light green evokes water. Where this color congealed along the edges (below the hips and at the sides of the sheet near the edge), Rodin later reworked it and contoured it in pencil to suggest floral growths, the leaves of some strange aquatic plant. The impression is very poetic and well-nigh surreal—a vision of Venus Anadyomene, born of the sea, who has hardly emerged from the waves when she is transformed into a living vase.

The third drawing in this group—which we, not Rodin, have arranged in compositional sequence (plate on p. 247)—represents the third step in the metamorphosis, a total abstraction of a girl's body into the shape of a vase. This shape floats on the light-colored paper surface as if cut out, yet itself seems three-dimensional thanks to its color variation and interior drawing. Arms are no longer visible, and the chin is there only because we know it to be. This time Rodin has chosen a brown hue for the body, like a terracotta vessel. The process of transformation has reached an end. Horizontal lines, bands, and friezes "etched" with pencil into the torso mark tiers like those of red-figure Greek vases. At the waist, a frieze of figures, dancing or perhaps fleeing from Pan, is given in sharp foreshortening. Band-shaped stripes with sketched ornaments complete the vase's decoration. A very similar variation of this drawing served as the basis for a frontispiece lithograph (executed by Auguste Clot) for the deluxe edition of Mirbeau's *Le Jardin des supplices* of 1902, whose illustrations were prepared for printing about 1899–1901. In other words, Rodin's vase idea had its roots in the 1890s. Further variants witness to his continual preoccupation with this theme.[13]

The motif of girlfriends, "Lesbian" couples, is among the most fascinating in Rodin's drawing œuvre. During his later years he frequently had his models pose not alone but in twos or threes, because this encouraged uninhibited movement. He let them follow their own intui-

225

tions, in a word, and this may well be the source of those pairs of girls which are found not rarely in his portfolios. Yet already among the unused sketches for illustrations to *Le Jardin des supplices* (as early as 1899, in other words) we discover a drawing of two young women, one crouching with her arms raised as if in prayer or supplication, the other, above her, seeming just to have lowered herself to her knees.[14] This is the scene in Mirbeau's novel[15] where Clara, the principal character, suddenly recognizing another girl, cries "A superb creature, whom I loved the night before!" Here we have a relatively early reference to the motif and its literary allusions. It should also be remarked at this point that the variant of this drawing, shown in 1979 at the Rodin exhibition in East Berlin, is among the drawings in the present Weimar collections that go back to the artist's gift of 1905 (Fig. 5). This was the donation arranged by Kessler which, when it was exhibited in Spring 1906, led to the notorious, embarrassing scandal.[16] Yet Rodin had by no means chosen particularly daring examples from his series of nudes, except perhaps for one drawing of a seated woman with raised, slightly spread thighs.[17] The newspaper attack on Rodin's drawings—and by implication on Kessler's museum policy —nevertheless called them "offensive" and "disgusting", which led to the closure of the show and eventually to Kessler's demission. This moral outrage, whether hypocritical or prudishly real, extended from the educated philistine all the way up to the Kaiser himself, and it reflected the astonishment and incomprehension with which the art public in Germany greeted the drawings of the aging Parisian sculptor. William II is said to have stated in 1907 that Rodin's international reputation was a mystery to him, and that "no one in France would consider looking at the drawings now on show at the Berlin Secession, but the good Berliners are all eyes and think them admirable..."[18] Paul Klee, by contrast, was amazed by drawings of this kind. During a stay in Rome to round off his training at the Munich Academy, he noted in his diary on April 12, 1902: "Yesterday I saw the Roman Salon, the annual exhibition at the Gallerie d'Arte moderna. The only good things were the drawings, etchings and lithos of the French artists. Especially Rodin, with caricatures of nudes—caricatures!—a species previously unknown in his case. And he's the best I've ever seen at it, astonishingly brilliant. Contours drawn with a few scant strokes of the pencil, flesh tones added with a full brush in watercolor, and sometimes drapery suggested with another color, greenish, say. That's all, and the effect is simply monumental."[19] Klee's use of the word "caricatures" in this connection, of course, was by no means pejorative. Rodin's nudes, drawn in full motion and with an "uncontrolled" line, must have offered the greatest imaginable contrast to what Klee had learned from Knirr and Stuck during his studies in Munich—static nudes in neo-classical poses. The "misdrawings" and deformations which Rodin so nonchalantly accepted must have struck Klee as incredibly daring, and opened his eyes to new possibilities in rendering the nude figure. In my opinion, the stimulus which Rodin's nudes likely gave to Klee's treatment of the subject from 1902 on, has yet to be sufficiently appreciated.

One final and special category within Rodin's pencil-and-watercolor drawings of nudes remains to be discussed, the category of *papier découpé*. These are works done by cutting out figures and pasting them singly or in new groupings on another sheet. Rodin treated his nude drawings like puzzles, taking their elements out of the original context and shifting, turning and recombining them as he pleased. Earlier, he had sometimes altered the center of gravity of his figures by turning the sheet on edge and writing the word "*bas*" below the new and perhaps even more interesting position, changing, say, a reclining figure into a flying or hovering one. Cutting the figures out gave him even more freedom to dispose them at will. It was probably the sculptor in him that suggested isolating figures from the plane surface and letting them float in space (plates on pp. 259, 260). Even more daring were his combinations of two nudes cut from different drawings, as in *Three Women Embracing* (plate on p. 261). The collage represents a quite remarkable constellation: a reclining figure seen foreshortened from below, and a seated figure from a "normal" point of vantage whose left arm has been cut off to make her jibe better with the first. Rodin has even let part of a third figure's face stand over the "amputated" upper arm, making the interlocking even more complex. What is disquieting about this collage is the sudden shift from one perspective to another—the reclining figure seems to advance in front of the seated one, yet at the same time this is demonstrably impossible... The use of his sketches as "pattern sheets" for these puzzle-games, as Elsen and Varnedoe have convincingly pointed out,[20] bears similarities to Rodin's penchant for making assemblages of fragments of his plaster castings. Here, too, he would separate parts of figures from their original context and combine them into new, often surprising configurations. In the field of drawing he began early on to paste cutouts together and to integrate into his compositions certain existing patterns or ornaments (from business letters, bills, advertisements). Hence Rodin deserves to be included in the early history of collage as employed by such classical moderns as Picasso, Max Ernst, Miró, Franz Roh, and others. However, most of the collages Rodin did during his late period were of his own drawings, seldom including found material from other sources such as the engraved illustrations Max Ernst used. Rodin, a sculptor foremost, was mainly interested in isolating and recombining figures from his own renderings. He achieved astonishing effects by this method, which reveal the force of a visual imagination which provided him with infinite formal variations throughout his lifetime.

Finally, mention must be made of the fact that Rodin made copies of many of his nude drawings, sometimes by tracing. The idea was to obtain a "clean copy", that is, to reduce his sheaves of tentative contour lines to a single, lucid, convincing one. Wherever such extremely "clean" lines are met with in the figures, it is worth considering whether these have not resulted from tracings of earlier sketches.

The Cambodgiennes

At the colonial exhibition arranged by the French government at Marseille in 1906, one of the highlights was the appearance of Cambodian court dancers, overseen by King Sisowath and his eldest daughter, Princess Soumhady. Cambodia had become a French protectorate in 1884, and the king travelled with a large retinue. He, his court and dancers were guests of the French Republic during their six-week stay. On July 1, 1906, a gala was held in their honor at the Elysée Palace, to which Rodin was invited. Here he saw the dancers for the first time, and in his enthusiasm reportedly invited them to his house in Meudon, to draw them and make a portrait of their King. This, however, did not transpire. On July 10 the Cambodians performed a second time, in the Bois de Boulogne, an event arranged by King Sisowath in honor of the French Colonial Minister. Here Rodin saw and admired the ballet again. On July 12, thanks to the aid of high ministerial officials, Rodin was able to visit the Cambodian delegation at their hotel and execute a few studies, probably including portrait drawings of the king and some of his dignitaries. The appearance, costumes and gestures of the Cambodians had set him aflame. Hearing that they were to return to Marseille that same evening, he immediately decided to take the same train. Rodin himself has given us a description of the elated mood in which he sketched the dancers in Marseille,[21] working in part on silky grey wrapping paper from a bakery, since he had no drawing materials when he arrived and the shops were closed. This paper, he said, was ideal—"le papier sur les genoux et le crayon à la main, émerveillé de leur beauté singulière et du grand charactère de leur danse. Ce qui surtout m'étonnait et me ravissait, c'était de retrouver dans cet art d'Extrême-Orient, inconnu de moi jusqu'alors, les principes mêmes de l'art antique" ("The paper on my knees and pencil in hand, marvelling at their singular beauty and the superb quality of their dancing. But what astonished and ravished me most was to discover in this art of the Far East, of which I knew nothing up to then, the principles of the art of antiquity.")

The sculptor goes on to explain this connection in detail. What slept in fragments of Greek sculpture, he says, was real and present and incredibly alive here. The reason for this was the same link of art to religious faith: "En effet, ces danses sont religieuses parce qu'elles sont artistiques: leur rythme est un rite, et c'est la pureté du rite qui leur assure la pureté du rythme... La même pensée avait donc sauvegardé l'art à Athènes, à Chartres, au Cambodge, partout, variant seulement par la formule du dogme..." ("Indeed these dances are religious because they are artistic—their rhythm is rite, and the purity of the rites insures that their rhythms will be pure... The same thinking infuses the art of Athens, of Chartres, of Cambodia, the only difference being their form of dogma...").

The series of drawings collectively entitled *Cambodgiennes* contains a few portraits besides the depictions of dancers. Rodin drew King Sisowath (plate on p. 274) and some of the male members of his court and retinue. Another portrait drawing (plate on p. 275) represents a Cambodian whose name and title have not been recorded. The pencil contours are of the most extreme simplicity. A few lines, set down with astonishing conviction and elegance, record the contours of head, nose and brows, eyes and lips, and suggest in broad curves the forms of shoulders and chest. The beginning of a second portrait, upside down and unfinished, is visible below. Rodin tinted his drawing in two colors—the flesh a greyish pink or beige, the hair an opaque dark grey with a slight bluish cast, playing into brown. The cream-colored paper lends the drawing the look of a sketch for a Persian miniature. Its simplicity of manner has something lasting and permanent; the sharp yet delicate pencil strokes seem almost engraved.

Most of the drawings of the Cambodia series are devoted to single figures, and of these most are of dancers in costume. Again and again Rodin endeavored to capture the motions transmitted from torso to arms and legs and the delicate gestures of hands and feet. The drawings reproduced on pages 278, 279 and 282 show positions in which the dancers' raised arms and hands vibrate to the fingertips. It has often been remarked that their supple grace makes one forget that they are real people with a skeleton and sinews. Many an arm in the drawings indeed seems almost to coil and vibrate like a snake (plates on pp. 277, 280, 284, 285, etc.). But besides extremely tranquil figures (e. g., plate on p. 287) there are some whose gestures are extremely ecstatic. The *Cambodian Dancer en face* (plate on p. 285) is a good example, her legs whirling even faster and higher than those of two other dancers caught in similar positions (plates on pp. 281, 283). Interestingly, the most violent steps are performed by almost masculine-looking women of the court ballet, while the lyrical role is taken by the slenderer, more delicate girls. The first-named drawing (page 285) records a very extreme pose, the dancer hopping on her left foot, having propelled herself upwards, raised her right knee and thrown her arms into the air, twirling her hands. Rodin has captured the kinesics of this sequence of movements in line after line, evidently noting the changing positions of the limbs five or six times. After tentatively sketching their first position he continually increased the pressure on his pencil, making darker and broader strokes, interrupting and beginning again time after time, until gradually the final contour emerged from this web of attempts. But none of them satisfied him; striking again and again, Rodin finally let several "key lines" stand adjacent to one another, in order to visualize the motor movement of the dance and its rapidly changing positions—especially leg positions. A closer look at this drawing shows that the dancer's left, supporting leg was originally bent at less of an angle and positioned closer to the center line of the body, indeed that Rodin had already given it a wash of greyish-red incarnadine. In a later phase of work he corrected and increased the expressive force of this leg, setting the "finished" linear construction in motion again and finding an even more extreme position for the spread thighs and angled calves. It was this reworking that created the impression of the dancer's stamping, leaping, whirling legwork. Around her body flutter her costume, sash, and veil in sweeping, flowing lines. The colored wash places a few accents—mere suggestions of the hue of costume and skin, and of the surrounding space, which seems to emanate in waves from the figure.

As this description shows, Rodin's technique of capturing rapid evanescent movement took him into an area that only a few years later the Futurists would explore, in a programmatic and well-nigh scientific manner—the depiction of rapid, motoric sequences of motion. They made use of the optical discoveries of stroboscopic (kinetic) photography, developed by the Parisian psychologist Etienne Jules Marey (1831–1904) and by the Americans Muybridge and Eakins in their experimental photographs of running horses and human beings in action, and eventually of birds in flight, which they began making in 1878–80 and initially published only in specialized periodicals.[22] The work of Seurat already contains certain effects of this discovery, as in the details of his painting of vaudeville dancers, *La Chahut*, 1889–90 (Otterlo), which presumably go back to chronophotographs he had seen. The representation of successive phases of a figure's motion also plays a role in the caricature of the period (from Wilhelm Busch to Charles Dana Gibson).[23] Finally, Frantisek Kupka, the Futurists Ballà, Russolo, Boccioni, Severini, and others, and Marcel Duchamp (*Nude Descending a Staircase*, 1911–12, Philadelphia Museum of Art) began to treat this theme in a systematic manner. Rodin's drawings of figures in motion were made independently of these endeavors, though he did know Muybridge's key volume of 1887 (in the preface to his second book in 1901, Muybridge proudly listed the artists who had subscribed, and Rodin was among them). Rodin's drawings grew out of his early interest in depicting movement in sculpture, which began to take on more and more importance with the beginning of his work on *The Gates of Hell* in 1880. In many of his studies associated with this work, the "black drawings", he had already begun to let *pentimenti* stand, which increased the impression of movement (e.g., in *Embracing Couple*, pencil and pen-and-ink, c. 1880, Philadelphia, Rodin Museum).[24] This graphic method, consciously applied, reached its culmination in the dynamic representation of dance in the *Cambodgiennes*. With these drawings Rodin made a significant if inadvertent contribution to the pre-Futurist art of depicting the sequential movements of individual figures. This is certainly one reason why they were considered so astonishingly modern when they were exhibited in 1907–08 in Paris and shortly thereafter outside of France.

However, there are other reasons to admire this group of works, particularly the wonderful colors of many of the drawings. Looking through them, one can distinguish several different levels of color employment, very much as in the later nudes with watercolor wash. While some of the *Cambodgiennes* are limited to pencil outlines, others possess only the single tone of a brownish-beige, ocher-yellow, or greyed pink incarnadine, which often flows freely across the figure, sometimes in disregard of the contouring pencil lines. Then we find almost mono-chrome images (as that on p. 277) in which all the color nuances appear to be developed from a single ocher tone, which, now brownish, now mixed with white to produce a lighter yellow, plays diaphanously around the figure. The next category is that of watercolors in two hues, an example of which is the drawing reproduced on page 282. This too has an almost monochrome effect, because the darker grey tone of the dancer's costume has been lightened to a greyish pink in the skin, and appears again in the coiffure. By the way, this sheet is a good example of reworking *after* the application of watercolor (which generally represented a second or third, in any case final phase of work). Over the wash Rodin has applied heavy pencil textures to hair and costume, throwing the entire figure into greater relief. In other drawings he even used pen-and-ink over the watercolor to heighten the definition (plate on p. 281).

A related watercolored drawing (p. 287) has, in addition to the grey nuances, a touch of dull green in the dress and a greyish pink with violet overtones which, having been mixed with white, is semi-opaque. The costumes of other dancers scintillate through the delicate hues of blossoms—rose, bluish-red, blue and yellow (p. 279). Usually these colors are greyed, subdued, reserved, which heightens the brilliance of occasional touches of glowing mauves and magentas. On the whole, the watercolor and gouache washes lend these drawings an impression of hovering delicacy, a suggestion of unreality, of strange exotic charm. They embody a completely unprecedented nuance of Orientalism in European art. They are infused with the mystery of a very ancient culture, which developed over the centuries between India and China and revealed itself to European artists only in flashes. The ceremonial gestures of the temple dancers that Rodin united in a number of groupings possess this strange beauty and grace (plates on pp. 288, 289). Particularly fascinating is the series of five figures ascending a flight of low steps as if towards a temple, with gestures whose meaning remains a mystery to us but which we can assume signify supplication, worship, prayer, and evocation. In this drawing Rodin has placed the brown bodies with their yellow, ocher, and greenish costumes before a light blue, cloudy background, a combination of hues that rings out like a sonorous hymn of praise; the brown limbs of the dancers stand out against the blue like the arabesques on a ceramic. At the right, above their heads, Rodin has written, only partially intelligibly, "…action creuze (?) … attachées à une harmonie … fait valoir le corps possible …" and, by themselves, the words "Fleur humaine … ami … cultivé." Halting words of admiration, it seems, which Rodin felt for the apparitions from some magical Oriental fairy-tale come true— "Fleurs humaines", flowers transformed into womanly shape.[25]

Though it cannot be excluded that he drew some of these Cambodian dancers later, from memory, Rodin created the series in a very short time, as if in a fever, and we certainly believe him when he says "I looked at them ecstatically… what a void they have left behind! When they departed I was left in darkness and cold, I thought they had carried the beauty of the world away with them… I followed them to Marseille. I would have followed them to Cairo!"[26]

Rilke immediately recognized the new mastery of these colorful drawings, and many still consider them the finest in Rodin's late œuvre. He created them in his sixty-sixth year. One cannot say that his work culminated here, however, since the gifted sculptor was still to model such powerful portraits as that of Hanako (1908), that of Gustav Mahler (1909), of Clemenceau (1911), and of Pope Benedict XV (1915), as well as the striking statuette of Nijinski leaping (1912), not to mention other works. His work in drawing continued to develop, too, the years immediately preceding the First World War probably bringing many of those nude drawings which he no longer accentuated with watercolor but solely by rubbing the pencil to produce painterly and sculptural effects.[27] Nevertheless, the *Cambodgiennes* represent a special and superb achievement within Rodin's liberated, most mature art of drawing, in which he gave himself over totally to a depiction of movement, gesture, and the evanescent apparition of the human form in physical expressions bordering on the ritualistic.

Rodin knew Michelangelo's injunction to the artist, "... to attempt in the sweat of his brow to create a work with diligence and zeal such that it appears to have been designed rapidly and easily and as if without effort." Rodin's late drawings and watercolors of nudes and dancers fulfill this demand with astonishing perfection. But they also fulfill another of the artist's purposes, being metaphors for the transience of animate life. The flowing watercolor washes, the open, tentative contours, the vibrating multiplicity of lines and strokes, all contribute to the same evocation of fleetingness. Yet Rodin's art can no longer be equated with that capturing of quick movements in Impressionistic sketches which we know from the work of Manet and Degas, Liebermann and Slevogt. Rather, Rodin's late graphic style transcended this approach to enter a sphere of symbolic allusion which arose from his personal philosophy of life. Rilke recognized this, as did, partially, Roger Marx (in his essay "Rodin dessinateur", *Gazette des Beaux-Arts,* 1912) and—clairvoyantly interpreting the sculpture—the philosopher and sociologist Georg Simmel.[28] He saw revealed in Rodin's work the "Heraclitican" principle of modern culture at the onset of the twentieth century, the flux of all perceptions, the transitory, ever-changing, ineffable nature of life. Where this quality transcends the purely visual and perceptual approach of Impressionism to combine with the significances of symbolism, such as in the music of Debussy, probably also in Monet's *Water-lilies,* and certainly in Rodin's late drawings and watercolors, it achieves a higher degree of artistic compulsion, a potentiated expressive force. Where human bodies grow transparent and reveal their animate existence, or where, as in the *Cambodgiennes,* their aura becomes visible, they evoke a harmony with the pantheistic cosmos which Rodin sensed and which before him hardly any other European artist had even begun to detect.

Notes

1 J. Kirk T. Varnedoe, "Rodin as a Draftsman – A Chronological Perspective." In: Albert Elsen and J. Kirk T. Varnedoe, *The Drawings of Rodin. With additional contributions by Victoria Thorson and Elisabeth Chase Geissbuhler.* London, 1972, pp. 25–120.

2 Victoria Thorson, *Rodin Graphics: A catalogue raisonné of Drypoints and Book Illustrations.* The Fine Arts Museums of San Francisco, 1975, p. 66 ff.

3 J. Kirk T. Varnedoe, *op. cit.,* p. 75, fig. 61.

4 Clément Janin, "Les dessins de Rodin." In: *Les maîtres Artistes,* October 15, 1903.

5 On the development and execution of the monument to *The Burghers of Calais,* see: J. A. Schmoll gen. Eisenwerth, "Rodins 'Bürger von Calais' und ihr Kompositionsproblem ..." In: *Saarbrücker Hefte,* no. 10, 1959, pp. 59–70; and Claudie Judrin, Monique Laurent and Dominique Viéville, *Auguste Rodin—Le Monument des Bourgeois de Calais (1884–1895) dans les collections du Musée Rodin et du Musée des Beaux-Arts de Calais.* Paris and Calais, 1977.

6 Museum of Fine Arts, Budapest, Inv. No. 1935–2776. Purchased in 1935 from the Pál Majovszky Collection, Budapest. Last reproduced in the exhibition catalogue *Auguste Rodin—Plastik, Zeichnungen, Graphik,* ed. Claude Keisch, Staatliche Museen zu Berlin/DDR (Nationalgalerie), 1979, no. 88, p. 195.

7 Jacques de Caso and Patricia B. Sanders, *Rodin's Sculpture. A critical study of the Spreckels Collection.* California Palace of the Legion of Honor, The Fine Arts Museums of San Francisco (Charles E. Tuttle Co., Inc., Rutland, Vermont and Tokyo), 1977, p. 293.

8 Monique Laurent and Claudie Judrin (eds.), *Rodin et les écrivains de son temps, sculptures, dessins, lettres et livres du fonds Rodin.* Exhibition catalogue, Musée Rodin, Paris, 1976, p. 126 ff., where the drawing reproduced here (and three others of Séverine) are illustrated.

9 On the reverse is still another rapid sketch of a standing female nude with many *pentimenti,* and also the note: "Offert par Mr. Fenaille au Musée Rodin le 16 juin 1927." Fenaille was a patron and admirer of Rodin who suggested the facsimile edition of his drawings in 1897 and oversaw their selection. Rodin did several portraits of his wife. The bust in marble, with its so lyrical and meditative expression, entered the Musée Rodin along with the same gift as the portrait drawing of an unknown model under discussion.

10 J. A. Schmoll gen. Eisenwerth, *Malerei nach Fotografie, von der camera obscura bis zur Pop Art.* Exhibition catalogue, Münchner Stadtmuseum, 1970, p. 56.

11 Elsen and Varnedoe, *The Drawings of Rodin, op. cit.,* p. 95, fig. 83 (reversed by mistake). See also Rodin's erotic drawings reproduced there, figs. 101, 103, and 105.

12 I owe the reference to Helene von Nostitz's newspaper article to her son, Oswalt von Nostitz, whom I should also like to thank for his kind aid regarding other details of this essay as well.

13 Some of these variants are reproduced in Elsen and Varnedoe, *The Drawings of Rodin, op. cit.* (note 1). Fig. 80: *Kneeling Woman with Vase on her Head,* pencil and watercolor, Washington, National Gallery; fig. 96: *The Inception of the Greek Vase,* pencil and watercolor, New York, Metropolitan Museum, purchased 1913.

14 Reproduced in the catalogue to the Rodin exhibition, Staatliche Museen zu Berlin/DDR, 1979 (see note 6), no. 100; and Claudie Judrin, *Auguste Rodin, 100 Zeichnungen und Aquarelle.* German edition: Herder, Freiburg i. Br., Basel and Vienna, 1982, no. 53 (color plate).

15 See fig. 117 in: Victoria Thorson, *Rodin Graphics, op. cit.* (see note 2), p. 112. See also the catalogue *Rodin et les écrivains, op. cit.* (note 8), pp. 90–115.

16 See Volker Wahl, "Die Jenaer Ehrenpromotion von Auguste Rodin und der 'Rodin-Skandal' zu Weimar 1905/06." In: *Auguste Rodin—Plastik, Zeichnungen, Graphik, op. cit.* (see note 6), pp. 58–67. Also Claude Keisch, "Chronologie des Weimarer 'Rodin-Skandals'", *ibid.,* pp. 68–74.

17 Reproduced in the East Berlin catalogue, *ibid.,* no. 113, p. 217.

18 Jules Huret in an article in *Le Figaro,* Paris, March 26, 1907, describing the situation at the Berlin court and quoting various of its members. See also *Auguste Rodin—Plastik, Zeichnungen, Graphik, op. cit.* p. 29; also J. A. Schmoll gen. Eisenwerth, "Rodin und Kaiser Wilhelm II." In: *Rodin-Studien,* Munich, 1983, pp. 329–346.

19 Felix Klee (ed.), *Tagebücher von Paul Klee 1898–1918.* Cologne, 1957 (first ed.), p. 114.

20 Elsen and Varnedoe, *The Drawings of Rodin, op. cit.,* p. 99 and other places.

21 Monique Laurent and Claudie Judrin (eds.), *Rodin et l'Extrême-Orient.* Exhibition catalogue, Musée Rodin, Paris, 1979, pp. 67–99.

22 On chronophotography, see: a) Otto Stelzer, *Kunst und Photographie.* Munich, 1966; b) Aaron Scharf, *Art and Photography.* London, 1968; c) J. A. Schmoll gen. Eisenwerth, *Malerei nach Fotografie...* Exhibition catalogue,

Münchner Stadtmuseum, 1970; d) Herbert Molderings, "Film, Photographie und ihr Einfluß auf die Malerei in Paris um 1910." In: *Wallraf-Richartz-Jahrbuch 1975;* e) Margit Rowell, *Frantisek Kupka*. Exhibition catalogue, The Solomon R. Guggenheim Museum, New York. 1975, and (expanded), Kunsthaus Zürich, 1976; f) Jean Clair, *L'œuvre de Marcel Duchamp, Catalogue raisonné.* Centre Georges Pompidou, Paris, 1977; g) J. A. Schmoll gen. Eisenwerth, "Die Bewegungsphotographie inspiriert Maler." In: Erika Billeter (and J. A. Schmoll), *Malerei und Photographie im Dialog*... Exhibition catalogue, Kunsthaus Zürich and Buch Verlag Benteli, Bern, 1977 and 1979; reprinted in: J. A. Schmoll gen. Eisenwerth, *Vom Sinn der Photographie, Texte aus den Jahren 1952–1980.* Munich, 1980, pp. 175–186.

23 Otto Stelzer, *Kunst und Photographie.* Munich, 1966 (first ed.), pp. 128–131.

24 Reproduced in: Elsen and Varnedoe, *The Drawings of Rodin, op. cit.* (see note 1), fig. 28.

25 Rilke mentions this note of Rodin's on watercolor D. 4517, which was exhibited at Bernheim Jeune, Paris, in October 1907, in a long passage of a letter to his wife, Clara Rilke-Westhoff: "Naturally, soon after I'd thought of it, I read 'Fleurs humaines' somewhere in his joyous handwriting. How sad that he doesn't trust us to draw such conclusions—they're really quite obvious. Then again, it moved me that I had understood him so literally, as I often do." Claudie Judrin quotes this letter extensively in: *100 Zeichnungen und Aquarelle, op. cit.* (see note 14), p. 17. See also the color plates and notes on the *Cambodgiennes* there.

26 Quoted in: Laurent and Judrin (eds.), *Rodin et l'Extrême-Orient, op. cit.,* p. 67.

27 Claudie Judrin (*100 Zeichnungen und Aquarelle, op. cit.,* p. 21) thinks Paul Gsell was probably right when he said that after 1910, in a third phase of his late drawing style, Rodin no longer employed watercolor but executed more delicate nude drawings, rubbing the pencil to create veiled effects. Some of these can possibly be dated, since their model was the dancer Alda Moreno, who appeared at the Opéra Comique in Paris; a letter of 1912 refers expressly to the fact that she modelled for Rodin's drawings.

28 J. A. Schmoll gen. Eisenwerth, "Simmel und Rodin". In: *Ästhetik und Soziologie um die Jahrhundertwende: Georg Simmel.* Ed. H. Böhringer und Karlfried Gründer. Frankfurt am Main, 1976, pp. 18–39; reprinted in: *Rodin-Studien,* Munich, 1983, pp. 317–328.

121 *Portrait of Séverine; D.5644*

5941.

M.R

M.R

122 *Portrait of a Woman; D. 5941*

123 *Portrait of a Woman; D.2861*

124 *Dancer*

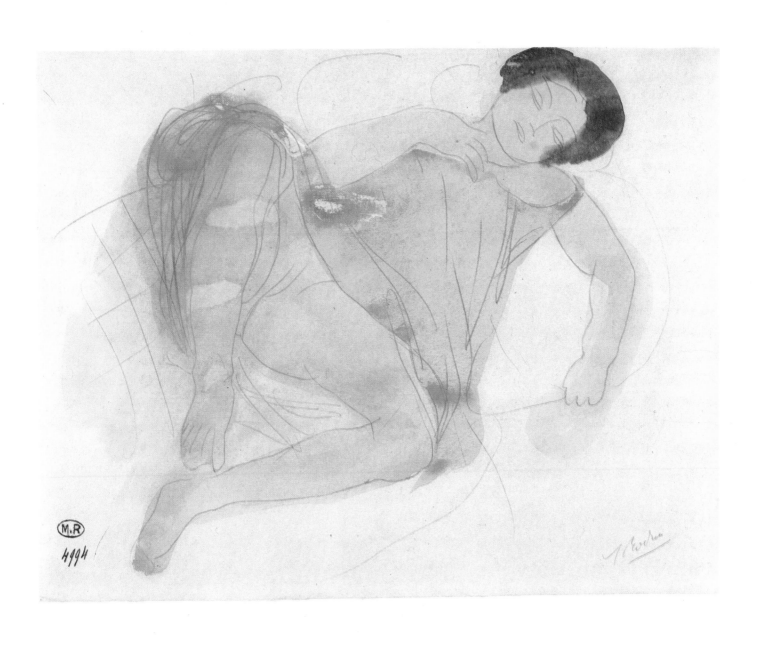

125 *Reclining Woman with Exposed Legs; D. 4994*

126 *Sleeping Girl Seen Obliquely from Below*

127 *Clothed Woman Lying on Her Side; D.5657*

128 *The Muse and the Poet*

242

129 *Clothed Woman Seated between Her Heels; D.5003*

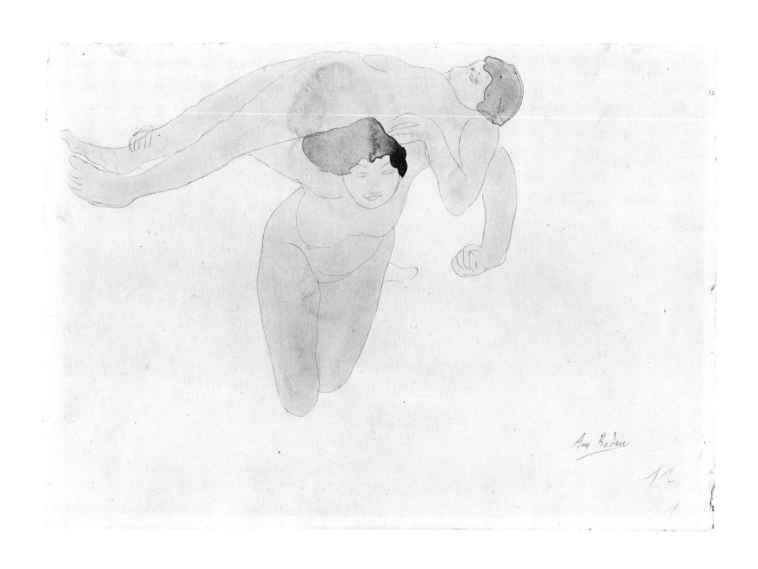

131 *Nude Kneeling Woman Holding Her Arms behind Her Back; D.4620*

132 *Kneeling Woman, Her Head Thrown Back; D.4772*

133 *Vase Woman; D.4771*

134 *Reclining Female Nude, One Foot Propped on Her Thigh; D.2479*

135 *Reclining Female Nude, One Hand under Her Raised Leg; D.1379*

136 *Nude Woman from the Side, One Knee on the Floor, Bent Backwards, Holding Her Foot with One Hand; D.1741*

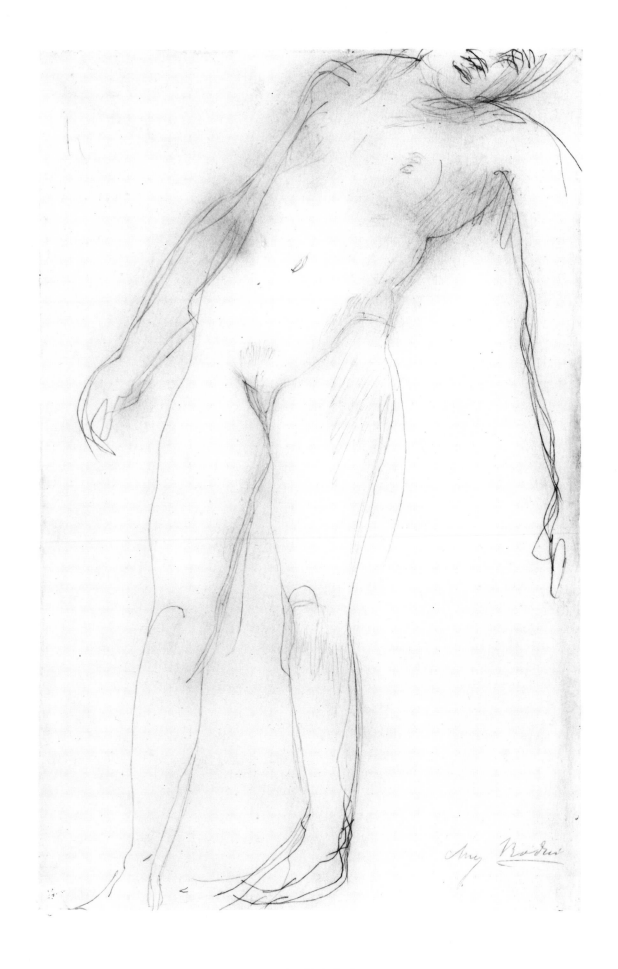

137 *Nude Study*

138 *Two Seated Women, Holding Hands; D.3919*

139 *Female Nude*

140 *Female Nude from the Back*

141 *Seated Woman*

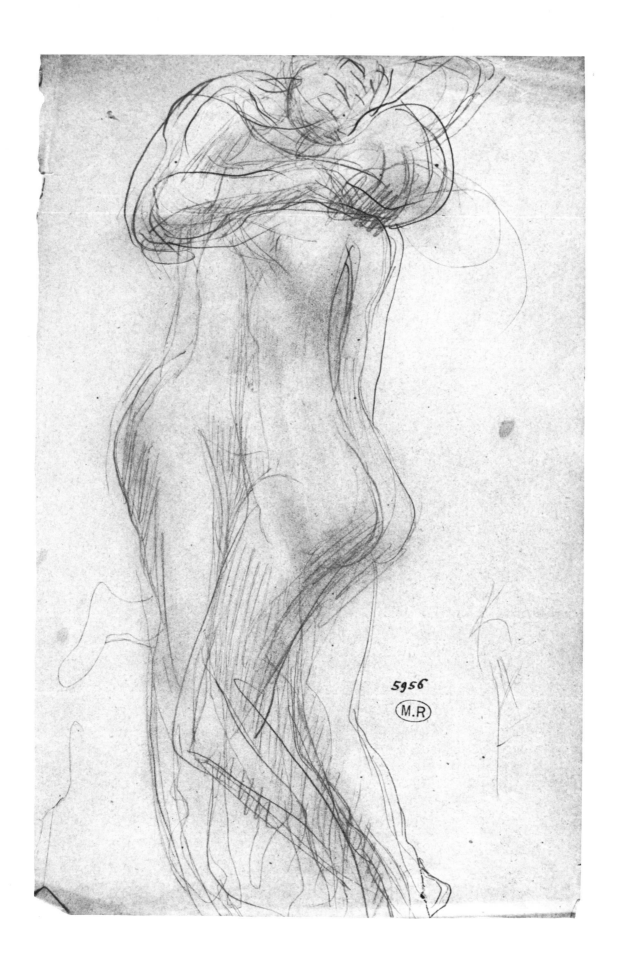

142 *Embracing Couple, also known as Desire; D.5956*

143 *Two Women Embracing; D.7195*

144 *Seated Man (Neptune)*

145 *Reclining Woman, a Hand behind Her Head; D.5239*

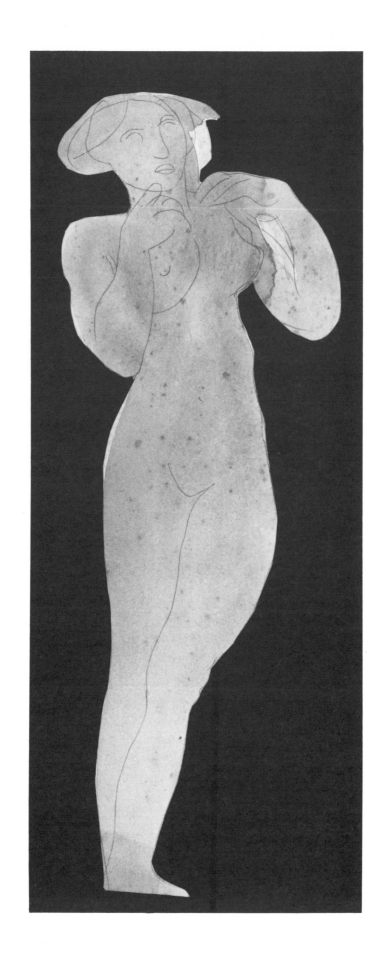

146 *Female Nude with Angled Arms; D.5201*

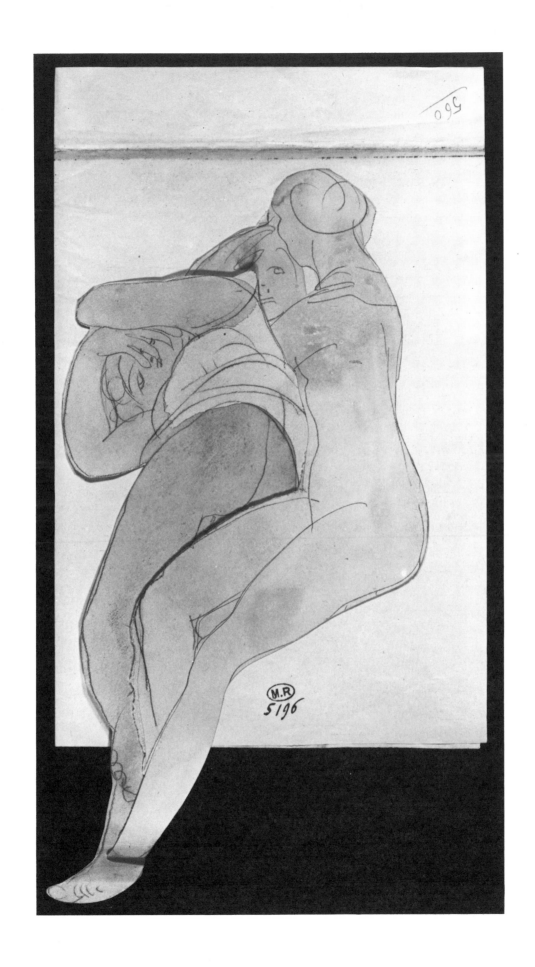

147 *Three Embracing Women; D.5196*

148 *Nude Woman Bent Over Her Raised Leg, the Other Leg Stretched Out Behind Her; D.7181*

149 *Reclining Nude Woman from Behind; D.1537*

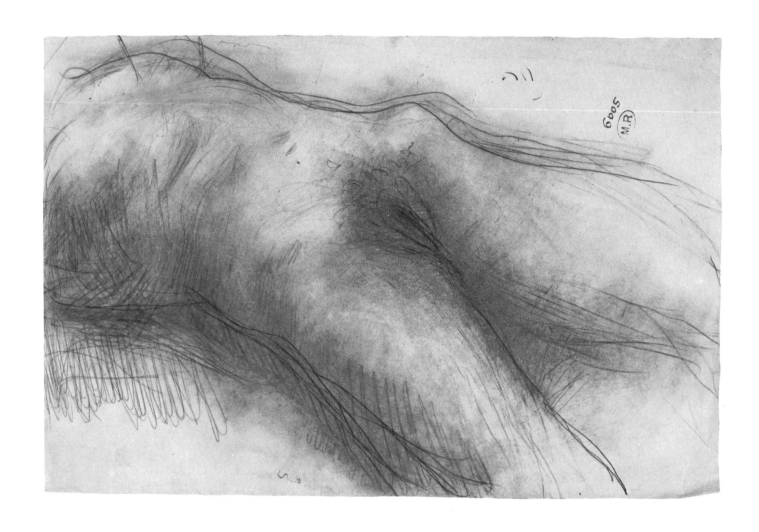

150 *Reclining Nude Female Torso; D.6005*

151 *Reclining Female Torso, a Hand on Her Breast; D.2909*

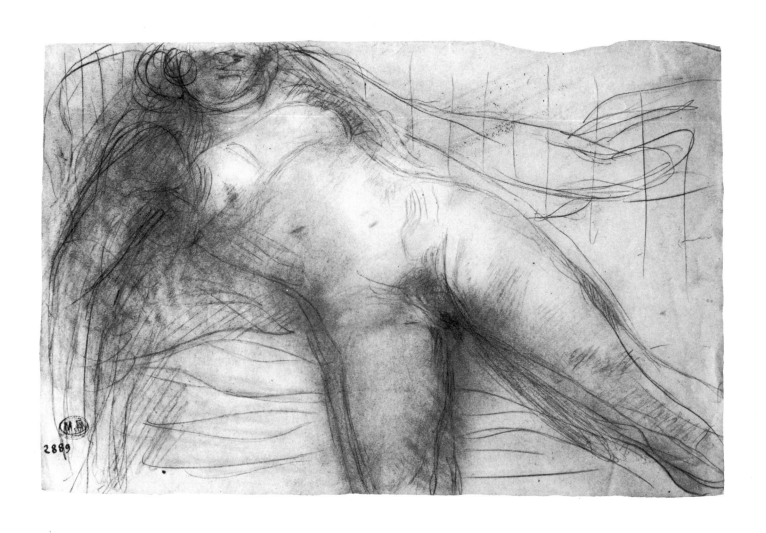

152 *Reclining Female Nude; D.2889*

153 Salammbô, Woman Lying on Her Back, Stretching Herself; D.6012

154 *La lune, Psyché*

The Cambodian Dancers

Rodin drawing a Cambodian dancer in Marseille, 1906

THE DANCERS OF KING SISOWATH OF CAMBODIA

Auguste Rodin

I have spent the four most wonderful days of my life with my pretty friends. The little Javanese girls who were here at the exhibition had already pleased me, and now the delightful Cambodian princesses have reawakened my old impressions and increased them a hundred times. They have brought antiquity to life again for me. They have shown me, in reality, the beautiful gestures, the beautiful movements of the human body which the ancients knew how to capture in art. They suddenly immersed me in nature, revealed a completely new aspect and taught me that artists here below have no other task than to observe nature and find sustenance at its source. I am a man who had devoted his entire life to the study of nature and who infinitely admires the works of antiquity; so you can imagine how such a superb spectacle must have affected me, a spectacle that opened my eyes to antiquity again. These monotonous, slow dances to the rhythms of strange music have an extraordinary, a perfect beauty, like the beauty of Greece but with its own special quality. The Cambodian dancers have revealed movements to me that I have never found anywhere before, either in the art of sculpture or in nature. For instance, that longitudinal motion they create by stretching out their arms, turning their hands up, and spreading their fingers, producing a slow undulation from one end of the cross they form to the other, a wave motion that is also transmitted to chest and shoulders and which creates a continual opposition of the curves of their arms, one forming a convex and the other a concave arc. Or the pose I have sketched here, showing the dancer crouched down almost to the ground, leaning forward, one bent knee touching her breast and her feet thrown out behind her. Isn't this wonderfully lovely and new? This is what convinces me that my little girlfriends are as beautiful as the art of the ancients. And if they are beautiful, it is because their movements are right, in a perfectly natural way.—What makes a movement right is impossible to define. A wrong movement in sculpture is the same thing as a false note in music. But what is a false note? You have to have an ear for it... Well, and in our case you have to have an eye. All you can say is that all movements of the body, if they are harmonious and right, can be inscribed within a geometric pattern whose lines are simple and few. The Greeks had a good feeling for this law, and my little friends do, too. They have a natural knowledge of harmony and truth—or someone has it for them, because I suppose Princess Samphoudry, who directs them, and King Sisowath, who supports them, must be great artists [?] in their own right. Where do they derive this knowledge? They simply obey nature, their own nature, instead of striving for the rare and artificial. I immediately recognized their superiority the evening I saw them at the Pré-Catalan. They had stopped dancing; they were being applauded, but lukewarmly, because Paris audiences are no longer capable of recognizing true beauty. After them came so-called "Greek dances"—a crying shame, really a crying shame, because everything about them was false, contrived, artificial... Until the 18th century we had, besides a respect for tradition, a love of classical harmony. Then a school arose which, abjuring nature, changed all that, and which we have to thank for our present bad taste. And this bad taste is spreading everywhere, onto the streets and into our houses, into art as much as furniture! ... In my beginnings, when I had a model come I always used to ask her right off what studios she had "worked" in. I saw immediately if she had come from the Academy.

As soon as she climbed onto the podium I saw her assume one of those attitudes she had learned there, and it was always wrong. How could it be otherwise? What do they teach you at the Academy? Composition! But composition is theatrics, the dramatic science of lies. So let's stick with nature—it contains true, eternal science and is a source that never fails. In nature truth is always to be found. It is a sign of weakness to rely on imagination. Imagination is only the gift of combining memories. But our memories are limited and our imagination is limited; infinite nature, by contrast, continually offers us a great store of new sensations. And if I love Sisowath's little dancers, it is because the rhythmic movements of their bodies have revealed a little corner of nature I had yet to discover... If I were younger, I would have gone back with the dancers to their own country, studied them in peace, and would have tried to make something of their costumes, which bring out their poses and figures so wonderfully... But now it's too late. And I regret this very much, because I'm convinced that an observation of their movements, which appear so new to us, would introduce elements of innovation and intense life into our sculpture. As far as I'm concerned, I can only say that I have learned from them...

THE DANCE GESTURE IN ESSENCE

Rainer Maria Rilke

Among the drawings I was familiar with (or thought I was familiar with, for how new they appear each time; or rather, how new they make oneself feel from case to case), I discovered a scattering of about fifteen sheets from a later period. They were made about a year ago, when Rodin travelled in pursuit of the King of Cambodia's dance troupe, and they contain, captured in the most remarkable way, that most uncapturable thing: dance. The dance gesture of ancient rhythmic cultures in essence, to delineate which with his means keyed to nuance, to that all-important nothingness that links two momentary poses, Rodin had already so longed when the Javanese girls appeared in Paris [1900]. Too preoccupied with his troublesome exhibition on Place de l'Alma, he had to forgo those models; but now one senses an outbreak of all of his long-restrained readiness in the rapid grasp and regrasp with which he mastered this astonishing subject six years later.

With an assurance that only apparently casually throws everything into confusion to get a hold on that one key thing, he extracts from the tangle of movements the end of the thread that explains them all. Undistracted by the emergence of ever-new aspects, he has time to recognize how the long, slender arms, formed seemingly in a single piece, extend through the rotund Buddha torso, and, by tracing their motions, he comes quite naively upon the hands, and sees that they, standing up at the wrists like actors just come on stage, are the real dancers for the sake of whose balance and freedom every movement of hips and feet takes place. And in them he now locates, with passionate precision, the dance itself, distilled and contained. Here as always everything succumbs to the impetuosity of his attack, down (or up) to the accident of his selecting a mummy-brown paper to draw on, which when mounted casts itself into countless tiny folds whose corruscations distantly recall the ornamental look of Oriental calligraphy. Onto this or a somewhat lighter ground the central gesture has then been brushed, in opaque, enamellike rose-white, as solemn as an illuminated initial and accompanied by that soft landscape blue or that almost odorous heliotrope familiar from Persian miniatures. Their incredibly frank reds also appear, torn past by the whirl of a pirouette, since they have been inherited and passed on, and also because the dancers wore them; and that transparent, immature tree-green—sensed in a moment of impassioned vision and brushed in blindly with the most primitive rightness.

Pages of an herbarium, one is tempted to say, as one passes from one to the next. Flowers have been collected here and, gently dried, their unconscious gestures have drawn into themselves to assume a final intensity which contains, as though in a symbol, their former existence entire.

155 *Portrait of a Man (King Sisowath of Cambodia)*

156 *Portrait of a Cambodian (Court Official of King Sisowath); D.4482*

157 *Cambodian Dancer*

158 *Cambodian Dancer en face; D.4437*

159 *Cambodian Dancer en face; D.4498*

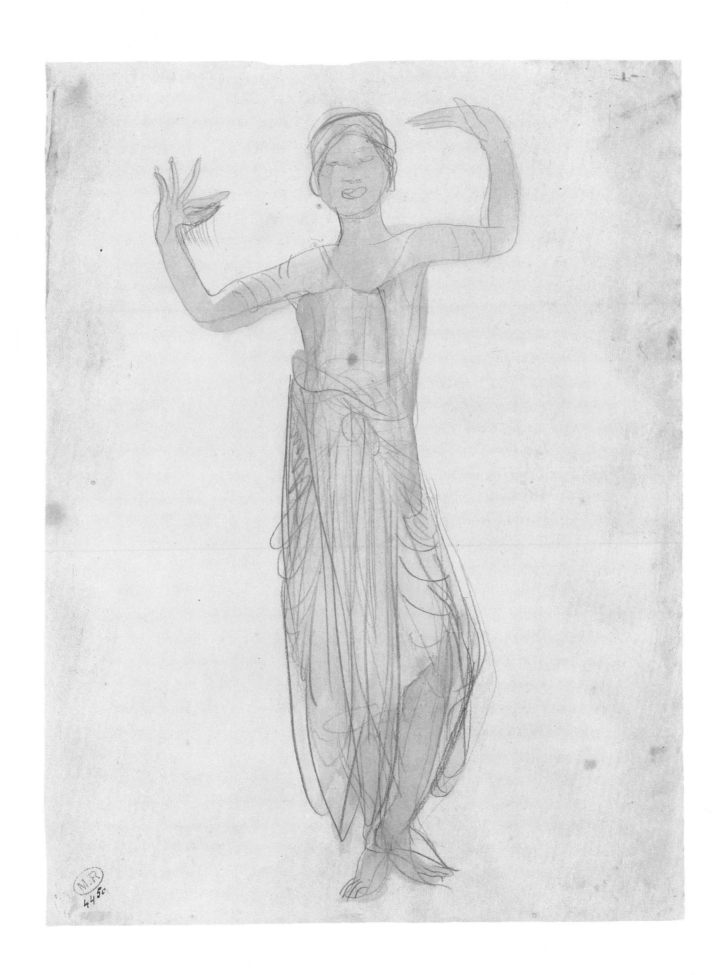

160 *Cambodian Dancer en face; D. 4450*

161 *Cambodian Dancer en face; D.5077*

162 *Cambodian Dancer en face; D.4511*

163 *Cambodian Dancer en face; D. 4449*

164 *Cambodian Dancer en face; D.4429*

165 *Cambodian Dancer from the Side; D.4432*

166 *Cambodian Dancer en face; D. 4455*

167 *Cambodian Dancer; D.4430*

M.R 5700

168 *Cambodian Dancer en face; D.5700*

169 *Six Studies of Cambodian Dancers; D.5076*

170 *Five Studies of Cambodian Dancers; D. 4517*

171 *Cambodian Dancer*

Rodin working with a model, about 1895

Biography

2 Rue de l'Arbalète, Paris

3 Marie Rodin née Cheffer

1840

François-Auguste-René Rodin is born on November 12, in Paris.

His parents, Jean-Baptiste and Marie Rodin *née* Cheffer, live on Rue de l'Arbalète, 12th Arrondissement.

Auguste Rodin's father, Jean-Baptiste, was among those who were caught up in the first wave of industrialization and rushed from the provinces to the capital about 1830. Born in Yvetot, he came of a family of cotton-goods vendors who, even before travel had become a common thing, were continually on the road offering their wares in the surrounding countryside. Jean-Baptiste had spent a few years in the Brethren of the Christian Doctrine and before coming to Paris he had even been a lay brother. Upon his arrival he exchanged a sequestered life for that of a subaltern official of the Prefecture of Police, a department to which he remained faithful to the end of his life... At the age of thirty-four he married a second time. Marie Cheffer—a typical Lorraine name—came of an old family long established on the Moselle. She was born in Laundorff, in German-speaking Lorraine. Marie was an irreproachable, hard-working wife, but not very sociable and not exactly blessed with physical charms.
(Bernard Champigneulle, *Rodin*. Quoted from the German translation by Brigitte Kahr, Gütersloh, n.d., p. 10)

1847

Attends the Ecole des Frères de la Doctrine Chrétienne, on Rue du Val-de-Grâce.

1851–1853

Goes to a boarding school in Beauvais, the headmaster of which is his uncle, Alexandre Rodin.

His dictations bristled with spelling errors. Unlike the others he never succeeded in learning Latin. In arithmetic he was a zero. Drawing was the only subject that interested him... He drove his teachers to despair and spent most of his time making pencil copies of paintings that he chanced to come across. As far as he could remember, he had always occupied himself with drawing. The owner of a general store where Mme. Rodin did her shopping, used to wrap his plums in paper cones which he rolled from the

pages of illustrated magazines. These pictures were Auguste's first models.
(Champigneulle, *Rodin*, p. 12)

4 Auguste Rodin
and his sister
Maria

1854–1857

Enrolls at the Petite Ecole (Ecole Spéciale de Dessin et des Mathématiques). His teacher there is Horace Lecoq de Boisbaudran.

Most students of this institution—called the "little school" to distinguish it from the great Ecole des Beaux-Arts—received a training there which enabled them to work later for etchers and steel engravers, illustrators, goldsmiths and jewellers, textile manufacturers, and for the embroidery and lace industry. The "little" academy also possessed a sculpture studio devoted as much to woodcarving for furniture and the interior decoration of churches and palatial residences as to actual sculpture—stonecarving, albeit decorative as well, for the adornment of public and private buildings. Like the rest, the students of the sculpture class began their training by drawing, which they had to master absolutely before going on . . . to work in three dimensions.
(Champigneulle, *Rodin*, p. 14)

The sculptor Etienne-Hippolyte Maindron, seeing Rodin's drawings, recommends he enroll at the Ecole des Beaux-Arts. Rodin fails the entrance examination three times; though his drawings please the commission, his sculpture, oriented to the eighteenth century, finds less approval.

1858–1862

Works for various decorators and commercial sculptors, including Blanche, Bièze, Cruchet, and Roubaud, to support his family. Meets Jules Dalou.

1862

His sister Maria dies at the age of twenty-four. A mental crisis leads Rodin to join the congregation of Priests of the Holy Sacrament, founded by Father Pierre-Julien Eymard.

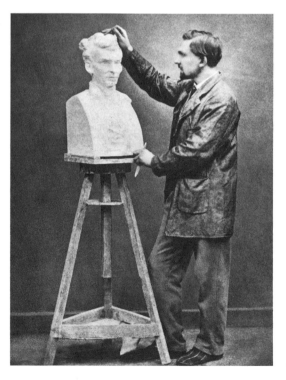

5 Rodin working
on the bust of
Father Pierre-
Julien Eymard,
about 1863

6 *Father Pierre-Julien Eymard*, 1863

In his daily intercourse with these pious men and in the monastic atmosphere, imbued with spiritual faith, Auguste regained not only his mental poise but his love of work. He was given a shed in the little back garden of the monastery where, as far as the observances of the order left him time, he worked on his sculptures.
(Champigneulle, *Rodin*, p. 24)

1863

Models bust of Father Pierre-Julien Eymard.

Father Eymard had not remained oblivious to the passionate artistic devotion of his novice, nor perhaps to his talent either. He nevertheless knew that despair can produce much that does not necessarily prove a true calling. But when he sat to Rodin for his bust, he had ample opportunity to converse with him and recognize the artist in him. And to convince him that his place was certainly not in a monastery. His vocation—must he not see it in the art to which he devoted himself with such abandon?
(Champigneulle, *Rodin*, p. 26)

Rodin leaves the order and becomes a member of the Union Centrale des Arts Décoratifs, which was founded by the sculptor Jules Klagmann and whose members included Delacroix, Ingres, and Lecoq de Boisbaudran. There Rodin meets the sculptor Jean-Baptiste Carpeaux, among others. Begins work on the sculpture *Man with Broken Nose*.

7 *Man with Broken Nose*, 1863–1864

One senses what must have moved Rodin to model this head, the head of an aging, ugly man, whose broken nose increased still further the tormented expression of his face—it was the abundance of life concentrated in these features; it was the circumstance that there were no symmetrical surfaces in this countenance, that nothing repeated itself, that no spot remained empty, dull or indifferent. This face had not been marked by life, it had been kneaded by it through and through, as if a merciless hand had plunged it into fate as into the maelstrom of a rising, corroding sea.
(Rainer Maria Rilke, *Auguste Rodin*, Leipzig, 1922, p. 23)

1864

Participates in a course in animal anatomy, held by Antoine Louis Barye at the Musée d'Histoire Naturelle, and studies anatomy at the Ecole de Médecine. Barye was an advocate of "silent instruction", which, as Rodin recalled to his biographer, amounted to this:

We felt uncomfortable surrounded by amateurs and ladies, and the waxed parquetry floor of the library where the classes were held definitely intimidated us. After a long search we finally discovered in the Botanical Garden a kind of cellar vault whose walls sweated with dampness, and there we gleefully installed ourselves. On a stick rammed into the ground we placed a board to use as a modelling board; since it was not revolvable, however, we ourselves revolved around the board and the models we were copying. They were kind enough to tolerate us there, and allowed us to take from the lecture rooms parts of animal cadavers, lion's paws, and similar things. We worked like madmen, becoming as good as wild animals ourselves. The great Barye sometimes dropped by. He would look at what we had done and then depart, usually without having wasted so much as a single word.
(Champigneulle, *Rodin*, p. 20)

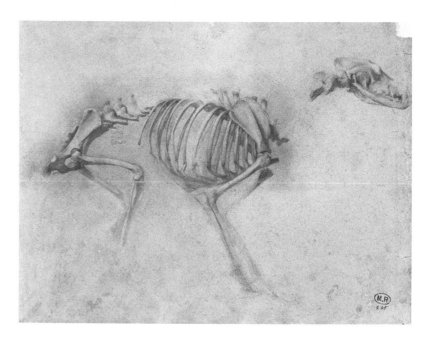

8 *Skeleton of a Dog*, D. 245

1864–1865

Meets Rose Beuret, who is to become his lifelong companion.

Auguste was generally shy, but this young girl's open face and frank trusting gaze robbed him of his bashfulness. And he embarked upon an adventure, probably his first. The adventure lasted fifty-two years. Rose Beuret was born in the Haute-Marne region, in a little place near Joinville, on the banks of the Marne. Her parents were farming people.
(Champigneulle, *Rodin*, p. 27)

Works during the following years in the studio of Albert Carrier-Belleuse on Rue de la Tour d'Auvergne.

[Carrier-Belleuse] managed his atelier on Rue de la Tour d'Auvergne with technical skill and business acumen, almost like a factory. He had realized that his true talent lay in the arts and crafts, and employed about twenty assistants who copied their master's models down to the last

9 *Mignon* (Rose Beuret), 1867–1868

10 Auguste Beuret
and his wife "Nini"
in the Meudon
studio

11 *Landscape*, D.60

*detail. He was a respected and much-patronized supplier
of the bourgeoisie, who revelled in statuettes, vases, center-
pieces, candelabras, and grandfather clocks.*
(Champigneulle, *Rodin*, p.33)

1866

Birth of his son, Auguste-Eugène Beuret (dies
April 23, 1934).

1871

Executes ornamental work for Albert-Ernest
Carrier-Belleuse on the Palais de la Bourse,
Brussels.

*Carrier-Belleuse supervised a crew of artists and artisans,
stonemasons and stucco-workers. If he had left Paris it
was because the war had suffocated all artistic activity
there and emigrants had a chance abroad to temporarily
create a respected and lucrative position for themselves.
Besides the sculptors he had hired on the spot, Carrier-
Belleuse had his assistant Van Rasbourg along, whom
Rodin knew well from their Paris days. Rodin found lodg-
ings in a rundown inn on an old sidestreet of the Bourse
quarter, and turned over every penny in the hope of sending
his family a little money.*
(Champigneulle, *Rodin*, p.36)

1872

Rose Beuret follows Rodin to Brussels.

1873

Carrier-Belleuse returns to Paris. Rodin col-
laborates with Van Rasbourg on architectural
sculptures, and does paintings and landscape
drawings in his spare time. Makes friends with
Constantin Meunier, Julien Dillens, Gustave
Biot, and Paul de Vigne.

1875–1876

Travels over Mont Cenis to Turin, Genoa, Pisa,
Florence, Rome, and Naples. Sees Michel-

angelo's Medici Tombs in the sacristy of San Lorenzo in Florence.

Nothing I have seen in photographs or plaster copies conveys the slightest idea of the sacristy of San Lorenzo. You have to view the tombs from the side and in three-quarter profile. I spent five days in Florence and did not see the sacristy until today, and I must say everything left me cold during those five days. I have had only three lasting impressions: Reims, the Alps, and the sacristy. When you stand before it, you do not analyze what you see at first. It will probably not come as a surprise to you when I tell you that ever since I have been in Florence I have studied Michelangelo, and I believe the great magician will probably reveal a couple of his secrets to me... Nights, in my room, I have been making drawings, but not after his works—of the scaffoldings I have been building in my imagination in an attempt to understand him.
(Letter by Rodin to Rose Beuret, quoted in Champigneulle, *Rodin*, p. 41)

After returning from Italy Rodin begins work on *The Bronze Age*.

That gesture that grew and gradually developed to such grandeur and force, emerged here like a spring trickling softly down this body. It awoke in the obscurity of the beginnings of time, and, growing, it appears to traverse the breadth of this work as if traversing the millennia, far beyond us to those who will come. Hesitantly it unfolds in the raised arms; and these arms are still so heavy that the hand of the one must fall back to rest on the top of the head. Yet it is no longer asleep, it is gathering itself; high up, at the very apex of the brain, where loneliness is, it is preparing itself for work, the work of centuries, which knows neither respite nor end. And in the right foot stands a first step, waiting.
(Rilke, *Rodin*, 1922, pp. 28–29)

1877

Returns from Brussels to Paris. Begins his study of French cathedrals.

The cathedrals give rise to a feeling of confidence, trust, peace. Why is this so? Because of their harmony. A few technical notes are necessary here. The harmony of the living body arises from an equilibrium of animated masses. Cathedrals are constructed in the image of the living body. Their proportions, their relations of balance correspond

12 Michelangelo, *Medici Tombs*, Sacristy of San Lorenzo, Florence, 1520–1534

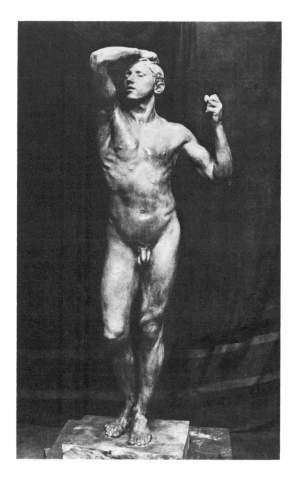

13 *The Bronze Age*, 1875–1876

14 *John the Baptist*, 1878

exactly to natural order, derive from general laws. The great masters who built these miracles of the architectural art had a full grasp of natural science and knew how to apply it, since, derived from natural sources, it had remained living in them.
(Auguste Rodin, *The Cathedrals of France*. Quoted from the German edition, *Die Kathedralen Frankreichs*, Berlin, n.d., p.1)

1878

Executes the sculpture *John the Baptist*.

The body of this man is no longer untried—deserts have brought it to white heat, hunger has hurt it, all thirsts have put it to the test. It has passed and grown hardened. His gaunt ascetic body is like a wooden grip into which the spread fork of his pacing legs has been inserted. He walks as though all the world's distances were within him and he were measuring them out with his pace. He strides. His arms tell of this stride, and his fingers splay and seem to make the sign of striding in the air.
(Rilke, *Rodin*, pp.29–30)

15 Design for *La Défense*, 1879

Works on architectural sculpture in Nice and Marseille under the sculptors Cordier and Fourquet.

1879

Competition held by the City of Paris for a memorial of the Franco-Prussian War of 1870–71. Rodin's *La Défense* goes unnoticed.
Works on a freelance basis for Sèvres Porcelain Manufactory (director Carrier-Belleuse) until 1882.

Sèvres mainly supplied the President of the Republic and the Ministries with horrifyingly tasteless objects of art, and produced endless series of those famous Sèvres vases, all based on the same model, whose inimitable blue figured as a trademark and which, insofar as you might not win them in the lottery, were distributed as complimentary gifts to winners of competitions and laureates. Rodin modelled small decorative figures and executed a large centerpiece, The Hunt, *after Carrier-Belleuse's designs.*
(Champigneulle, *Rodin*, p.62)

1880

Commissioned to execute a sculpture of d'Alembert for the Hôtel de Ville in Paris; has his studio in the national Dépôt des Marbres, 182, Rue de l'Université. Begins work on the portal of a planned Musée des Arts Décoratifs, with thematic allusions to scenes from Dante's *Divine Comedy*. *The Gates of Hell* are to occupy Rodin to the end of his life.

In search of an impressive subject, it was easy for him to confuse the great poetic possibilities of earlier centuries with the quite basically different demands of his own time. In his projected Gates of Hell, *a configuration of immense size and populated with myriads of figures, he attempted to represent in sculpture a new philosophy of suffering; but by propping this modern idea on a notion of the entrance to Hell which by this time had lost its force, he entangled himself inextricably in an historical preoccupation.*
(Carl Burckhardt, *Rodin und das plastische Problem*, Basel, n.d., p. 27)

16 Design for the *Gates of Hell* with separate relief fields, D. 1970

1881–1882

Journeys to London. Works on *The Gates of Hell* and on portraits, of Alphonse Legros, Jean-Paul Laurens, and Albert-Ernest Carrier-Belleuse among others.

1883

Rodin meets Camille Claudel, who becomes his student, mistress, and model for about fifteen years.

This young girl, Paul Claudel's sister, was four years older than the poet. She had an influence on the young man which, as he himself said, was "frequently cruel". She taught him to despise traditional values, and the ties of family and religion. She read Shakespeare aloud to him and put him in a state of ecstatic transport. And she gave him feelings of inferiority, since without ever having enjoyed artistic training she knew how to model in clay. Her encounter with Rodin was to awaken forces that slumbered unconsciously within her. The artist's genius blinded her; the quiet force of the man made her a prisoner. Too proud to show any signs, she subordinated herself to him. Soon she was working in the atelier on Rue de l'Univer-

17 Camille Claudel, *Bust of Rodin*, 1888

18 Camille Claudel ▷

19 Third maquette for *Gates of Hell*, 1880

sité. Absolutely under the master's influence, she became his secretary and assistant.
(Champigneulle, *Rodin*, pp. 157–161)

1884

Takes studio at 117, Rue de Vaugirard, and begins work on *The Burghers of Calais*, continuing at the same time to develop his *Gates of Hell* in the Dépôt des Marbres.

A dramatically gripping representation of the special state of inward and outward excitation felt by a group of men going to a death they fear yet themselves voluntarily chose—that was the primary thing for Rodin. By emphasizing the unpathetic attitude, the confusion and self-imposed impassibility, even the fear and horror in the faces and gestures of these men, he wished to communicate to us the whole import of their almost superhuman sacrifice.
(Burckhardt, *Rodin und das plastische Problem*, pp. 31–32)

1886

His design for a Jules Bastien-Lepage monument is accepted. Works on illustrations to Baudelaire's *Les Fleurs du Mal*.

1889

Receives commissions for monuments to Claude Lorrain in Nancy and to Victor Hugo in the Panthéon. Exhibits with Monet at Galerie Georges Petit. Critical support begins to come from Camille Mauclair, Gustave Geffroy, Octave Mirbeau, and Roger Marx.
Makes architectural sketches in Toulouse, Albi, and Clermont-Ferrand.

1890

Architectural studies in Anjou and in the Touraine, Rodez and Saumur.

Only gradually have I come to our old cathedrals, penetrated the secret of their lives, which undergoes a continual renewal under a changing sky. Today I can say that I owe my best friends to them. Romanesque, Gothic, Renaissance! Today I know that several lifetimes would not be enough to exhaust the treasures of joy which our old buildings offer to the honest admirer of beauty. And I am faithful to them; snow, rain and sun find me before them again and again, me, the vagabond of France.
(Rodin, *The Cathedrals of France*, p. 15)

1891

Commissioned to execute a Balzac monument by the Société des Gens de Lettres.

The hair splayed out against the back of the muscular neck, and the face leaned back into the hair, seeing, in an intoxication of vision, foaming with creation: the face of an element. This was Balzac in the fecundity of his profusion, the founder of generations, the profligate of destinies. This was the man whose eyes required no things to see; had the world been empty, his gaze would have furnished it. This was the man who hoped fabulous silver mines would make him rich and a foreign woman happy. This was creativity itself, that had chosen Balzac's shape in which

21 *Portal in Toulouse*, D.5902

22 *Balzac Monument*, 1891–1897

23 Rodin with long coat in the Balzac style, February 1914

to materialize; the superciliousness, arrogance, giddiness and drunkenness of creation. The head, which was thrown back, lived at the apex of this figure like those balls which dance on the jets of fountains. All massiveness had grown light, rose and fell.
(Rilke, *Rodin*, pp. 69–70)

Travels to Jersey and Guernsey.
The director of Hamburg Kunsthalle, Alfred Lichtwark, visits Rodin.

1895

Purchases Villa des Brillants in Meudon.
The Burghers of Calais is erected, against Rodin's wishes, on a pedestal.

But in Calais they declined to use a low pedestal because it was not customary, and Rodin suggested another kind of installation. Build a tower, he declared, right at the edge of the sea, polygonal, with the circumference of the base, plain, hewn walls, and two stories high, and up there place the six citizens, amid the solitude of winds and sky. Predictably, this suggestion too was rejected.
(Rilke, *Rodin*, p. 64)

1897

First book on Rodin is published, *Les Dessins d'Auguste Rodin*, with an introduction by Octave Mirbeau.

1898

The *Balzac* rejected by the Société des Gens de Lettres, who consider it unfinished. Rodin takes the plaster sculpture to Meudon. No bronze casting of it is ever made during his lifetime.

In 1898, Rodin's circle of friends was large and strong enough to pick up the gauntlet thrown at their feet by the Société des Gens de Lettres. Gustave Geffroy, Octave Mirbeau, Camille Mauclair, Georges Rodenbach spoke out, defended Rodin, praised his work, and heaped fiery coals on the heads of that Society. Nor did the debate remain limited to the local newspapers. The Balzac Affair became the talk of the town. And soon the battle for and against the Balzac statue reverberated even farther afield.

24 Rodin on Guernsey, 1897

25 Installation of *The Burghers of Calais* in the Jardin Richelieu, Calais, 1895

116 CALAIS. — Le Jardin Richelieu et le Monument des Bourgeois. — LL.

26 Rodin Exhibition in the Pavillon de l'Alma, Paris, 1900

27 Rainer Maria Rilke and Clara Westhoff, 1904

Albert Mockel in Belgium and Arthur Symons in London joined forces with the maestro. Rodin's name was in the air everywhere.
(Otto Grautoff, *Auguste Rodin*, Bielefeld and Leipzig, 1908, p. 37)

Travels to Holland and Belgium.

1900

A retrospective of 150 works is held on the occasion of the Paris Universal Exposition, and reaps wide acclaim.

Much had been said about him over the past years both good and bad. Now his work had been recognized by those of his contemporaries who by all rights ought to represent his true audience. The turn of the century had brought fame and prosperity to the now sixty-year-old artist. For his students and admirers, whose number increased daily, the Villa des Brillants became a shrine, captivating artistic Paris and emanating to the far corners of the earth. Rodin became an international star.
(Champigneulle, *Rodin*, p. 211)

Out of studies for *John the Baptist* Rodin develops *Striding Man.*

1901

Executes portrait busts, marble replicas of his sculptures, and above all drawings.

1902

The photographer Edward Steichen visits Rodin in Meudon. Rodin travels to England, Prague, and Vienna. Meets Rilke. Engages Alexis Rudier to cast his statues.

1903

Books on Rodin by Rilke and Judith Cladel are published.

28 *Striding Man*, 1900–1907; erected 1912 in the courtyard of Palazzo Farnese (Michelangelo) in Rome, seat of the French Embassy. Photograph with Rodin's corrections

29 Rodin with Ignacio Zuloaga and Sergei I. Shtshukin, Pamplona, 1906

30 Rodin sketching a Cambodian dancer in Marseille, 1906

1904

Exhibitions in Düsseldorf, Weimar, Dresden, Leipzig, Krefeld.

1905

Receives honorary doctorate from the University of Jena. Rilke becomes Rodin's secretary.

This relationship quite naturally led to Rodin's asking me one morning whether I wanted to stay with him as his private secretary; I pointed out how bad my French was—this seemed no obstacle to him, and so I finally accepted, and now I'm in the second month of performing this office, to his satisfaction.—You can imagine that writing the letters ... takes me ten times as long as it would a Frenchman ...Rodin wants me to have a lot of time for myself, because he gave me this position in order to help me. I'm still being treated like a guest ... and receive a monthly salary of 200 francs into the bargain.—It was a great relief to be able to take the pressure off my father like this ... sadly, though, I can't help Clara, at least not for the moment.
(Rilke in a letter to Ellen Kay, Swedish author and teacher, November 6, 1905)

1906

Journeys with Rilke and the painter Ignacio Zuloaga to Toledo, Madrid, Cordoba, Seville, and Pamplona.
Quarrels with Rilke and dismisses him.
Visits the Royal Cambodian Ballet performances in France. Executes drawings of Cambodian dancers.

These Cambodian girls gave me everything I admired about antique marbles, and beyond that the strangeness and suppleness of the Far East. What a delight to realize how humanity remains true to itself through time and space! Yet this constancy has one prerequisite: a sense of tradition and faith.
(Rodin, quoted in Champigneulle, *Rodin*, pp. 221–222)

Sketches in Isadora Duncan's dancing school in Paris.

31 Edward Steichen,
Balzac—
Towards the Light,
Midnight, Meudon,
1908

32 Rodin looking
at an Egyptian
statuette, February
1914

1908

Steichen takes photograph of the *Balzac* sculpture
in the moonlight at Meudon. Rodin lives at the
Hôtel Biron, Rue Varenne.

1909

An unaltered version of the *Victor Hugo Monument*
is erected in the garden of the Palais Royal.

1914

Rodin's *Les Cathédrales de France* is published.

*The means to understanding them are all around you. The
cathedrals are the synthesis of the country. I repeat—
cliffs, forests, gardens, the sun of the North, all of these
are contained in their gigantic volumes; all of France is in
our cathedrals, just as all of Greece was in the Parthenon.*
(Rodin, *The Cathedrals of France*, p. 11)

Travels to England, then to Italy.

33 Installation of
*Victor Hugo Monu-
ment* in the garden
of the Palais Royal,
1909

1915

Continues his journey to Rome and Florence.

1916

Rodin makes three bequests to the French nation. Hôtel Biron becomes a Rodin museum.

1917

Marries Rose Beuret on January 29. She dies on February 14. Death of Rodin, November 17; funeral in Meudon, November 24.

Let the artist give a great example.
He worships his work; the joy of doing it right is a divine reward. Nowadays the workers are unfortunately being told that they ought to hate their work and do it shoddily. Mankind will not be happy until all men have the souls of artists, that is, until every man's work gives him pleasure. And art sets a superb example of honesty.
The true artist always expresses what he thinks, at the risk of flying in the face of all ingrained prejudice. This is how he teaches others courage and candor.
Now, just imagine what a miraculous step forward we would suddenly take if absolute truthfulness prevailed among men!
O how rapidly society would liberate itself from ingrained error and ugliness, and how quickly our earth would become a paradise.
(Auguste Rodin, *A Testament*. Quoted from the German edition, *Das Testament*, Überlingen, 1946, unpaginated)

34 Rodin in Rome, 1915

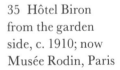

35 Hôtel Biron from the garden side, c. 1910; now Musée Rodin, Paris

36 Rodin's funeral,
November 24,
1917. On his grave,
The Thinker

LIST OF PLATES

The Early Years
Plates on pages 31–60

Notes by Kirk Varnedoe on a number of the drawings discussed in his essay are printed here, following the technical information. These texts are signed K.V. Professor Varnedoe was not responsible for the selection of works.

1

Portrait of a Man with Cap
Graphite pencil on cream-colored paper, pasted on mount, $3\frac{3}{8} \times 2\frac{1}{4}''$
From *Album I*, dispersed in March 1930
Paris, Musée Rodin, D.119
Probably a fragment of a lost sketching album, this tiny portrait was more likely saved by Rodin as a remembrance of a friend than as an achievement of draftsmanship. One might consider dating it in the early 1860s, in part because of its loose connection with the drawings from life in the Mastbaum sketch album in the Philadelphia Museum of Art. K.V.

2

Skeleton of a Dog
Graphite pencil on sand-colored paper, $9\frac{5}{8} \times 12\frac{1}{4}''$
From *Album II*, dispersed in March 1930
Paris, Musée Rodin, D.245
The logical date for this work would be in the early 1860s, when Rodin studied with the great animal sculptor Antoine-Louis Barye, at the Jardin des Plantes, Paris. Barye was a master of animal anatomy, and this kind of precise study of the inner structure of a dog would have been a training exercise dear to his heart. Rodin's fulfillment of the task is highly competent, but curiously and perhaps typically partial—focussed on the difficult spatial configuration of the rib cage and little concerned with the extremities. K.V.

3

Human Skeleton
Lead pencil on sand-colored paper, $7\frac{7}{8} \times 4\frac{1}{2}''$
From *Album I*, dispersed in March 1930
Paris, Musée Rodin, D.139
More loose and informal than the other surviving Rodin studies after human or equine skeletons, this drawing was almost certainly done for the artist's own purposes rather than as a classroom exercise. The oblique viewpoint suggests a rendering from an actual skeleton, instead of from anatomical illustrations. (See Musée Rodin D.100 and 102 for more precise, frontal renderings of the human skeleton from the same period.) K.V.

4

Study after "Madonna and Child" by Michelangelo
Charcoal on cream-colored paper,
$25\frac{1}{8} \times 19\frac{1}{4}''$
Paris, Musée Rodin, D.5116

5

Study after "Morning" by Michelangelo
Charcoal on cream-colored paper with watermark, $19 \times 24\frac{5}{8}''$
Paris, Musée Rodin, D.5117

6

Study after "Day" by Michelangelo
Charcoal on cream-colored paper with watermark, $19\frac{1}{8} \times 24\frac{5}{8}''$
Paris, Musée Rodin, D.5118

7

Study after "Night" by Michelangelo
Charcoal on cream-colored paper with watermark, $19\frac{1}{8} \times 24\frac{5}{8}''$
Paris, Musée Rodin, D.5119
The origin and dating of this series of drawings are considered at length in my essay on Rodin's

early drawings (pp. 13–28). The studies were almost certainly made around 1877, in Paris, from casts of Michelangelo's sculptures. Unfortunately, all but one of these drawings have been ruined by ill-advised attempts at restoration. By comparing their present condition with photographs taken prior to 1960 (such as those published in Joseph Gantner's *Rodin and Michelangelo*; also that reproduced here, p. 27, fig. 33), we can readily see that the crude clumsiness of line and unconvincing rendering of volume now evident in Musée Rodin D. 5117, 5118, and 5119 are attributable to the work of a restorer. The change in these drawings is so devastating that one is in truth no longer justified in attributing them to Rodin. Only the study of Michelangelo's *Madonna and Child* (D. 5116) still bears witness to the subtleties of the original drawings, even though it too has suffered, from abrasion and paper mold (apparently, and mercifully, no attempt was made to restore this sheet). K. V.

8

Life Study of a Bearded Man
Charcoal on cream-colored paper with watermark, 23⅞ × 18⅛″
Paris, Musée Rodin, D. 5105
Though unfinished and in poor condition, this early life study is instructive in showing us the extent to which the young Rodin learned the human anatomy initially in terms more painterly than sculptural. The musculature and bone structure are seen here through surface modelling, and depicted in pockets of light and shadow that undermine any sense of the organic unity of the body as sculptural form. A sense of fluid movement throughout the human frame, and special force of tension at points of thrust and support, would come to be prime attributes of Rodin's renderings of the body; but here they are not yet present to the eye or the hand of the young artist. K. V.

9

Male Nude from the Back, a Hand on his Head
Charcoal on cream-colored paper with watermark, 24 × 18¼″
Paris, Musée Rodin, D. 5108
Rodin's surviving academic studies of the nude are not a distinguished group; unlike the student work of such other artists as Degas or Seurat, they give little evidence of future mastery. In some instances, as here, the blocky, schematic quality of the light-and-dark patterning may owe in part to abrasion and to restoration attempts. The pose contains elements of the torsion and self-address that would become major aspects of Rodin's gestural language in sculpture; but here they convey only a stiffened inertia. K. V.

10

Female Nude Seated on a Pedestal
Lead pencil on cream-colored paper with watermark, 22⅛ × 17⅛″
Paris, Musée Rodin, D. 5101
This, the only academic rendering of a female nude among Rodin's preserved early life studies, is one of the most completely achieved and appealing of his *académies*; but its style raises intriguing questions. The cross-hatched rendering of the background is an affectation that appears as well in another, male *académie* (D. 5102); it recalls the manner of earlier artists such as Van Loo, whose studies from the model were frequently used in the instruction of students in Rodin's day. Furthermore, the manner of lighting the figure, as well as its strict profile head and tightly coiffed hair, suggest the style of the earlier nineteenth century. All these features contrast sharply with the more aggressively realist, and more typically Second Empire, manner of rendering in the majority of Rodin's student life studies. One might conclude that this female nude is either a drawing after an earlier artist's *académie*, or that it was conceived as an exercise in a specific set of stylistic devices. K. V.

11

Antique Scene. Goddess of Victory Crowning an Athlete
Graphite pencil and watercolor on cream-colored paper, 9½ × 7⅛″
From *Album 1*, dispersed in March 1930
Paris, Musée Rodin, D. 109
The format suggests that the original model in antique art was not sculpture but perhaps a painted basin interior or plate surface, or a cameo. In any event, the antique source has been thoroughly transformed, and the accent of mid-nineteenth century style lies heavily on Rodin's image: in the polychromy, in the modelling and physiognomy of the figures, and in the softened, atmospheric conception of line. The distance from the antique in all likelihood owes, as it does

in the Parthenon "copies", to intermediary renderings from which Rodin copied. Such watercolor studies, relatively accomplished in execution, may have grown out of Rodin's work as an apprentice decorator in the 1860s—though they lack the vigor and conviction we associate with the rococo vein of Rodin's sculptural essays in decorative style. The only sculptural monument which seems to bear some relation to these neo-Greek exercises is the early facade work on the small theater (now known as *Le Rodin*) on the Avenue des Gobelins. K.V.

12

Girls Bearing Offerings. Copy after a Parthenon Frieze
Graphite pencil and watercolor on cream-colored paper, 8⅜ × 11⅛"
From *Album I*, dispersed in March 1930
Paris, Musée Rodin, D.87
A group of copies after antique subjects, in fine pencil and delicate watercolor, show Rodin working in the neo-Hellenistic vein of the Second Empire. The idea of "restoring" the polychromy to the Parthenon frieze is particularly in tune with the archaeological interests we associate with neo-Greek style, and with the students and followers of Ingres. Note how much more suave and refined this vision of the maidens' procession appears than the comparable tracing, with its more blunt, more sculptural accents (plate 14, D.52). K.V.

13

Procession. Copy after a Parthenon Frieze
Graphite pencil and watercolor on cream-colored paper, 6¾ × 10"
From *Album I*, dispersed in March 1930
Paris, Musée Rodin, D.88
The chiselled monochrome of this fragment of classical Greek sculpture (one of the panels removed by Lord Elgin, and now in the British Museum) has been here transformed into something more painterly, both in the coloration and modelling of the figures and in the relative weightlessness of the scene as a whole. The vision of classical antiquity suggested is no longer that of Flaxman and David, but more that of Boulanger or Gérôme. In all likelihood Rodin drew, not from any cast of the British Museum's frieze, but from some intermediate graphic representation such as a suite of color lithographs reconceiving the original frieze in terms of mid-nineteenth century "his-

torical accuracy" (note for example the restoration of the helmet to the head of the background horseman, a detail absent from Rodin's other copy of this scene in the Musée Rodin, plate 15, D.61). K.V.

14

Girls Bearing Offerings. Copy after a Parthenon Frieze
Pen and brown ink on cream-colored paper, 4⅜ × 7¼"
From *Album I*, dispersed in March 1930
Paris, Musée Rodin, D.52
This tracing is identical in style and format to plate 15, but the subject is a more intriguing one. First, there is a close similarity between this section of the Parthenon frieze and that found in the fragment owned by the Louvre; and that association helps to reinforce our awareness of the extent to which the rendering here represents not a confident translation from a three-dimensional object but a timidly servile copying of a previous graphic representation. (Though Rodin copied numerous antiquities at the Louvre, he preserved no drawing directly from the museum's fragment of the Parthenon procession.) Secondly, Rodin's attraction to the strict isocephalic composition, with its insistently repetitious rhythms of drapery, adds another dimension to our understanding of the complex origins of his innovations in the later sculptural group of *The Burghers of Calais*. K.V.

15

Procession. Copy after a Parthenon Frieze
Pen and brown ink on tracing paper, permanently mounted, 4⅜ × 7⅝"
Inscribed twice at the left, in graphite pencil: *non*
From *Album I*, dispersed in March 1930
Paris, Musée Rodin, D.61
Rodin preserved a series of small, schematized renderings of the Parthenon frieze, in pen and pencil on tracing paper. These may be tracings from his own drawings, or—as is more likely in view of their technique—tracings from engravings. The reductive, schematic character of these linear renderings contrasts sharply with the fuller, more decorative aspect of his student watercolors of the same subjects (see plate 12, D.87 and plate 13, D.88, for example). While the latter are more typical of Second Empire taste, these spare tracings look back to a more austere classicizing style. K.V.

16

Landscape

Sanguine on cream-colored paper,
6⅝ × 10⅜″

From *Album I*, dispersed in March 1930

Paris, Musée Rodin, D.46

17

Landscape

Sanguine on sand-colored paper,
6¾ × 8½″

From *Album II*, dispersed in March 1930

Paris, Musée Rodin, D.195

18

Landscape

Sanguine heightened with graphite pencil, on cream-colored paper, torn at bottom, right and center, 7⅜ × 10⅜″

From *Album I*, dispersed in March 1930

Paris, Musée Rodin, D.60

Rodin described to his biographers the infrequent days of relaxation he permitted himself at the time he worked in Brussels, in the mid-1870s. On such days he and his consort Rose would escape to the countryside. A series of small landscape sketches in sanguine, of which these three are characteristic examples, have always been associated with those days in the country. Their style and subject are so totally disconnected from the rest of Rodin's draftsmanship that, were it not for such slender clues, one would be almost completely at a loss in attempting to position them meaningfully within his œuvre. K.V.

19

Head of a Young Woman

Charcoal on cream-colored paper,
5¾ × 3⅞″

From *Album II*, dispersed in March 1930

Paris, Musée Rodin, D.147

While this little fragment has the liveliness of direct observation, the material (charcoal) and the character of the features suggest a quick notation *de chic*, from memory, somewhat in the manner of Constantin Guys. The simplicity of the accents around the head, and the rapidity of execution, suggest an artist well past the first experiments of his student years. K.V.

20

Nude Infant with Raised Arms

Graphite pencil and stump on sand-colored paper, 5½ × 3⅛″

From *Album II*, dispersed in March 1930

Paris, Musée Rodin, D.244

In contrast to the other sketches of infants discussed above, this sheet can be quite firmly dated and associated with Rodin's sculptural work, by virtue of its very close relation to Rodin's drawings for the *Vase des eléments*, a ceramic he made at the Sèvres Porcelain Manufactory in 1879 (see Elsen and Varnedoe, *The Drawings of Rodin*, 1971, p.49, fig.27). The differences between this and the earlier conceptions of infants are striking, not only in the greater confidence of execution, but in the feeling for fluid movement that animates the chubby volumes. The emphasis on light and shadow in the drawing reflects the concerns of Rodin's style of ceramic modelling, which exploited the possibilities of applied-paste reliefs for a high drama of tenebrism. Here the rococo putto type of Clodion becomes party to a very non-rococo sense of drama and forceful action. Another rendering of an infant form, similar in style, appears on the mounted assemblage of drawings illustrated in plate 25, D.82. K.V.

21

Three Nude Infants

Graphite pencil, pen and black wash on cream-colored paper,
5⅜ × 4⅛″

From *Album I*, dispersed in March 1930

Paris, Musée Rodin, D.36

Far more confident in execution than plate 22 below, this sheet seems to represent either more aggressive appropriations from the putti of another artist, or, as is perhaps more likely given the boldness of the execution, free-form improvisation on Rodin's part. Cherubs have their own stylistic history in art, and the type that Rodin favored —particularly chubby, virtually without ankles, and with exceptionally prominent bald crania— seems quite close to those found in Clodion. This connection is most insistent late in Rodin's life, in the *Jardinière* with a relief of infant figures that he conceived for Baron Vitta. The present drawing is very close in style and feeling to one found on the mounted assemblage of drawings discussed below (plate 25, D.81). K.V.

22

Semi-reclining Nude Infant
Graphite pencil heightened with pen and black
ink, on cream-colored paper, cut out irregularly
and firmly pasted on mount,
2½ × 3¾"
From *Album I*, dispersed in March 1930
Paris, Musée Rodin, D.115
A relatively tentative copy, perhaps partly made
by tracing, after a representation of a putto. Such
chubby little winged cherubs were the stock-in-
trade of any decorative artist of Rodin's day, and
he no doubt saved this little scrap for its possible
usefulness as a guide to some future decorative
composition. K.V.

23

Three Nude Infants
Graphite pencil, pen and grey ink on
mildewed cream-colored paper,
3⅜ × 6⅜"
Note in pen and black ink: *St. Marcel 12/Adèle
Poulain* (?)
From *Album I*, dispersed in March 1930
Paris, Musée Rodin, D.38
Showing the same basic infant type found in
plate 21, this sheet would similarly seem to represent a series of experimental sketches from memory, in which Rodin explored the postural
possibilities of the comically inflated volumes of
the infant form. K.V.

24

Elevation of the Cross with Three Figures
Pen and brown wash on cream-colored paper,
5⅜ × 3¾"
From *Album I*, dispersed in March 1930
Paris, Musée Rodin, D.143
The loose, cursive style of pen rendering seen here
is one that we find often in Rodin's work when he
draws entirely from memory or imagination. The
central figure is no doubt a variant on a pose seen
by Rodin in some previous work of art, with the
surrounding figures now added in an attempt to
envision the possibilities of a new sculptural
group. The motif suggests eventual derivation
from a group representing the descent from the
cross, though in the present instance the overtones of struggle or violence seem to indicate a
changed iconography. K.V.

Rodin's Assemblages of Drawings
Rodin began carefully editing and preserving his
own drawings at an early age. He made up albums of his work, but these have for the most part
been disassembled since his death. Only a few
pages like this remain to indicate the way in which
the artist ordered, edited, and reconsidered his
drawings. In the case of the pages at hand (plates
25 and 26), the drawings assembled are predo-
minantly those that he did during his trip to Italy
in 1875. K.V.

25

Assemblage of Drawings
10⅜ × 13⅜"
From *Album I*, dispersed in March 1930
Paris, Musée Rodin, D.80–86
From left to right and top to bottom:

Running Draped Female Figure
Graphite pencil, tracing, on cut paper, firmly
mounted. D.80

Infant Nude from the Right
Graphite pencil, pen and ink with wash, on cut
paper, firmly mounted. D.81

Seated Figure
Graphite pencil

Corinthian Capital
Graphite pencil, pen and ink with wash, on cut
paper, firmly mounted. D.84
Inscribed in pen and ink: *Ste Sophie*

Seated Draped Female Figure with Hand to Chin
Graphite pencil heightened in pen and ink, on
cut paper, firmly mounted. D.85
This figure, in antique garb, may be related to
those seen in other neo-Hellenic studies from Rodin's youth (plate 11, D.109; plate 12, D.87;
plate 13, D.88). Rodin saved such drawings over
long periods of time, turning to assemblages such
as this one for ideas when beginning new projects.
In this regard, it is interesting to note the small
pencil sketch, without number, that Rodin added
above and to the left of this drawing, showing
another figure with hand to chin and legs crossed.
This latter gesture of contemplation would not
have been unrelated to his exploration of
possibilities for the representation of the figure of

Dante in *The Gates of Hell*—the contemplative creator that eventually became the *Thinker*. K.V.

Contour of a Standing Nude Infant
Graphite pencil on torn paper

Nude Infant
Graphite pencil and blue colored pencil, on cut sand-colored paper, mounted. D.82

Nude Infant with Raised Arms
Pen and ink on cut paper, firmly mounted. D.83

Draped Female Figure with Raised Arms
Graphite pencil with grey wash and traces of red pencil on paper, mounted laterally. D.86
Probably a copy after an allegorical figure, as yet unidentified. K.V.

26
Assemblage of Drawings
Graphite pencil, pen and grey wash, on various papers, mounted by the artist on a larger sheet, 10⅜ × 13½″
Inscribed in graphite pencil: *traits plus petits · cheval de Marly · Michelange ·*
From *Album II*, dispersed in March 1930
Paris, Musée Rodin, D.160–175
From top to bottom and left to right:

Two Studies of Heads, one of Michelangelo's "Moses"
D.160
This is a page from a sketchbook that Rodin disassembled after his Italian trip. Another page in the Musée Rodin (plate 27, D.192) shows the torso of the *Moses*, with special attention to the right hand which grasps the beard. K.V.

Six Figure Studies
D.161
These quick notations seem to have been inspired by—though not scrupulously copied from—the Michelangelo figures known as the *Boboli Captives* in the Accademia museum in Florence. K.V.

Reclining Woman Playing a Lute, with Crescent Moon Above
D.162
No source has as yet been identified for this work, which is almost certainly a copy from a painting or sculpture seen on the Italian journey. K.V.

Reclining Woman with Infant
D.163
This little sketch provides a clear example of Rodin's process of adapting older art to new iconographies. In this case, the female figure is that of the mother of Angelo Cesi, drawn from a figure carved by Vincenzo di Rossi for the Cesi tombs in Santa Maria della Pace in Rome. Rodin has adapted the Christian motif to a seemingly pagan subject, adding a flowing urn and a child to suggest a sort of river goddess or water nymph. K.V.

Man on Horseback
D.164

Man on Horseback
D.165
Studies done after Donatello's *Gattamelata* equestrian figure, in front of the church of San Antonio in Padua. In these and several other studies (see plate 26, D.168, 173 and 174) Rodin recorded all aspects of the monument from diverse points of view within the surrounding square. The artist never spoke of a visit to Padua, but these drawings are apparently from the same sketchbook in which he recorded his impressions of the Michelangelo *Moses* in Rome (see plate 26, D.160). Another page from the same book holds an annotation from the relief panel of the *Miracle of the Ass* by Donatello, from the altar of San Antonio in Padua (Musée Rodin, D.310). K.V.

Composition with Two Figures
D.166
Though a precise source has yet to be identified, this drawing was likely done from a motif seen on the Italian journey of 1875; given the low vantage point and foreshortening, the source motif may lie in a ceiling painting. K.V.

Two Figures
D.167
The two figures would appear to be supporting a globe above them; like D.166 above, they await precise identification among the works Rodin studied during his Italian sojourn. K.V.

Man on Horseback
D.168
Like D.164 and 165 above, this is a study after Donatello's *Gattamelata*. K.V.

Landscape

D.169

Probably a study from nature instead of a copy of a painting; but the locale is not identified. K.V.

Sketch

D.170

The subject here resists identification. The fact that Rodin saved this little fragment is evidence of his use of the most reduced little ciphers as *aides-mémoires*. K.V.

Two Figures, One with a Horse

D.171

Especially given Rodin's annotation on this sheet, the drawings represent a memory of the French sculptures, now on the Champs-Elysées, known as the *Chevaux de Marly*. In the context of these Italian sketches, they might also remind us how earlier French travellers—notably Géricault—had been led to remember the *Chevaux de Marly*, with their struggling horse-tamers, by the spectacle of riderless horse races in Rome. K.V.

Landscape

D.172

Apparently, like D.169, a study from nature, of an unidentified locale. K.V.

Man on Horseback

D.173

Man on Horseback

D.174

Two further studies after Donatello's *Gattamelata* (see D.164, 165, 168). The ink reworkings were likely added some time after the initial pencil sketch done on the site. K.V.

Mother and Child

D.175

Though Rodin has written the name "Michelange" on the mount sheet immediately adjacent to this oval cut-out, the drawing is not a direct copy of a precise motif in Michelangelo; instead it is either a free variant, or—more likely—it is based on the work of another Italian artist, and only served to remind Rodin of general properties of Michelangelo's compositions. K.V.

27

Assemblage of Drawings

Graphite pencil, pen and brown wash on various papers, mounted by the artist on a larger sheet, 10⅜ × 13⅜"

Various inscriptions: *seule · jeune fille sarcophage · le nu des draperies se modelera d'abord sur le nu de l'académie et les plis seront toujours coupés en biais · Musée du Vatican · Salle des Nils · sarcophage · bas reliefs saillants et en biais ·*

From *Album II*, dispersed in March 1930

Paris, Musée Rodin, D.180–194

This sheet is also dominated by drawings from Rodin's Italian journey, and was likely assembled in the late 1870s. K.V.

From left to right and top to bottom:

Two Figures

D.180

Apparently a scene of seduction, with an enticing figure approaching from the rear left, partially wrapped around a frontal figure. K.V.

Leda and the Swan

D.181

The figure, directly derived from Michelangelo's figure of *Night* on the Medici tombs, is seen from the radically foreshortened viewpoint that Rodin wrote had most excited him in seeing these sculptures in person. K.V.

Figure with Hands on Hips

D.182

Unidentified sketch, likely a pencil copy from the Italian trip, with later additions in ink. K.V.

Three Heads

D.183

These are almost certainly based on antique sculpture seen in Rome. K.V.

Scene with Horse and Chariot

D.184

The composition is directly taken from a scene of Luna and Endymion frequently found on Roman sarcophagi. Such a sarcophagus, with a scene corresponding exactly to the Rodin sketch, is in the collections of the Capitoline Museum in Rome. K.V.

Figure of a Woman
D.185
Given the annotation by Rodin, the sketch is likely taken from a Roman sarcophagus. K.V.

Standing Man with a Shield
D.186
Apparently a memory-sketch based on the figure of Donatello's *St. George*, in Florence. K.V.

Leda and the Swan
D.187
The sketch is based on a sculpture in the Museo San Marco, Venice. K.V.

Man on Horseback
D.188
A profile view of Verrocchio's *Colleoni* equestrian monument in Venice. K.V.

Figure with Clasped Hands
D.189
A loose copy of the female allegorical figure to the left of Michelangelo's *Moses* in the partial version of the Julius tomb in San Pietro in Vincoli, in Rome. K.V.

Nude Woman with Flowing Urn and Two Standing Figures
D.190
This is not a freehand sketch, but has been transferred to the page. Its source motif has not been identified. K.V.

Man on Horseback
D.191
A foreshortened view from the rear of Donatello's *Gattamelata* monument in Padua. K.V.

Torso
D.192
This was formerly a complete study of the upper body of Michelangelo's *Moses*, but Rodin tore away the head portion before he mounted the sketch. When compared to the original motif, Rodin's sketch seems to have somewhat distorted the proportions of the *Moses*, giving a skewed diagonal impetus to the torso and arms. He has concentrated particularly on Moses' semi-involuntary gesture of grasping his beard, a motif that would later be of primary interest to Sigmund Freud as well. K.V.

Man on Horseback
D.193
Nearly identical to D.191, and drawn from the same source. K.V.

Seated Woman with Upraised Arm, and Inverted Half-length Figure
D.194
This is a page from the sketchbook Rodin used on his 1875 Italian journey, but the motifs he copied here have not been identified. K.V.

28
Oriental Landscape
Graphite pencil, pen and brown ink, and water-color on cream-colored paper, $4 \times 4\frac{5}{8}''$
From *Album II*, dispersed in March 1930
Paris, Musée Rodin, D.224
This and the following two scenes form part of a small ensemble of orientalizing images Rodin preserved from his early drawings. Though miniature in dimension, they are remarkably complete copies, especially in light of Rodin's general tendency, more marked as he matured, to copy from a given source only the essential outlines he needed as a cue for his memory. The care of tracing and coloration here, and consequent subservience to the model in each case, suggest a very early date in the artist's career; though the confidence in rendering chiaroscuro speaks for a date past the initial student years (compare the relative freedom of execution here with the restraint of the copies after the antique, above). The models for these scenes will certainly someday be found, among the innumerable paintings and illustrations of North African subjects by artists such as Fromentin. Napoleon III's adventures in Algeria raised the level of interest in such subjects in the 1860s. Rodin's copies are likely from Salon paintings, but may have derived as well from book illustrations, or wood-engravings from the illustrated press. K.V.

29
Oriental Scene in a Landscape not Far from a City
Pen and brown ink, watercolor and gouache on cream-colored paper, cut out in a semi-oval, $4 \times 7\frac{1}{8}''$

From *Album I*, dispersed in March 1930
Paris, Musée Rodin, D.63

30
Oriental Scene
Graphite pencil, pen and brown ink on cream-colored paper, $3\frac{1}{4} \times 2\frac{5}{8}''$
From *Album II*, dispersed in March 1930
Paris, Musée Rodin, D.222

The *Gates of Hell* Period
Plates on pages 83–130

Claudie Judrin has written comments on a number of drawings treated in her essay. These, printed after the technical information, are signed C.J.

31
Self-portrait
Charcoal on cream-colored paper, $16\frac{1}{2} \times 11\frac{3}{4}''$
Signed lower right in charcoal: *Rodin*
Given to the Musée Rodin in July 1919 by Olivier Sainsère; Paris, Musée Rodin, D.7102
Self-portrait drawings are very rare in Rodin's œuvre. This likeness resembles a photograph taken by Bergerac in 1886. Could it have been the source of a woodcut made in 1889 by Ernest Florian for Maillard's book on Rodin? C.J.

32
Reclining Woman Embracing a Child, and Sketch of Gates of Hell
Graphite pencil, pen and brown wash on paper, mounted on moiré paper, $5\frac{5}{8} \times 6\frac{1}{4}''$
Annotated below on the mount in pen and brown ink: *bas-relief accentuer*
Paris, Musée Rodin, D.1966

33
Design for The Gates of Hell
Graphite pencil, heightened in pen and brown ink, on paper, mounted on page from an account book, $7\frac{3}{4} \times 6''$
On the mount, two sketches of *The Gates of Hell* and notes in pen and ink: *Panneau divisé comme celui-ci au lieu du panneau entier*
Paris, Musée Rodin, D.1963

34
Relief Panel for The Gates of Hell
Pen and brown ink on cream-colored hand-laid paper, $7 \times 4\frac{1}{2}''$
Paris, Musée Rodin, D.3657

35
Sketch for The Gates of Hell
Graphite pencil on cream-colored paper, $4\frac{7}{8} \times 3\frac{1}{2}''$
Paris, Musée Rodin, D.5478

36
Woman Moving in a Dance, and Two Sketches for The Gates of Hell
Graphite pencil, pen and brown ink on cream-colored hand-laid paper, $7\frac{1}{8} \times 9''$
Paris, Musée Rodin, D.3498

37
Sketch for The Gates of Hell
Graphite pencil and pen and ink on cream-colored paper, $4\frac{3}{8} \times 2\frac{3}{4}''$
Annotation in graphite at bottom: *porte 1897 · septembre (?) Le Monde moderne 5 rue St Benoit*; annotation from top to bottom in pen and ink: *Monsieur*
Paris, Musée Rodin, D.1961

38
Dante and Beatrice
Graphite pencil, pen and black ink on cream-colored paper, $7\frac{5}{8} \times 5''$
Annotated upper left with pen and black ink: *Prends ton luth*; left of center in graphite: *fuyer renversé et remords*
On the reverse, in pencil and blue wash: Man holding a woman up in his arms
Paris, Musée Rodin, D.5598

39
Charon's Boat
Graphite pencil, pen and grey wash, gouache on light sand-colored cardboard, $8\frac{3}{8} \times 6\frac{1}{8}''$
Signed lower left in pen and grey ink: *A. Rodin*
Given to the Musée Rodin in 1917 by Marcel Guérin; Paris, Musée Rodin, D.2057

40
Study for The Gates of Hell
Pen and blue ink over lead pencil,
4¾ × 3⅜″
Signed on cardboard mount: *Rodin*
Private collection
These anonymous shades were apparently among the 170 drawings that Rodin sent to Düsseldorf for the International Exhibition in 1904 (May 1 to October 23). The following year, a group of artists offered the drawings to Arthur Kampf, head of the Königliche Kunstakademie, who later passed them on to Arno Breker. Rodin was elected to membership in the Königliche Akademie, Berlin, on May 7, 1906. C.J.

41
Shade
Graphite pencil, pen and brown ink on torn paper, 4½ × 2¼″
Annotated upper right in graphite: *limbes* (?)
Paris, Musée Rodin, D.5613

42
Minos
Graphite pencil, pen and brown wash on cream-colored paper, 3 × 3⅞″
On the reverse, in graphite: Contour drawing of legs
Paris, Musée Rodin, D.5593

43
Mask of Minos
Graphite pencil, pen and grey wash, gouache on cream-colored paper, cut out and mounted on cardboard, 6½ × 4⅜″
Paris, Musée Rodin, D.1933

44
Reclining Couple, Embracing
Pen, grey and brown wash, and gouache on cream-colored paper, 4⅜ × 6¾″
Paris, Musée Rodin, D.1912

45
Embracing Couple
Graphite pencil, pen and brown wash on cream-colored paper, mounted on lined paper, 6⅜ × 4″
Annotated at top in ink and graphite: *Françoise Paolo · Virgile et Dante · Contemplation*; on lined paper mount below, in brown ink: *l'amour profond comme les tombeaux · Baudelaire · Abruzzesi · très beau*
Paris, Musée Rodin, D.5630

46
Shades Speaking with Dante
Pen and brown wash heightened with gouache, on sand-colored paper, pasted on mount, 7⅞ × 5¾″
Annotated upper left in pen and brown ink: *Ombres parlant à Dante*; on the mount: *Adam et Eve parlant à Dieu dans l'état de pureté · Ombres parlant à Dante*
Paris, Musée Rodin, D.3760

47
Paolo and Francesca da Rimini
Graphite pencil, pen and brow ink heightened with gouache, on cream-colored paper, firmly mounted, 7⅝ × 5¾″
Paris, Musée Rodin, D.3763

48a   48b

48a
Sketch of Group of Figures
Lead pencil heightened with pen and ink, 7⅜ × 5⅜″
Annotated upper left in pen and brown ink:
Dante Virgile une ombre embrasse les genoux quand... reverra les plaines... Ulysse embrasse les genoux de la po...
On the reverse: *Deposition* (48b)
Leipzig, Museum der Schönen Künste, I.4962
This drawing was apparently lent to the journal *Pan* and reproduced in its issue for November 1897–April 1898, p.190. The loan had been arranged by the painter Carl Koepping, and Rodin permitted him to keep all or some of the drawings. In a letter of October 3, 1897, from Riva on

the Lago di Garda, Koepping sent Rodin his warmest thanks and promised to send him etchings soon—which he did, for besides this correspondence the Musée Rodin possesses an impression of a Sibylle, a Maenade, and a seated female nude. It is possible that the notes on the edge of the sheet refer to the XXVI canto, where Odysseus, on Virgil's inquiry, reports how he deceived his companions and gave them over to the sea. C.J.

48 b
Deposition
Lead pencil, 7⅜ × 5⅝″
Annotated top: *médecin*; at right: *descente du Christ*
On the obverse: 48 a
Leipzig, Museum der Schönen Künste, I. 4962
The reverse, more frequently reproduced than the obverse, contains a double allusion: to the deposition of Christ and to a physician aiding and supporting a patient. C.J.

49
Rain, Circle of Vexation
Pen and grey wash, heightened with gouache, on lined paper pasted to mount, 8¼ × 5⅝″
Collection of Octave Mirbeau; Sotheby Parke Bernet auction, Monaco, Nov. 25, 1979, No. 23; Paris, Musée Rodin, D. 7605

50
Shade of an Avaricious Man
Pen and brown ink on cream-colored paper, pasted to mount, 6½ × 4⅜″
Annotated in pen and brown ink top and on mount: *ombre · avare*
Paris, Musée Rodin, D. 2071

51
Pluto (?)
Graphite pencil, pen, brown wash and gouache on cream-colored paper, firmly mounted on lined paper, 5½ × 4″
Annotated at bottom in graphite: *Le transport de Plutus*
Paris, Musée Rodin, D. 1936

52
Medusa
Graphite pencil, pen, with black and violet wash and gouache on cream-colored squared paper, lower left corner torn, 4¼ × 3¼″

Annotated upper left in graphite: *Méduse*
On the reverse, in graphite: Outline drawing and tethered horse
Paris, Musée Rodin, D. 1996

53
If Medusa saw you, you would have ceased to live
Graphite pencil, pen and brown ink on sand-colored paper, torn lower left, 6 × 4⅝″
Annotated upper right in pen and brown ink: *Si Méduse te voyait, tu aurais cessé de vivre*
On the reverse, in graphite: Two embracing men
Paris, Musée Rodin, D. 3781

54
Blasphemy
Graphite pencil, pen and brown wash on cream-colored paper, mounted on a page from an account book, 6⅜ × 5½″
Annotated at bottom in graphite and pen and ink: *ch · bas*
On the reverse, in graphite: Figure holding a ball
Paris, Musée Rodin, D. 3772

55
Centaur Embracing Two Women
Pen, brown wash and gouache on paper, mounted on another sheet, 6⅝ × 8¼″
Annotated lower right in pen and brown ink: *Blanc?*; upper left: *vieux centaure · jeune faune*
Paris, Musée Rodin, D. 5429

56
Icarus and Phaeton
Graphite pencil, pen and brown wash, heightened with gouache, on lined paper, firmly pasted to mount, 5½ × 4⅝″
Annotated lower right in pen and brown ink: *Icare · Phaeton*
Paris, Musée Rodin, D. 3759

57
Dante and Virgil on a Ghostly Horse
Graphite pencil, pen and brown wash on paper, pasted to mount, 6½ × 5″
Annotated on mount bottom right in pen and brown ink: *Dante et Virgile · Le cheval plus chimérique · Pégase*
Paris, Musée Rodin, D. 3769

58
Medea
Graphite pencil, pen, brown wash and gouache on cream-colored paper, pasted to mount, 3¾ × 5⅝″
Annotated upper right in graphite: *Médée*; on the mount below: *au feu*; signed upper left in pen and brown ink: *A. Rodin*
On the reverse, in graphite: Woman embracing two children
Paris, Musée Rodin, D. 2056

59
Dans la m...
Graphite pencil, pen, grey, violet and red wash, heightened with gouache, on paper, mounted on lined paper, 7⅛ × 5⅜″
Annotated at right in pen and ink: *dans la m...*
Formerly collection of Maurice Fenaille; Paris, Musée Rodin, D. 7616

60
Demon Holding Up a Shade Who Has Fallen in Tar
Graphite pencil, pen, brown and grey wash, on the back of printed, cream-colored paper, pasted on mount, 6⅜ × 5¼″
Annotated at left in pen and brown ink: *anatomie ecce homo / Promethée*; on the mount: *Dante / regarde / en horreur / le démon / l'a rattrapé sur / l'abime de poix*; annotated on reverse of mount in pen and ink: *lignes greques*
Paris, Musée Rodin, D. 5594

61
Cloak of Lead
Graphite pencil, pen and brown ink on paper, pasted firmly to mount, 7⅝ × 4¾″
Annotated upper right in pen and brown ink: *chape de plomb / se sauve des regards de Dante*
Paris, Musée Rodin, D. 5086

62
The Horrifying Union
Graphite pencil, pen, brown and grey wash, heightened with gouache, on cream-colored paper, mounted on lined page of an account book, 6⅝ × 4⅝″
Annotated on mount in pen and brown ink: *l'horrible mélange*
Paris, Musée Rodin, D. 2069

63
Boso and the Snake
Graphite pencil, heightened with pen and brown ink, on cream-colored paper, torn bottom right, mounted on lined sheet, 5½ × 5⅜″
Annotated upper left in pen and brown ink: *serpent / Bose*; at right: *je veux que Bo...*; on the mount, in graphite: *bas-relief du bas*
On the reverse, in graphite: Nude figures
Paris, Musée Rodin, D. 1932

64
Shade of Count Guido
Graphite pencil, pen and brown ink on sand-colored paper, pasted firmly to mount, 3⅞ × 2⅝″
Paris, Musée Rodin, D. 3762

65
Damned Souls around Count Guido
Graphite pencil, pen and brown ink on lined paper, mounted firmly on cardboard, 5⅞ × 7¼″
Annotated upper right in pen and ink: *dans le... bas-rel...*
Paris, Musée Rodin, D. 5617

66
Satan and St. Francis Fighting over Count Guido
Graphite pencil, pen and brown ink on cream-colored paper, 2½ × 2⅞″
Annotated at bottom in pen and brown ink: *Oreste lit*
Paris, Musée Rodin, D. 5591

67
Count Guido
Graphite pencil and brown wash on lined, sand-colored paper, pasted to mount, 6⅝ × 8⅜″
Annotated top in graphite: *Comte Guidon porte bas soubassement*
On the reverse of mount, drawing and notes in graphite:
Un panneau · harpie
Paris, Musée Rodin, D. 1928

68
Count Guido between Satan and St. Francis
Graphite pencil, pen and brown ink on sand-colored paper, mounted on cardboard, 6⅛ × 3½″

Annotated upper left in pen and brown ink:
Guidon; at right: *St Francois*; below: *Guidon*
Paris, Musée Rodin, D.3767

69
Count Guido
Graphite pencil, pen and brown wash on cream-colored paper, mounted on paper,
4⅛ × 4⅞″
Annotated upper right in graphite: *Baudelaire angoisse*; in pen and ink on mount: *Comte Guidon*; in graphite, at bottom of drawing and mount: *tombeau*
Paris, Musée Rodin, D.5590

70
Mohammed with Dangling Intestines
Graphite pencil, pen and brown wash, heightened with gouache, on paper, mounted firmly on cardboard, 6¾ × 2″
Annotated upper right in pen and brown ink:
Mahomet intestines pendants
Paris, Musée Rodin, D.5633

71
Ugolino
Graphite pencil, pen and brown and red ink, grey wash, heightened with gouache, on lined, cream-colored paper, torn lower left,
6¾ × 5⅜″
Annotated upper right in pen and brown ink:
Ugolin; signed lower right in pen and brown ink:
Aug. Rodin
On the reverse, in graphite: Horseman surrounded by three figures
Paris, Musée Rodin, D.7627

72
Depiction of an Entombment
Graphite pencil, pen and grey wash, heightened with gouache, on sand-colored paper, mounted on cardboard, 4¾ × 6½″
Annotated and signed in brown ink on the cardboard mount: *à Fourcault son ami A. Rodin*
Formerly collection of Maurice Fenaille; Paris, Musée Rodin, D.7629
This scene was published in 1883, under the title *La vision du Sculpteur*, in an article by Dargentry on the Salon National (*L'Art*, vol. IV, p.35). It may correspond to No.81 in the auction of Louis de Fourcaud's collection (March 29, 1917), where it

was entitled *Mise au tombeau* (Entombment). The critic Louis de Boussès de Fourcaud (1853–1914) contributed to the *Gazette des Beaux-Arts*, *Le Figaro*, and particularly to *Le Gaulois*, where in an article on the Exposition des Arts Libéraux of 1883 he wrote that Rodin was "an incomparable draftsman, with tendencies that alternately recall the Gothic and Michelangelo." C.J.

73
Entombment
Graphite pencil, pen, grey and violet wash, heightened with gouache, on paper, pasted on mount, 5⅜ × 7¼″
Annotated on the mount, above, in pen and black ink: *panneau du bas*; below: *I bas*
Paris, Musée Rodin, D.7614
Maurice Fenaille, who encouraged the publication of the Goupil Album but modestly declined to have his name mentioned in Octave Mirbeau's preface, owned a few drawings by Rodin in addition to sculptures. A letter of April 26, 1913 shows that he received many as a gift (Musée Rodin Archive, Paris). The note *panneau du bas* links this entombment, a theme very close to Rodin's heart, to the original *Gates of Hell*. C.J.

74
Mephisto
Graphite pencil, pen and brown wash on tracing paper, right corners torn,
6⅝ × 4½″
Annotated upper right in pen and brown ink: *à faire un / groupe rond de bosse / avec la figurine accroupie / Mephistos*; on the reverse, in graphite:
Villette · Galimart et Rochefort
Paris, Musée Rodin, D.5609
The National Museum of Western Art, Tokyo, possesses a similar drawing. Rodin certainly chose tracing paper in order to repeat a pose that fascinated him and that appears in the lower section of the right wing of *The Gates of Hell*. The isolated couple embraces here, as the title says, with *Vaine Tendresse* (Vain Tenderness). In conjunction with D.5630 (plate 45) the drawing was published by Camille Mauclair in the *Revue des revues* of June 15, 1898; and a year later, with a few changes, it was used to illustrate the poem dedicated to Rodin in Henry de Braisne's book *Parmi le fer, parmi le sang*. The names listed on the back of the drawing indicate some of the contacts Rodin

maintained at this period. In 1884, he made the bust of Henri Rochefort, a journalist and pamphleteer; he was acquainted in 1887 with Paul Gallimard, who commissioned the vignettes for Baudelaire's *Les Fleurs du Mal*; the caricaturist Adolphe Willette drew Rodin for the cover of the *Courrier français* in 1902, and again in 1910, for the menu of a banquet held to celebrate Rodin's nomination as Grand Officer of the Legion of Honor. C.J.

75
Embrace
Graphite pencil, pen and brown wash on lined, cream-colored paper, mounted on paper, 8⅜ × 6¾"
On the reverse of the mount, in graphite pencil and red pencil: Sketch of a reclining woman next to an animal
Paris, Musée Rodin, D. 1904
This anonymous embracing couple might be Paolo and Francesca, or then again, Dante and Virgil. The many depictions of embraces Rodin made culminated in 1886, with *The Kiss*. This drawing was probably done after the sheet had been affixed to the mount, as can be seen from the overlaps of the graphite and ink lines and the brushed wash. C.J.

76
Group with Three Figures
Pen, brown and violet wash, and gouache on cream-colored paper, pasted to mount, 8½ × 6¾"
Annotated at top in pen and brown ink: *groupe à mettre dans la niche ce groupe avec mes figures de terre estampe*
Paris, Musée Rodin, D. 1930
Rodin must have done this drawing in two phases, first applying the pen-and-ink lines and pasting it to the mount, and then executing the passages in wash, which flows over both surfaces. The note indicates that Rodin wished to place his composition in a niche and associate it with a sculptural group. C.J.

77
Head of a Woman
Graphite pencil and black wash, heightened with gouache, on cream-colored paper, three corners cut off, 7⅜ × 5⅜"

On the reverse, in graphite: Outline of a figure and arm of a skeleton
Paris, Musée Rodin, D. 2049

78
Demon in Space
Pen and ink with wash, on cut-out cream-colored paper, 1½ × 5⅛"
Paris, Musée Rodin, D. 5665

Architectural Drawings
Plates on pages 148–167

79
Church Portal in Nantes
Graphite pencil, pen and grey wash, heightened with gouache, on squared cream-colored paper, 3½ × 5¾"
On the reverse, in graphite, pen and ink, grey wash, and gouache: Triangular pediment of vestibule
Paris, Musée Rodin, D. 5764

80
Church Facade in Mantes
Graphite pencil and gouache on cream-colored paper, 7¾ × 6⅛"
On the reverse, in graphite: Sketch of a vestibule
Paris, Musée Rodin, D. 5806

81
Facade of the St. Jacques et St. Christophe Church in Houdan
Pen and brown ink on cream-colored paper, 6⅞ × 4⅛"
Paris, Musée Rodin, D. 5828

82
Facade of the St. Jacques et St. Christophe Church in Houdan
Pen and grey wash on cream-colored paper, 5¼ × 7⅞"
Paris, Musée Rodin, D. 5778

83
Moldings and Door in Charles VIII Style
Graphite pencil, pen and brown ink on envelope, 4¾ × 5¾"

Annotated in graphite and pen and ink: *pilastres porte la sculpture renaissance s'ajustant toujours porte Charles VIII.*
On the reverse, in graphite: Facade of a palace
Paris, Musée Rodin, D. 5856, 5857

84
Buttresses of a Church
Pen and brown ink on squared paper with letter-head of Hôtel de la Coupe d'Or, Houdan, 8⅜ × 10½″
On the reverse, in pen and ink: Perspective sketch of a church facade; annotated in graphite: *Batissiere H de l'arche*
Paris, Musée Rodin, D. 5889, 5890 v

85
Vestibule in Toulouse
Pen and brown ink, heightened with gouache, on cream-colored paper, 7 × 4⅝″
Paris, Musée Rodin, D. 5904

86
Church Portal in Tonnerre
Graphite pencil and violet wash on lined paper, 5⅜ × 7¼″
Various annotations in graphite, from left to right: *ma porte · contrefort cassé flanqué de tours · ronde · épaisseur · pilastre · inclus · portail · console · entable-ment très saillant · fruits · console · tête d'ange · écusson blond*
On the reverse, in graphite: Section of a buttress and a beam; with annotations: *contrefort · entable-ment · noir · lignes fines*
Paris, Musée Rodin, D. 5942, 5943

87
Portal in Toulouse
Pen and brown wash on cream-colored paper, 6½ × 5⅞″
On the reverse, in pen and brown ink: Church facade
Paris, Musée Rodin, D. 5902

88
Facade in Toulouse (?)
Pen and brown wash on cream-colored paper, 4½ × 7″
Paris, Musée Rodin, D. 5920

89
Facade with Portal in Auxerre
Graphite pencil, pen and grey wash on squared paper, 7⅛ × 5⅝″
On the reverse, in graphite and grey wash: Niche
Paris, Musée Rodin, D. 5916, 5917, 5918

90
Portal of St. Pierre Abbey in Auxerre
Graphite pencil, pen, brown wash and gouache on sand-colored paper, 12¼ × 7⅞″
Annotated in pen and ink: *noir · blanc*
Paris, Musée Rodin, D. 5925

91
Two Studies of Niche for Henley Bust
Graphite pencil, pen and brown ink on cream-colored paper, 5⅜ × 3⅞″
Annotated bottom in pen and ink: *Henley*
On the reverse, in pen and ink: Pilaster capital
Paris, Musée Rodin, D. 5877, D. 5878

92
Sculpture before a Portal
Pen and brown ink on cream-colored paper, 11⅜ × 7⅜″
Annotated below center in graphite and ink: *réduit · ombre*
On the reverse, in pen, brown ink and gouache: Moldings
Paris, Musée Rodin, D. 5921

93
Corbels in Dijon
Pen and brown ink on cream-colored squared paper, 2⅛ × 3¼″
Annotated in graphite and ink: *chapiteau · partie grosse bas · portes… haut*
On the reverse, in graphite and ink: Corner-turrets
Paris, Musée Rodin, D. 5912, 5913

94
Corbel in Quimperlé (?)
Graphite pencil, pen and brown wash on cream-colored paper, 4¾ × 3⅛″
On the reverse, in pen and brown ink: Architec-tural motif
Paris, Musée Rodin, D. 5879

95
Renaissance Cornice
Pen and brown ink on cream-colored paper,
6½ × 4⅛″
Paris, Musée Rodin, D.5884

96
Cornice in Chambord (?)
Pen and brown ink on cream-colored paper,
12¼ × 8⅜″
Annotated at bottom in pen and ink: *encadrement*;
in graphite: *réduction*
On the reverse, in pen and brown ink: Door with
shell pediment; annotation in graphite: *porte*
Paris, Musée Rodin, D.5887, 5888

97
Columns of the Church in Champeaux
Graphite pencil, pen and ink, and gouache on
cream-colored paper, 5¼ × 4⅛″
Paris, Musée Rodin, D.5812

98
Ussé
Graphite pencil, pen and brown ink, heightened
with gouache, on cream-colored paper,
12¼ × 7⅛″
Paris, Musée Rodin, D.5818

The Transition Period
Plates on pages 186–207

Ernst-Gerhard Güse has written comments on a
number of the following drawings. These are
signed E.-G.G.

99
Four Sketches for the Nude Balzac and a Church Facade
Graphite pencil, pen and brown ink on cream-
colored paper, 9 × 7⅛″
On the reverse, in graphite and pen and brown
ink: Three sketches for the *Balzac* and a church
facade
Paris, Musée Rodin, D.5324, 5325; reverse,
D.5321, 5322, 5323
The four sketches of Balzac show him in the nude,
standing before a chair with his legs spread, his
right hand resting on the chair and his left behind
his back. The sheet also contains a sketch of the

facade of the Eglise Saint-Jacques et Saint-Christophe in Houdan. Claudie Judrin dates the
drawing to 1895. E.-G.G.

100
Balzac Study
Pen and brown ink on cream-colored paper,
10¾ × 6⅜″
Paris, Musée Rodin, D.5329
The drawing corresponds in every respect to the
Balzac figure exhibited in 1898. It was possibly
done after the sculpture was finished. E.-G.G.

101
*Standing Nude Woman with Head Bent Forward and
Hands in Her Hair*
Pen and brown and red ink with red wash, on
cream-colored paper with watermark,
6⅞ × 4⅜″
Paris, Musée Rodin, D.4304
This nude figure belongs to the category of delicate contour drawings which led to the drawings
with watercolor wash of Rodin's late style. A clue
to the dating of these sheets is given by the etching
Ames du Purgatoire (ill. p.177), which was published in 1893. E.-G.G.

102
Nude Woman with Long Veil, a Shell at Her Feet
Pen and brown ink with grey wash on cream-
colored paper with watermark,
6⅞ × 4⅜″
Paris, Musée Rodin, D.4283
The shell motif characterizes the figure as Venus
Anadyomene. This is a clean rendering after
sketches made directly from the model, for exam-
ple D.4277. E.-G.G.

103
Woman Putting On a Garment
Graphite pencil, pen and ink, brown and red
wash, heightened with gouache, on cream-
colored paper with watermark, 7 × 4½″
Paris, Musée Rodin, D.4282

104
*Clothed Woman, Her Hands in the Folds of Her
Garment*
Graphite pencil, pen and brown wash on cream-
colored paper with watermark, 7 × 4½″
Paris, Musée Rodin, D.4276

105

Two Clothed Women
Pen, brown and red wash on cream-colored
paper with watermark, 7 × 4¾″
Paris, Musée Rodin, D.4379

106

Clothed Woman with Outstretched Arm
Graphite pencil, pen and brown and red wash,
watercolor and gouache on cream-colored paper
with watermark, 6⅞ × 4¼″
Paris, Musée Rodin, D.4296

107

Woman Seen from the Side, in a Dancing Pose
Graphite pencil, pen and brown wash, heightened with gouache, on cream-colored paper,
7 × 4½″
Paris, Musée Rodin, D.4363

108

Woman Dancing with Veils
Pen and black wash on cream-colored paper
with watermark, 7 × 4½″
Paris, Musée Rodin, D.4349
The dark colors and intensely vital line still owe
much to the gouaches of the 1880s. They suggest a
date of c. 1890 for this drawing. Stylistic proximity is evinced by D.4363 and 4379. E.-G.G.

109

*Standing Young Woman from the Front, Her Head Low-
ered, Arms Crossed Over Her Body, and Bare Breasts*
Lead pencil, green and white watercolor,
brown hair, on brownish paper, 7 × 4⅜″
Kunsthalle Bremen, No. 1962/263, a

110

Standing Female Nude with Veils
Lead pencil and red ink, heightened with white
and with yellow watercolor wash, on paper with
watermark, 6⅞ × 4¼″
Signed lower right in lead pencil: *Aug. Rodin*
Kunsthalle Bremen, No. 1962/229, a

111

Naked Woman with Open Garment
Graphite pencil, pen and brown and red ink, red
wash, watercolor and gouache on cream-colored
paper, 6⅞ × 4¼″
Paris, Musée Rodin, D.4305

112

*Standing Woman with Garment Lifted to Her
Hips*
Graphite pencil, red wash, watercolor, heigh-
tened with chalk, on cream-colored paper with
watermark, 7 × 4½″
Paris, Musée Rodin, D.4373

113

Nude Woman Swirling Her Veils
Graphite pencil, pen, brown and red wash,
watercolor and gouache on cream-colored paper
with watermark, 6⅞ × 4¼″
Paris, Musée Rodin, D.4309

114

Semi-nude Woman Bending to the Side
Graphite pencil, pen and red ink on cream-
colored paper with watermark,
6¼ × 3⅞″
Paris, Musée Rodin, D.4266

115

Sapphic Couple in an Embrace
Graphite pencil, pen and brown ink, watercolor
and gouache on cream-colored paper with watermark, 7 × 4½″
Paris, Musée Rodin, D.4275

116

Twilight
Graphite pencil, stump, pen and ink, brown
wash, and watercolor on cream-colored paper,
7 × 4½″
Annotated lower right in graphite: *le crépuscule*
Paris, Musée Rodin, D.4278
The subject of girls embracing is a frequent one
with Rodin, in both his drawing and sculpture.
His group *Femmes damnées* was executed in 1885.
Rodin was acquainted with Pierre Louys's *Songs
of Bilitis*. The theme took on great importance to
him during the 1890s thanks to his preceding involvement with *Les Fleurs du Mal*. E.-G.G.

117

*Nude Woman Bending Forward in Front of a Standing
Woman with Open Hair*
Graphite pencil, pen and brown ink, wash,
watercolor and gouache on cream-colored paper
with watermark, 7 × 4½″
Paris, Musée Rodin, D.4261

118
Nude Woman Bending Forward in Front of a Standing Woman
Graphite pencil, pen and brown and red ink, red wash, watercolor and gouache on paper with watermark, 7 × 4½″
Paris, Musée Rodin, D. 4370

119
Standing Woman (Torso), Pulling on a Garment
Graphite pencil, red wash and gouache on cream-colored paper with watermark, 7 × 4½″
Paris, Musée Rodin, D. 4371

120
Nude Standing Woman from the Side, a Garment in Her Hand
Graphite pencil and watercolor on cream-colored paper with watermark, 7⅞ × 5″
Paris, Musée Rodin, D. 4340

Around 1900
Plates on pages 235–268, 274–290

J. A. Schmoll gen. Eisenwerth has written comments on a number of the following drawings. These texts are signed S. g. E. In those cases where the Musée Rodin provided technical information, it is given here, even when the author is of different opinion about the means and media used by Rodin. The author has requested us to print his commentaries as given even though his description of Rodin's techniques sometimes diverges from that of the Musée Rodin.

121
Portrait of Séverine
Charcoal on cream-colored paper, 12⅜ × 9⅞″
Signed at the right in charcoal: *A. R.*
Purchased by the Musée Rodin at the Pontremoli Auction on November 25, 1924
Paris, Musée Rodin, D. 5644
The collection of Charles Pontremoli, an architect of Egyptian origin, includes works by Rodin and Camille Claudel. This drawing, with its ample, sweeping line, is from a series of portrait sketches of the writer Caroline Rémy, whose pen-name was Séverine (1855–1925). A similar drawing is at Budapest, in the Museum of Fine Arts (reproduced in the catalogue of the Rodin exhibition, Nationalgalerie Berlin/DDR, 1979, No. 88). In the same year, 1883, Rodin modelled a mask of Séverine (see ill. p. 217; bronze castings in Paris, Musée Rodin, and San Francisco). Both the sculpture and the drawings convey the unusual temperament of this socially critical and committed woman, who fervently admired Rodin's art and publicly supported it even at times of extreme difficulty. This and other drawings from the series at the Musée Rodin (see the exhibition catalogue *Rodin et les écrivains de son temps*, 1976, p. 126 ff.) are unusual for a sculptor, being highly expressive and spontaneous. They are considered preliminary studies or accompanying works to the modelled portrait mask, which also captures the intense expression of the eyes and volatile lips, open as if to speak. S. g. E.

122
Portrait of a Woman
Lower right: *Rapid Sketch of a Face (?)*
Graphite pencil and stump on cream-colored paper, 12⅛ × 7⅞″
Signed lower right in graphite: *Aug. Rodin*
On the reverse, in graphite: Female nude from the back
Gift of Maurice Fenaille to the Musée Rodin, June 16, 1927
Paris, Musée Rodin, D. 5941
Three-quarter profile of an unknown woman's head, her eyes turned sharply to the right (from the observer's point of view). The profile line and other contours have been gone over repeatedly for emphasis, hatched with lead pencil and softened to shadows with the stump. Highlights have been picked out with an eraser. This is a spontaneous sketch, recording principal lines and masses. The woman portrayed bears a certain resemblance to Tilla Durieux, an actress and wife of the Berlin art dealer and publisher Paul Cassirer, who in the decade before the First World War exhibited and sold many Rodin drawings in Berlin. The connection would be worth looking into. Below the bust is a contour line, a profile drawing of the head reversed, which was probably a first, rejected attempt to capture the profile without looking at the paper. S. g. E.

123
Portrait of a Woman
Graphite pencil and stump on cream-colored paper, 7 × 7⅞″
Violet signature stamp lower right
Paris, Musée Rodin, D. 2861
Blocked out with extremely delicate pencil lines, then emphasized to bring out the principal lines, and the contours and hatching gone over with the stump to increase the 'painterly' and 'sculptural' values. The veiled expression exudes eroticism. S. g. E.

124
Dancer
Lead pencil with watercolor, 12⅞ × 7½″
Purchased with the Strecker Collection, 1958
Cologne, Wallraf-Richartz-Museum, No. 1958/61

125
Reclining Woman with Exposed Legs
Graphite pencil and watercolor on cream-colored paper, 9⅞ × 12⅝″
Signed lower right in graphite: *A. Rodin*
Paris, Musée Rodin, D. 4994
The treatment, and extremely confident contours, are similar to plate 127, D. 5657. The woman, resting on pillows suggestions of which are visible, has raised her right leg, letting her chemise slip back to reveal her open thighs. This is the naively voluptuous pose seen in many drawings, but here without shading to emphasize the pubic area. The incarnadine is of an ocher-yellow tint, the watercolor wash flowing in many areas beyond the contours, particularly around the legs. The dress is of an Indian yellow hue with a greenish cast, and the paint has run together in places, concentrating the color. The hair, a greyish-black whose effect approaches the bluish-black of the *Cambodgiennes* of 1906, suggests a dating to the same period. S. g. E.

126
Sleeping Girl Seen Obliquely from Below
Lead pencil and delicate yellow watercolor wash, on slightly yellowed paper, 12⅝ × 9¾″
Brown line lower right
Bremen, Kunsthalle, No. 1962/9, a

127
Clothed Woman Lying on Her Side
Graphite pencil and watercolor on cream-colored paper, 9⅞ × 12⅝″
Signed lower right in graphite: *A. Rodin*
Paris, Musée Rodin, D. 5657
The model is of a type resembling the woman in the portrait drawing of plate 123, D. 2861, and her smiling expression has been achieved with a minimum of means. The rendering is delicate, the lines concise and of flowing, supple beauty. Before drawing the contours in lead pencil, Rodin blocked in the forms with watercolor, the hair in a greyish-black, the incarnadine delicate yellow, and the garment light blue. Color application is transparent, growing more dense in the hair and dress (over the breast), and the puddles and edges of the color areas have been integrated into the overall impression, as is often the case in Rodin's drawings. See also the watercolor from the Helene von Nostitz Estate (plate 154). S. g. E.

128
The Muse and the Poet
Watercolor and lead pencil, 12¾ × 9⅞″
Signed lower right (probably not by the artist): *Rodin*
Berlin, Georg-Kolbe-Museum

129
Clothed Woman Seated between Her Heels
Graphite pencil and watercolor on cream-colored paper with watermark, 12⅝ × 9⅞″
Signed lower right in graphite: *Rodin*
Paris, Musée Rodin, D. 5003

130
Kneeling Female Nude Carrying Another Across Her Shoulders
Lead pencil and watercolor, 12¾ × 18½″
Signed lower right: *Aug. Rodin*
Stuttgart, Graphische Sammlung der Staatsgalerie, No. C 51/326

131
Nude Kneeling Woman Holding Her Arms behind Her Back
Graphite pencil, stump and watercolor on cream-colored paper, 13 × 10⅛″
Signed lower right in graphite: *Rodin*
Paris, Musée Rodin, D. 4620

A loose lead-pencil drawing worked over with a stump to provide sculptural modelling in the shadows. The flesh tones are a delicate rose, and across them run horizontal stripes of the blue watercolor that give the impression that the figure is submerged in the sea. Where the watery blue runs over the pink incarnadine the two tones merge into delicate variations of violet. The last color applied was the brown of the helmet of hair, which is heightened in places with touches of yellow. The hair, falling over the face, increases its masklike look. This and the two following drawings represent three phases in a metamorphosis of the female body into a vase-shape. S. g. E.

132

Kneeling Woman, Her Head Thrown Back
Graphite pencil, stump and watercolor on paper with watermark, 12⅝ × 9¾"
Signed upper left in graphite: *A. Rodin*
Paris, Musée Rodin, D. 4772
The woman's head is bent back so far that we see only the underside of her chin and the arch of her jaw. This, combined with her almost completely hidden arms, makes the figure into a torso—the second stage of a transformation into a vase-body. Contours and hatching in lead pencil have been slightly modelled with the stump to create a "relief" effect. Lateral hatching at the height of the thighs and adjacent to the figure evoke space and water. A yellowish watercolor wash has been used for the flesh tones, and a delicate green starting below the hips suggests a rising sea. Where the paint has puddled at the sides and below the junction of the legs, Rodin has traced around the dried edges in pencil to suggest water plants. The effect is almost surreal, a poetic sublimation. One is tempted to entitle this drawing *Venus anadyomene*, Venus born of the foam, emerging from the waves. S. g. E.

133

Vase Woman
Graphite pencil and watercolor on cream-colored paper, mounted on cardboard, 19⅜ × 12¾"
Paris, Musée Rodin, D. 4771
The last phase in the metamorphosis of a female body into a vase. The contour, flowing from knees over thighs, waist, shoulders and upper arms to raised chin, evokes the smooth, rounded volume of a vase, a vessel whose anthropomorphic origin in Greek antiquity Rodin illustrated—indeed argued for—in this series of nudes. Like an antique vase, the torso is divided into levels by delicate lead-pencil marks, a sequence of horizontal bands, friezes, scenes with figures. Yet indications of the female body from which the form derives are not lacking, either: suggestions of nipples in the upper curves, lines at the crotch and thighs, and the beautifully observed bend of the knees. The brownish-red watercolor evokes a terracotta vessel; its more transparent, lighter passages and the shading beneath it create an impression of volume, which is further heightened by the silhouette-like isolation of the color-volume on the light background. Metamorphoses of this kind are profound expressions of Rodin's visual imagination, which, by the way, was also inspired by numerous motifs from Ovid's and Dante's poetic metamorphoses. S. g. E.

134

Reclining Female Nude, One Foot Propped on Her Thigh
Graphite pencil on cream-colored paper, 12⅛ × 7⅞"
On the reverse, in graphite: Seated female nude with raised leg; repetition of the foot
Paris, Musée Rodin, D. 2479, 2480 v
The lead-pencil contours, first delicately applied and tentatively repeated, were then emphasized to bring out key lines of the body. The pose, with one raised leg crossed over the other, in a way recalls Michelangelo's reclining figures on the Medici tombs in Florence, which Rodin sketched several times. The observer's viewpoint not only emphasizes the erotic aspect of the pose but even more important, represents an unusual formal solution, with the pyramidal configuration formed by the angled leg. S. g. E.

135

Reclining Female Nude, One Hand under Her Raised Leg
Graphite pencil on cream-colored paper, 8½ × 12¼"
Paris, Musée Rodin, D. 1379
An example of the "kicking" pose, with the woman putting both hands to her crotch and turning her head obliquely to face the viewer. Repeated

contour lines mark shifts in position, particularly of the legs. Rodin has sketched the face spontaneously and with odd "distortions"; the glance seems troubled. This is one of a series of similar drawings of an intimate nature (see Claudie Judrin, *Auguste Rodin—100 Zeichnungen und Aquarelle*, 1982, Nos. 30/31 and 86). S.g.E.

136
Nude Woman from the Side, One Knee on the Floor, Bent Backwards, Holding Her Foot with One Hand
Graphite pencil on cream-colored paper, 9⅞ × 12¾″
On the reverse: Woman lying on her side, resting her face in one hand
Paris, Musée Rodin, D.1740, 1741 v
Repeated essays at capturing the contours of a model in movement and in a difficult pose. S.g.E.

137
Nude Study
Lead pencil, 12¼ × 7⅞″
Munich, Staatliche Graphische Sammlung, No.4487

138
Two Seated Women, Holding Hands
Graphite pencil, stump and watercolor on cream-colored paper, 12¾ × 9¾″
Violet signature stamp lower left
Paris, Musée Rodin, D.3919

139
Female Nude
Lead pencil and watercolor, 12¾ × 8¼″
Signed lower right: *A.Rodin*
Purchased for the Haubrich Collection, 1950
Cologne, Wallraf-Richartz-Museum, No.1950/214

140
Female Nude from the Back
Lead pencil, 12¼ × 7⅞″
Signed left: *Aug.Rodin*
Mannheim, Städtische Kunsthalle

141
Seated Woman
Lead pencil, 12⅛ × 8″
Frankfurt am Main, Städelsches Kunstinstitut und Städtische Galerie, No.2453

142
Embracing Couple, also known as Desire
Graphite pencil and stump on sand-colored paper, 12⅜ × 7⅞″
Paris, Musée Rodin, D.5956
The man, taller than his slender partner, raises her head up to his, tenderly supporting her neck. She seems to have run into his arms. Contours and shading have been rapidly notated, and certain original outlines left standing, for instance a raised left foot behind the man's right leg. This hasty study of movement shows many corrections and contours sharpened by repetition of the strokes. The subject is related to the lovers in *The Gates of Hell*, but must probably be associated with a later period in Rodin's career. S.g.E.

143
Two Women Embracing
Graphite pencil, watercolor and gouache on cream-colored paper, 12⅝ × 9½″
Annotated lower left in graphite: *hommage à ma grande amie Judith Cladel · Aug.Rodin 1911*
Acquired from the estate of Judith Cladel on February 12, 1961
Paris, Musée Rodin, D.7195

144
Seated Man (Neptune)
Lead pencil and watercolor, 13⅛ × 9¾″
Leipzig, Museum der bildenden Künste

145
Reclining Woman, a Hand behind Her Head
Graphite pencil and watercolor on cream-colored paper, cut out, 5⅞ × 11½″
Paris, Musée Rodin, D.5239
This and the two following *papiers découpés*— drawings of nudes cut out and pasted on another sheet—are examples of a technique with which Rodin apparently began to experiment in the 1880s in order to put parts of his own drawings in a new context. Around 1900 he developed this process further, gradually working out his own unique collage technique. He cut nudes out of his drawings, isolating them from the original surroundings, which allowed him to reposition them in completely new spatial relationships. In this way, a reclining figure might be transformed

into a floating or swimming figure, or even appear to fly acrobatically through empty space. Cutting the figures out as if from a printed sheet for model-building, Rodin then mounted them on a neutral sheet of paper, sometimes combining as many as two or three figures into a completely new group, as in plate 147. If the figures had been previously tinted with watercolor, he frequently diverged from the contours of the "color-volume" to include in the cut-out portion contour lines beyond the watercolor wash, which increased the effect of movement (see plate 145). In the group of plate 147 two cut-outs, the right-hand one including head and arm of a third figure, have been overlapped to create a very strange constellation with changing perspectives. These techniques of *découpage*, montage and collage recall Rodin's treatment of fragments of plaster sculptures, which he likewise repeatedly combined into ever-new configurations, thus multiplying the formal possibilities of his arsenal of "prefabricated" limbs and torsos and other elements of the body. Rodin manipulated these figures cut out of the drawings and released from their two-dimensionality in a similar way to his preparatory work when conceiving a sculpture in three dimensions, handling them almost like clay sketches in free space. S. g. E.

146
Female Nude with Angled Arms
Graphite pencil and watercolor on cut-out paper, 12¾ × 4⅝″
Paris, Musée Rodin, D. 5201

147
Three Embracing Women
Graphite pencil and watercolor on two pieces of cut-out and collaged paper, 14⅛ × 7⅛″
Paris, Musée Rodin, D. 5196

148
Nude Woman Bent Over Her Raised Leg, the Other Leg Stretched out Behind Her
Graphite pencil and stump on cream-colored paper, 9 × 14¼″
Annotated and signed at bottom in graphite: *bas · Rodin*
Acquired from the estate of Judith Cladel on February 12, 1961
Paris, Musée Rodin, D. 7181

149
Reclining Nude Woman from Behind
Graphite pencil, stump and watercolor on cream-colored paper with watermark, 12⅞ × 9¾″
Paris, Musée Rodin, D. 1537

150
Reclining Nude Female Torso
Graphite pencil and stump on cream-colored paper, 8 × 12¼″
Paris, Musée Rodin, D. 6005
The smeared graphite in this and the two following drawings, distributed with the fingertips, creates a strong sculptural effect. Rodin has concentrated on the torso, sectioning the body and leaving out head, lower legs, and sometimes arms. The simplification and density of the plastic volumes reveals the eye of the sculptor. The expressive approach neglects the beauty of line so characteristic of many of Rodin's other nude drawings, anticipating the work of younger artists, even down to some of Henry Moore's figure drawings of the 1940s. S. g. E.

151
Reclining Female Torso,
a Hand on Her Breast
Graphite pencil and stump on cream-colored paper, 7⅞ × 12¼″
Paris, Musée Rodin, D. 2909

152
Reclining Female Nude
Graphite pencil and stump on cream-colored paper, 7¾ × 13⅛″
Paris, Musée Rodin, D. 2889

153
Salammbô,
Woman Lying on Her Back, Stretching Herself
Graphite pencil and stump on cream-colored paper, 8 × 12¼″
Annotated lower left in graphite: *Salambo*; lower right: *Sᵗ Antoine*
Paris, Musée Rodin, D. 6012
The two titles refer to novels by Gustave Flaubert, *Salammbô* (1863) and *La Tentation de Saint Antoine* (1874). The latter also inspired Rodin to do a sculpture. The *Salammbô* was inscribed by Rodin very rapidly and without regard for accuracy.

Both titles allude to young women in their role of temptress, passionately offering themselves yet hiding their face as if in shame. The pose, with spread thighs, soles of the feet pressed together, and exposed sex, is daring and certainly unusual for the period, though the vehemence with which the living, breathing body unfolds is superb. A related drawing is in the Metropolitan Museum, New York, from the donation of the artist Georgia O'Keeffe. Here, however, the woman's lower legs have been redrawn into a semblance of goat's legs, making her a faun, as the title, *Satyresse*, indicates (illustrated in *The Drawings of Rodin*, London, 1972). S. g. E.

154
La lune, Psyché
Prior to 1907
Lead pencil and watercolor on yellowish paper, internal dimensions 9½×12⅜″
Signed lower right: *A. Rodin;*
annotated below signature in pencil:
la lune. Psychée
N 15
Rodin, who throughout his life made small spelling errors, has inadvertently added an *e* to *Psyché*, the mythological embodiment of the soul. This title, like most, was probably given to the drawing later, and it can be read alternatively as two separate titles, i. e., either as *la lune Psyché(e)* or as *la lune* on the one hand and *Psyché(e)* on the other. In the latter case, which frequently holds for Rodin's title annotations, the two words could be understood as alternatives; it is left up to the spectator to choose between them or give himself over to the mental associations suggested by their interplay. In thematic terms, the chemise lifted to the breasts and the cloudy grey watercolor wash above would justify the title *la lune*—the moon appearing in the cloudy night sky, an association very much in keeping with Rodin's symbolic visual poetry, of which there are many examples in his drawings. (Reproduced in Helene von Nostitz, *Rodin in Gesprächen und Briefen*, Dresden, 1927, opp. p. 52.) S. g. E.

The Cambodian Dancers
Plates on pages 274–290

When Rodin heard that the troupe of Cambodian dancers was to board the express from Paris to Marseille on the evening of July 12, 1906, he decided to follow them. The Cambodians had hoped to be able to stay longer in Paris and France. But the French government considered the expenses too high for King Sisowath's delegation, which totalled 149 persons and included his princesses, court officials, the dancers, and guards for jewellery and costumes, and they were requested to shorten their stay. Rodin remained in Marseille for only a few days, until the Cambodians boarded their ship, but he was able to make many drawings of individual members and groups in the ensemble in the park of the building where they were staying, the Villa des Glycines, not far from the site of the Colonial Exhibition. These "sessions" were recorded by M. Sanremo, a Marseille photographer (ill. p. 270). Rodin, seated on one of the park benches with a portfolio on his knees, would draw the dancers as policemen watched discreetly from the cover of the trees to ensure that none of the sculptor's models would attempt to slip away and stay in France, as they had done in Paris several times…
Rodin's drawings of Cambodian dancers represent a culmination in his late work, indeed in his oeuvre as a whole. In full possession of his means as a draftsman and colorist, he created sketches that for all their rapidity of execution are superb and delightful evocations of Far Eastern dance. Every variation in movement has been captured, from relaxed poses and graceful gestures of the hands to ecstatic, stamping dance steps. Faces, coiffures, costumes and jewellery—of which the dancers had an abundance—interested Rodin hardly at all, his sculptor's eye resting on such details only fleetingly. But their bodies, their movements, and their ritualistic gestures fascinated him, and he attempted to capture them, frequently with only a few swift strokes but even more frequently by "improving" on the forms again and again. We can assume that many of the drawings were not done in a single sitting. The watercolor washes may well have been applied, in every case, after the fact, either in the hotel immediately after the sessions, or perhaps even in Paris after Rodin had returned from his excursion

to Marseille. At any rate, there is evidence in many of the sheets that after the transparent watercolor had dried, Rodin went over the sketched forms again in heavier pencil, and sometimes in colored pencil or pen and ink, to emphasize principal lines and give them final form. A few drawings reveal up to seven or eight different stages of work, from a first tentative blocking-out in delicate pencil line to more solid contouring, and from initial applications of watercolor to the use of opaque gouache, followed by another two or three reworkings to give the configurations their definitive expression (see plates 165, where blue pencil was employed, and 163, 159, and particularly 162, 170, 168, and 161, which each show at least seven or eight "layers" of work). Another fascinating aspect is Rodin's notation of the figures' sequential phases of movement in many cases, a "pre-futuristic" technique that arose from the extreme rapidity of his transcription (for details, see p. 229).

It is astonishing that despite this repeated "processing" Rodin should have been able to retain an impression of spontaneity, an extreme lightness of touch that indeed is one of the miracles of Rodin's late draftsmanship. The impression is increased by the poetic sublimation of his color which, rather than being merely decorative or ornamental, captures the essence of the dancers, manifests the aura of their ritual, courtly dance, its nobility, and its religiosity, of which Rodin himself spoke many times (for instance in a newspaper interview with Georges Bois, published under the title "Le sculpteur Rodin et les danseuses cambodgiennes", in *L'Illustration*, July 28, 1906, and in the artist's later essay on Indian sculpture, "La danse de Civa", in *Ars Asiatica*, III, 1921).

Rilke, after seeing the exhibition of *Cambodgiennes* drawings at Bernheim Jeune, Paris, wrote to his wife, Clara Rilke-Westhoff, on October 15, 1907, that the color of these drawings reminded him of "dried flower petals." And the poet could only confirm a note which Rodin had written on the border of a drawing (plate 170, D.4517)—*fleur(s) humaine(s)*. S. g. E.

155

Portrait of a Man (King Sisowath of Cambodia)
Lead pencil and watercolor, 12½ × 9⅝″
Munich, Staatliche Graphische Sammlung,
No. 44488

156

*Portrait of a Cambodian
(Court Official of King Sisowath)*
Graphite pencil and gouache on cream-colored paper, 12⅜ × 9½″
Paris, Musée Rodin, D.4482
King Sisowath of Cambodia (reigned April 1906–1927) and his daughter Sounpady brought their court and a large dance company to Europe in the summer of 1906, invited by the French government, which had a protectorate of Cambodia, to participate in the great Colonial Exhibition at Marseille. On July 1, 1906, the king and his entourage were received by the French president at the Elysée Palace, where a gala performance of the Cambodian ballet took place. Though Rodin was probably not invited to this event, he may very well have been to the following performance on July 10 in the Bois de Boulogne, which had been arranged by the Colonial Minister in honor of King Sisowath. Minister Georges Leygues (1858–1933), in his youth a lesser-known poet of the Parnassiens group (exponents of an austere neo-classicism), was well disposed toward the arts, and he very likely arranged an invitation for Rodin, who modelled a portrait of him that same year (see Claudie Judrin, *Rodin et l'Extrême-Orient*, exhibition catalogue, 1979, p. 67 ff.). Inspired by the exotic charm of the dances and the expressive language of the performers' disciplined movements, Rodin tried to find some opportunity to sketch them. His desire to invite them to Meudon and to do a sculpture of King Sisowath could not be fulfilled due to the shortness of the official visit. However, he was able to meet the delegation in their Paris hotel on the afternoon of July 12. Perhaps the portrait sketches of the king and a few members of his court were made at this opportunity. Their economy of line and confidence of means put them among the most astonishingly spontaneous of the sculptor's portrait drawings. S. g. E.

157

Cambodian Dancer
Lead pencil and watercolor,
11⅞ × 7¾″
Signed lower right: *Aug. Rodin*
Gift of the Wallraf-Richartz-Gesellschaft, 1923
Cologne, Wallraf-Richartz-Museum, No. Z1779;
1923/68

158
Cambodian Dancer en face
Graphite pencil and watercolor on cream-colored paper, 12⅝ × 9¾″
Paris, Musée Rodin, D.4437

159
Cambodian Dancer en face
Graphite pencil, watercolor and gouache on cream-colored paper with watermark, 12⅝ × 9½″
Paris, Musée Rodin, D.4498

160
Cambodian Dancer en face
Graphite pencil, watercolor and gouache on cream-colored paper, 12⅝ × 9⅜″
Paris, Musée Rodin, D.4450

161
Cambodian Dancer en face
Graphite pencil, watercolor and lead pencil on cream-colored paper, 11⅞ × 7¾″
Annotated lower left in lead pencil: *Cambodgienne pour servir de gloire*
Paris, Musée Rodin, D.5077

162
Cambodian Dancer en face
Graphite pencil, pen and brown ink, watercolor and gouache on sand-colored paper, 12¼ × 7¾″
Paris, Musée Rodin, D.4511

163
Cambodian Dancer en face
Graphite pencil, watercolor and lead pencil on cream-colored paper, 12⅝ × 9¾″
Paris, Musée Rodin, D.4449

164
Cambodian Dancer en face
Graphite pencil, watercolor and lead pencil on cream-colored paper, 11⅞ × 7⅞″
Paris, Musée Rodin, D.4429

165
Cambodian Dancer from the Side
Graphite pencil, blue pencil, heightened with gouache, on sand-colored paper, 13⅛ × 9½″
Paris, Musée Rodin, D.4432

166
Cambodian Dancer en face
Graphite pencil, watercolor, gouache and lead pencil on cream-colored paper, 13⅜ × 10½″
Signed lower right in graphite: *A.Rodin*
Paris, Musée Rodin, D.4455

167
Cambodian Dancer
Graphite pencil and watercolor on cream-colored paper, 9¼ × 12⅝″
Paris, Musée Rodin, D.4430

168
Cambodian Dancer en face
Graphite pencil, grey wash, gouache and grease pencil on cream-colored paper, 12½ × 8⅝″
Signed lower left in graphite: *Aug.Rodin*
On the reverse, in graphite and watercolor: Cambodian woman
Paris, Musée Rodin, D.5700, 5699

169
Six Studies of Cambodian Dancers
Graphite pencil, watercolor and gouache on cream-colored paper with watermark, 10⅝ × 8⅜″
Annotated lower right in graphite: *cambodgiennes pour servir de gloire*
Paris, Musée Rodin, D.5076

170
Five Studies of Cambodian Dancers
Graphite pencil, pen and brown ink, watercolor and gouache on cream-colored paper, 12⅞ × 14″
Annotated upper left in graphite: *attachées à une harmonie…fait valoir le corps…*, and in ink: *fleur humaine… ami… cultivé*
Paris, Musée Rodin, D.4517

171
Cambodian Dancer
Lead pencil and watercolor, 12¾ × 9⅞″
Signed lower right: *A.Rodin* (probably not by the artist)
Berlin, Georg-Kolbe-Museum

LIST OF ILLUSTRATIONS IN THE TEXT

26 Cilio (?), *Narcissus*. London, Victoria and Albert Museum (fig. 32)

27 Auguste Rodin, study after *Night* by Michelangelo, unrestored. Paris, Musée Rodin, D. 5119 (fig. 33)

62 Auguste Rodin, about 1885

64 Auguste Rodin, first maquette for *Gates of Hell*. Terracotta, 9 × 5⅞ × ¾″. Paris, Musée Rodin, S. 1170 (fig. 1)

Auguste Rodin, design for *Gates of Hell* with separate relief fields. Paris, Musée Rodin, D. 1963; cf. p. 326, No. 33 (fig. 2)

Auguste Rodin, design for *Gates of Hell* with separate relief fields. Paris, Musée Rodin, D. 1970 (fig. 3)

Auguste Rodin, design for *Gates of Hell* with separate relief fields. Paris, Musée Rodin, D. 1969 (fig. 4)

Auguste Rodin, *Portal of St. Pierre Abbey in Auxerre*. Paris, Musée Rodin, D. 6951, 6952 (figs. 5, 6)

65 Auguste Rodin, *The Gates of Hell*, 1880–1917. Bronze, 280⅜ × 157⅛ × 33½″. Paris, Musée Rodin (fig. 7)

66 Auguste Rodin, sketch for *Gates of Hell* with Adam and Eve. Paris, Musée Rodin, D. 6940 (fig. 8)

Auguste Rodin, sketches for *Gates of Hell*. Paris, Musée Rodin, D. 6948 (fig. 9)

Auguste Rodin, sketch for *Gates of Hell*. Paris, Musée Rodin, D. 6956 (fig. 10)

Auguste Rodin, sketch for *Gates of Hell* with Adam and Eve. Paris, Musée Rodin, D. 6937 (fig. 11)

Auguste Rodin, third maquette for *Gates of Hell*. Terracotta, 43⅝ × 29⅛ × 11¾″. Paris, Musée Rodin, S. 1189 (fig. 12)

Auguste Rodin, detail from a page of sketches for *Gates of Hell* with Adam and Eve. Paris, Musée Rodin, D. 7197 (fig. 13)

67 Auguste Rodin, *Reclining Woman Embracing a Child*, and sketch for *Gates of Hell*. Paris, Musée Rodin, D. 1966; cf. p. 326, No. 32 (fig. 14)

Auguste Rodin, second maquette for *Gates of Hell*. Terracotta, 64⅞ × 53⅛ × 10¼″. Paris, Musée Rodin, S. 1169 (fig. 15)

Auguste Rodin, design for *Gates of Hell*. Paris, Musée Rodin, D. 3719 (fig. 16)

68 Auguste Rodin, design of stairs and setting of *Gates of Hell*. Paris, Musée Rodin, D. 3495 verso (fig. 17)

Auguste Rodin, *Woman Moving in a Dance* and two sketches for *Gates of Hell*. Paris, Musée Rodin, D. 3498; cf. p. 326, No. 36 (fig. 18)

Auguste Rodin, design for setting of *Gates of Hell*. Paris, Musée Rodin, D. 3502 (fig. 19)

Auguste Rodin, design for setting of *Gates of Hell*. Paris, Musée Rodin, D. 3505 verso (fig. 20)

69 Auguste Rodin, design for setting of *Gates of Hell*. Paris, Musée Rodin, D. 3505 recto (fig. 21)

Auguste Rodin, sketch of *Gates of Hell*. Paris, Musée Rodin, D. 1961; cf. p. 326, No. 37 (fig. 22)

Auguste Rodin, palace facades with *Gates of Hell*. Paris, Musée Rodin, D. 3518 verso (fig. 23)

Auguste Rodin, *The Gates of Hell* in marble and bronze. Paris, Musée Rodin, D. 7637 (fig. 24)

70 Auguste Rodin, sketch for *Gates of Hell*. Paris, Musée Rodin, D. 5478; cf. p. 326, No. 35 (fig. 25)

Auguste Rodin, *The Gates of Hell* framed with a fresco. Paris, Musée Rodin, D. 6128 (fig. 26)

Auguste Rodin, sketch for *Gates of Hell*. Paris, Musée Rodin, D. 5497 (fig. 27)

Auguste Rodin, fresco design for setting of *Gates of Hell*. Paris, Musée Rodin, D. 6136 (fig. 28)

72 Auguste Rodin, *Dante and Beatrice*. Paris, Musée Rodin, D. 5598; cf. p. 326, No. 38 (fig. 29)

Auguste Rodin, *Charon's Boat*. Paris, Musée Rodin, D. 2057; cf. p. 326, No. 39 (fig. 30)

Auguste Rodin, *Shade*. Paris, Musée Rodin, D. 5613; cf. p. 327, No. 41 (fig. 31)

Auguste Rodin, *Minos*. Paris, Musée Rodin, D. 5593; cf. p. 327, No. 42 (fig. 32)

Auguste Rodin, *Minos on his Throne*. Fig. 46 in Goupil Album (fig. 33)

73 Auguste Rodin, *Minos Surrounded by Infernal Judges*. Paris, Musée Rodin, D. 1965 (fig. 34)

Auguste Rodin, *Mask of Minos*. Paris, Musée Rodin, D. 1933; cf. p. 327, No. 43 (fig. 35)

Auguste Rodin, *Embracing Couple*. Paris, Musée Rodin, D. 5630; cf. p. 327, No. 45 (fig. 36)

Auguste Rodin, *Shades Speaking with Dante*. Paris, Musée Rodin, D. 3760; cf. p. 327, No. 46 (fig. 37)

Auguste Rodin, *Paolo and Francesca da Rimini*. Paris, Musée Rodin, D.3763; cf. p.327, No.47 (fig.38)

74 Auguste Rodin, *Reclining Couple, Embracing*. Paris, Musée Rodin, D.1912; cf. p.327, No.44 (fig.39)

Auguste Rodin, *Rain, Circle of Vexation*. Paris, Musée Rodin, D.7605; cf. p.328, No.49 (fig.40)

Auguste Rodin, *Shade of an Avaricious Man*. Paris, Musée Rodin, D.2071; cf. p.328, No.50 (fig.41)

Auguste Rodin, *Pluto (?)*. Paris, Musée Rodin, D.1936; cf. p.328, No.51 (fig.42)

Auguste Rodin, *Dante and Virgil in a Boat*. Paris, Musée Rodin, D.5373 (fig.43)

75 Auguste Rodin, *The Styx*. Illustrated on p.41 of the Goupil Album (fig.44)

Auguste Rodin, *Medusa*. Paris, Musée Rodin, D.1996; cf. p.328, No.52 (fig.45)

Auguste Rodin, *If Medusa saw you, you would have ceased to live*. Paris, Musée Rodin, D.3781; cf. p.328, No.53 (fig.46)

Auguste Rodin, *Centaur Embracing Two Women*. Paris, Musée Rodin, D.5429; cf. p.328, No.55 (fig.47)

Auguste Rodin, *Blasphemy*. Paris, Musée Rodin, D.3772; cf. p.328, No.54 (fig.48)

76 Auguste Rodin, *Dante and Virgil on a Ghostly Horse*. Paris, Musée Rodin, D.3769; cf. p.328, No.57 (fig.49)

Auguste Rodin, *Icarus and Phaeton*. Paris, Musée Rodin, D.3759; cf. p.328, No.56 (fig.50)

Auguste Rodin, *Medea*. Paris, Musée Rodin, D.2056; cf. p.329, No.58 (fig.51)

Auguste Rodin, *Dans la m...* Paris, Musée Rodin, D.7616; cf. p.329, No.59 (fig.52)

77 Auguste Rodin, *Demon Holding Up a Shade Who Has Fallen in Tar*. Paris, Musée Rodin, D.5594; cf. p.329, No.60 (fig.53)

Auguste Rodin, *Cloak of Lead*. Paris, Musée Rodin, D.5086; cf. p.329, No.61 (fig.54)

Auguste Rodin, *The Horrifying Union*. Paris, Musée Rodin, D.2069; cf. p.329, No.62 (fig.55)

Auguste Rodin, *Boso and the Snake*. Paris, Musée Rodin, D.1932; cf. p.329, No.63 (fig.56)

Auguste Rodin, *Battle Between a Man and a Snake*; also called *Transformation of Man and Snake*. Paris, Musée Rodin, D.7617 (fig.57)

78 Auguste Rodin, *Damned Souls around Count Guido*. Paris, Musée Rodin, D.5617; cf. p.329, No.65 (fig.58)

Auguste Rodin, *Count Guido*. Paris, Musée Rodin, D.1928; cf. p.329, No.67 (fig.59)

79 Auguste Rodin, *Count Guido between Satan and St.Francis*. Paris, Musée Rodin, D.3767; cf. p.329, No.68 (fig.60)

Auguste Rodin, *Shade of Count Guido*. Paris, Musée Rodin, D.3762; cf. p.329, No.64 (fig.61)

Auguste Rodin, *Demon Carrying Off His Prize (Count Guido)*. Paris, Musée Rodin, D.6903 (fig.62)

Auguste Rodin, *Mohammed with Dangling Intestines*. Paris, Musée Rodin, D.5633; cf. p.330, No.70 (fig.63)

Auguste Rodin, *Ugolino*. Paris, Musée Rodin, D.7627; cf. p.330, No.71 (fig.64)

Auguste Rodin, *Satan and St.Francis Fighting over Count Guido*. Paris, Musée Rodin, D.5591; cf. p.329, No.66 (fig.65)

Auguste Rodin, *Count Guido*. Paris, Musée Rodin, D.5590; cf. p.330, No.69 (fig.66)

80 Auguste Rodin, *Demon in Space*. Paris, Musée Rodin, D.5665; cf. p.331, No.78 (fig.67)

Auguste Rodin, *Three Embracing Women*. Paris, Musée Rodin, D.5196; cf. p.339, No.147 (fig.68)

132 Auguste Rodin, about 1906

134 Portal of Notre Dame Church in Tonnerre (fig.1)

Auguste Rodin, *Church Portal in Tonnerre*. Paris, Musée Rodin, D.5942; cf. p.332, No.86 (fig.2)

135 South facade of the St.Pierre of Beauvais Cathedral (fig.3)

Beauvais Cathedral: The stone forest (fig.4)

Beauvais Cathedral: Empty niches (fig.5)

Beauvais Cathedral: Stone branches, leaves and acorns (fig.6)

136 Auguste Rodin, *Moldings and Door in Charles VIII Style*. Paris, Musée Rodin, D.5856; cf. p.331, No.83 (fig.7)

Auguste Rodin, architectural drawing. Paris, Musée Rodin (fig.8)

137 Auguste Rodin, architectural drawing. Philadelphia, The Rodin Museum, Mastbaum Collection (fig. 9)

Auguste Rodin, architectural drawing. Philadelphia, The Rodin Museum, Mastbaum Collection (fig. 10)

138 South portal of St. Pierre Abbey in Auxerre (fig. 11)

Auguste Rodin, *Facade with Portal in Auxerre.* Paris, Musée Rodin, D. 5916, 5918; cf. p. 332, No. 89 (figs. 12, 13)

139 Notre Dame in Mantes (fig. 14)

Auguste Rodin, *Church Facade in Mantes* (Notre Dame, main and right side portals). Paris, Musée Rodin, D. 5806; cf. p. 331, No. 80 (fig. 15)

140 View of choir of St. Jacques et St. Christophe Church in Houdan (fig. 16)

Auguste Rodin, *Sketch of Choir Section of a Church.* Paris, Musée Rodin, D. 3460 (fig. 17)

141 St. Etienne Cathedral in Auxerre (fig. 18)

Auguste Rodin, *Church Portal in Nantes.* Paris, Musée Rodin, D. 5764; cf. p. 331, No. 79 (fig. 19)

Flying buttresses on the apse of St. Etienne Church in Caen (fig. 20)

Auguste Rodin, *Flying Buttresses of St. Etienne Church in Caen.* Paris, Musée Rodin, D. 5776 (fig. 21)

142 Renaissance pilaster, St. Etienne Church in Caen (fig. 22)

Auguste Rodin, architectural drawing: *"Le vieux Etienne".* Paris, Musée Rodin, D. 3488 (fig. 23)

143 Columns and pilasters, St. Martin Church in Champeaux (fig. 24)

Auguste Rodin, *Columns of the Church in Champeaux.* Paris, Musée Rodin, D. 5812; cf. p. 333, No. 97 (fig. 25)

144 Buttresses and capitals of Palace Chapel in Ussé (fig. 26)

Auguste Rodin, *Ussé.* Paris, Musée Rodin, D. 5818 (fig. 27)

Portal to courtyard of St. Pierre Abbey and Church in Auxerre (fig. 28)

Auguste Rodin, *Portal of St. Pierre Abbey in Auxerre.* Paris, Musée Rodin, D. 5925; cf. p. 332, No. 90 (fig. 29)

145 Facade of St. Jacques et St. Christophe Church in Houdan (fig. 30)

Auguste Rodin, *Facade of the St. Jacques et St. Christophe Church in Houdan.* Paris, Musée Rodin, D. 5778; cf. p. 331, No. 82 (fig. 31)

Buttresses and waterspouts, St. Pierre Church, Montfort Lamaury (fig. 32)

'Auguste Rodin, *Buttresses of a Church.* Paris, Musée Rodin, D. 5889; cf. p. 332, No. 84 (fig. 33)

170 Auguste Rodin, about 1895

172 Auguste Rodin, *Portrait of Henri Becque,* 1885. Drypoint, 6¼ × 8″ (fig. 1)

173 Auguste Rodin, *John the Baptist,* 1880. Pen and ink, 12¾ × 8¾″ (fig. 2, detail, and fig. 3)

174 Auguste Rodin, frontispiece to Charles Baudelaire, *Les Fleurs du Mal,* 1888. Pen and ink (fig. 4)

Auguste Rodin, illustrations for Charles Baudelaire, *Les Fleurs du Mal,* 1888. Pen and ink. "Le Guignon" (fig. 5), "La Beauté" (fig. 6)

175 Auguste Rodin, illustrations for Charles Baudelaire, *Les Fleurs du Mal,* 1888. Pen and ink with watercolor and gouache. "De profundis clamavi" (fig. 7), "La Mort des Pauvres" (fig. 8)

176 Auguste Rodin, *Group of Figures (Le Temps),* 1885–1890. Pen and ink with gouache (fig. 9)

177 Auguste Rodin, *Ames du Purgatoire,* frontispiece to Gustave Geffroy, *La Vie Artistique,* 1893. Drypoint (fig. 10)

178 Auguste Rodin, *Woman from the Front, Putting On a Garment.* Paris, Musée Rodin, D. 4311 (fig. 11)

Auguste Rodin, *Woman from the Front, Putting On a Garment.* Paris, Musée Rodin, D. 4294 (fig. 12)

179 Auguste Rodin, *Woman Bent Slightly Forward, Putting On a Garment.* Paris, Musée Rodin, D. 4302 (fig. 13)

Auguste Rodin, *Woman Bent Forward, Putting On a Garment.* Paris, Musée Rodin, D. 4321 (fig. 14)

180 Auguste Rodin, *Standing Female Nude with Veils.* Paris, Musée Rodin, D. 4277 (fig. 15)

Auguste Rodin, *Nude Woman from the Front with Veils.* Paris, Musée Rodin, D. 4367 (fig. 16)

Aubert, Marcel (ed.), *Quatorze aquarelles de Rodin.* Paris 1933.

Aubert, Marcel (ed.), *Images de Rodin.* Paris 1946.

Aubert, Marcel, *Douze aquarelles inédites de Rodin.* Paris 1949.

Ayrton, Michael, "The act of drawing". In: *The Studio* (London), CLVI, 1958, pp. 1–5, 38–43, 61.

Berlin: exhibition catalogue *Degas-Cézanne.* Galerie Paul Cassirer, November 1913, Berlin 1913.

Berlin: exhibition catalogue *Rodin-Aquarelle.* Galerie Alfred Flechtheim, Berlin 1930.

Bois, Georges, "Le sculpteur Rodin et les danseuses cambodgiennes". In: *L'Illustration* (Paris), no. 3309, July 28, 1906, pp. 64, 65.

Bourdelle, Emile Antoine, "Les dessins du sculpteur Rodin". In: *La grande Revue* (Paris), 1908, pp. 166–172.

Boutet, Henri, *10 Dessins choisis d'Auguste Rodin.* Paris 1905.

Bremen: exhibition catalogue *Handzeichnungen französischer Meister des 19. Jahrhunderts. Von Delacroix bis Maillol.* Ed. Günter Busch. Kunsthalle Bremen, March 9 – April 13, 1969, Bremen 1969, pp. 120–121, nos. 229–233.

Bucarelli, Palma, "Dessins d'Auguste Rodin à Rome". In: *Gazette des Beaux-Arts* (Paris), 6th series, vol. 76, no. 11, 1934, pp. 370–375.

Clutton-Brock, A., "Twelve Watercolours by Rodin". In: *The Burlington Magazine* (London), XXXVIII, 1921, pp. 144 f.

Coquiot, Gustave, "Rodin: Ses dessins en couleurs". In: *La Plume* (Paris), XII, 1900 (*Rodin et son œuvre*, special number devoted to Rodin), pp. 8–9.

Dayot, Armand, *Les dessins de Rodin.* Paris 1914.

"Dessins d'André Derain, d'Hélène Perdriat et d'Auguste Rodin". In: *L'Amour de l'Art* (Paris), November 7, 1920.

"Drawings of Auguste Rodin at the St. George Gallery (London)". In: *Apollo* (London), IX, no. 51, 1929, p. 194.

Elsen, Albert E., "Rodin's 'La Ronde'". In: *The Burlington Magazine* (London), no. 107, June 1965, pp. 290–299.

Elsen, Albert E., "Drawing and the True Rodin". In: *Artforum* (New York), X, no. 6, February 1972, pp. 64–69.

Elsen, Albert E., and Varnedoe, J. Kirk T., *The Drawings of Rodin.* With articles by Victoria Thorson and Elisabeth Chase Geissbuhler. New York 1971.

Elsen, Albert E., "Rodin's Drawings and the Mastery of Abundance". In: Elsen and Varnedoe, New York 1971, pp. 17–24.

Elsen, Albert E. (ed.), *Rodin rediscovered.* Exhibition catalogue, National Gallery of Art, Washington, D.C., June 1981 – May 1982, Washington 1981.

"Expositions". In: *L'Art Moderne* (Brussels), April 28, 1912.

Ganz, Hermann, "Kunstausstellungen in Paris". In: *Kunst und Künstler* (Berlin), XXVII, 1929, p. 74.

Geissbuhler, Elisabeth Chase, *Rodin. Later Drawings with Interpretations by Antoine Bourdelle.* Preface: Herbert Read. London 1963.

Geissbuhler, Elisabeth Chase, "Rodin's Abstractions: The Architectural Drawings". In: *Art Journal* (London), XXVI, 1966, pp. 22–29.

Geissbuhler, Elisabeth Chase, "Preliminary Notes on Rodin's Architectural Drawings". In: Elsen and Varnedoe, New York, 1971, pp. 141–156.

Geldzahler, Henry, "Two Early Matisse Drawings". In: *Gazette des Beaux-Arts* (Paris), 6th series, vol. 104, no. 60, 1962, pp. 491–505.

Goldscheider, Cécile, *Vingt-quatre dessins de Rodin.* Paris 1948.

Goldscheider, Cécile, *Dessins de sculpteurs.* Paris 1948.

Goldscheider, Cécile, *Aquarelles de Rodin.* Paris 1949.

Goldscheider, Cécile, "Rodin. Ausgewählte Zeichnungen und Aquarelle". In: exhibition catalogue *Auguste Rodin*. Institut Français, Innsbruck 1951.

Goldscheider, Cécile, *Aquarelles et dessins de Rodin*. Paris 1962.

Goldscheider, Cécile, "Rodin et la danse". In: *Art de France* (Paris), CXI, 1963, pp. 321–335.

Goldscheider, Cécile, *Danse—études de Rodin*. Paris 1967.

Gradmann, E., *Bildhauer-Zeichnungen*. Basel 1943, p. 94.

Grappe, Georges, "Filiation classique d'un maître moderne. Les dessins de Rodin pour 'La porte de l'enfer'". In: *Formes, Revue Internationale* (Paris), XXX, 1932, pp. 318–321.

Grappe, Georges, *30 dessins de Rodin*. Paris 1933.

Grappe, Georges, "Affinités électives—Ovide et Rodin". In: *L'Amour de l'Art* (Paris), XVII, no. 6, June 1936, pp. 203–208.

Grauthoff, Otto, "Der Herbstsalon Paris 1907". In: *Kunst und Künstler* (Berlin), VI, 1908, p. 92.

Grauthoff, Otto, "Rodins Handzeichnungen". In: *Kunst und Künstler* (Berlin), VI, 1908, pp. 218–225. (With a short essay by Rilke.)

Gsell, Paul "Le dessin et le couleur". In: *La Revue* (Paris), October 1, 1910, pp. 723–729.

Gsell, Paul, *Auguste Rodin. Die Kunst. Gespräche des Meisters gesammelt von Paul Gsell*. 1st ed., Leipzig 1912.

Gsell, Paul, "Zeichnung und Farbe, ein Gespräch mit Auguste Rodin". In: *Kunst und Künstler* (Berlin), X, 1912, pp. 192–202.

Gsell, Paul, *Douze aquarelles de Auguste Rodin*. Introduction. Geneva and Paris 1920.

H. [Heilbut, Emil], "Aus der achten Ausstellung der Berliner Secession". In: *Kunst und Künstler* (Berlin), II, 1904, pp. 139–146.

Heilbut, Emil, "Chronik. Nachrichten, Ausstellungen etc." In: *Kunst und Künstler* (Berlin), IV, 1906, pp. 358, 444, 531.

Heilbut, Emil, "Chronik. Nachrichten, Ausstellungen etc.". In: *Kunst und Künstler* (Berlin), V, 1907, p. 84.

Holzhamer, Wilhelm, "Der Herbstsalon 1904". In: *Kunst und Künstler* (Berlin), III, 1905, p. 178.

Jamot, Paul, "Le Salon d'Automne". In: *Gazette des Beaux-Arts* (Paris), 3rd series, vol. 48, no. 36, 1906, pp. 457, 459, 462, 464.

Janin, Clément, "Les dessins de Rodin". In: *Les Maîtres Artistes* (Paris), III, no. 8, October 15, 1903 (special number devoted to Rodin), pp. 285–287.

Jeanès, J. E. S., "Les dessins de Rodin". In: *Le Gaulois* (Paris), October 25, 1909.

Judrin, Claudie, "Rodin's drawings of Ugolino". In: Elsen, Washington 1981, pp. 191–200.

Judrin Claudie, *Auguste Rodin—100 Zeichnungen und Aquarelle*. Freiburg, Basel, and Vienna 1982.

Levy, Marvyn, *Drawing and Sculpture*. Bath 1970.

Leymarie, Jean, "Dessin de sculpteurs". In: *Quadrige* (Paris), 1946, pp. 19–24.

London: exhibition catalogue *Rodin: Sculpture and Drawings*. The Hayward Gallery, January 24 – April 5, 1970, London 1970.

Longstreet, Stephen, *The Drawings of Rodin*. Alhambra, California 1965.

Lumet, Louis, "Les dessins d'Auguste Rodin". In: *Les Arts Français* (Paris), February 14, 1918 (*Auguste Rodin 1840–1917*, special number devoted to Rodin), pp. 31–32.

Martinie, Henri, "Le dessin élément abstrait de l'art". In: *Le Dessin* (Paris), 1947, pp. 442–452.

Marx, Roger, "Cartons d'artistes—Auguste Rodin". In: *L'Image* (Paris), September 1897, pp. 293–299.

Mauclair, Camille, "Les dessins de Rodin sur un exemplaire des 'Fleurs du Mal'". In: Charles Baudelaire, *Les Fleurs du Mal*. Paris 1940, pp. I–XII.

Mauclair, Camille, "Le Salon d'Automne". In: *Revue politique et litteraire* (Revue bleue) (Paris), XXXXV, no. 2, 1907, pp. 463, 466.

Mellerio, André, "Les dessins de Rodin". In: *La Plume* (Paris), XII, 1900 (*Rodin et son œuvre*, special number devoted to Rodin), pp. 81–82.

Miomandre, Francis de, "Les dessins de Rodin". In: *L'Art et les Artistes* (Paris), XIX, no. 109, April 1914 (special number devoted to Rodin), pp. 73–84.

Mirbeau, Octave, *Les Dessins d'Auguste Rodin*. Paris 1897.

Montesquiou, Robert de, "A. Rodin". In: *Les Maîtres Artistes* (Paris), III, no. 8, October 15, 1903 (special number devoted to Rodin), pp. 262–265.

Neugass, Fritz, "Hochflut von Rodin-Fälschungen". In: *Weltkunst* (Munich), XXXV, 1965, p. 965.

Neugass, Fritz, "Rodin: echt oder falsch". In: *Weltkunst* (Munich), XXXXII, 1972, pp. 94–95.

New York: exhibition catalogue *Auguste Rodin*.

Fifty-eight drawings. Photo-Secession Gallery, January 2–21, 1908, New York 1908.

New York: exhibition catalogue *Auguste Rodin (Drawings)*. Photo-Secession Gallery, March 31 – April 16, 1910, New York 1910.

Norden, Julius, "Dritte graphische Ausstellung der Berliner Secession". In: *Gegenwart* (Berlin), vol. 64, 1903, pp. 380, 381.

Para-Perez, Rodolfo, "Notes on Rodin's Drawings". In: *The Art Quarterly* (Detroit), XXX, no. 2, summer 1967, pp. 126–138.

Paris: exhibition catalogue *Dessin de Rodin*. Galerie Bernheim Jeune, summer 1907 – late October 1907. Paris 1907.

Paris: exhibition catalogue *Exposition de dessins d'Auguste Rodin*. Salon d'Automne, Grand Palais, October 1–22, 1907, Paris 1907.

Paris: exhibition catalogue *Dessins de sculpteurs de Pajou á Rodin*. Musée du Louvre, Paris 1964.

Paris: exhibition catalogue *Un Siècle d'Art Français 1850–1950*. Petit Palais, Paris 1953.

Paris: exhibition catalogue *Rodin et les écrivains de son temps. Sculptures, dessins, lettres du fonds Rodin*. Compiled by Claudie Judrin. Musée Rodin, June 23 – October 18, 1976, Paris 1976.

Paris: exhibition catalogue *Rodin et l'Extrême-Orient*. Compiled by Claudie Judrin. Musée Rodin, April 4 – July 2, 1979, Paris 1979.

Paris: exhibition catalogue *Les Centaures*. Compiled by Claudie Judrin. Musée Rodin, Cabinet des Dessins, Dossier 1 (November 18 – February 15, 1981), Paris 1981.

Paris: exhibition catalogue *Ugolin*. Compiled by Claudie Judrin. Musée Rodin, Cabinet des Dessins, Dossier 2 (November 17, 1982 – February 14, 1983), Paris 1982.

Paris: exhibition catalogue *Dante et Vergile aux Enfers*. Compiled by Claudie Judrin. Musée Rodin, Cabinet des Dessins, Dossier 3 (November 23, 1983 – February 27, 1984), Paris 1983.

Pica, Vittorio, "Esposizione degli Amatori e Cultori di Belle Arti in Roma". In: *Emporium* (Bergamo), vol. 29, 1909, pp. 170, 173.

Pica, Vittorio, "I disegni di tre Scultori moderni. (Gemito, Meunier, Rodin)". In: *Emporium* (Bergamo), vol. 43, 1916, pp. 402, 418–425.

Rich, Daniel Catton, "The Stieglitz Collection". In: *Bulletin of the Art Institute of Chicago* (Chicago), 1949, pp. 64–71.

Rilke, Rainer Maria, *Auguste Rodin, dessinateur*. Vienna, n.d.

Rilke, Rainer Maria, "Auguste Rodin als Zeichner". In: *Morgen. Wochenschrift für deutsche Kultur* (Berlin), 15, September 20, 1907, p. 471.

Rilke, Rainer Maria, "Les dessins et les portraits de Rodin". (Excerpt from Rilke's book *Auguste Rodin*, translated by Maurice Betz, Paris 1928.) In: *L'Art Vivant* (Paris), 1928, pp. 580–584.

Riotor, Léon, "Rodin statuaire, son œuvre et ses aventures. Rodin dessinateur, caractères et projets-commentaires". In: *Les Maîtres Artistes* (Paris), III, no. 8, November 15, 1903 (special number devoted to Rodin), pp. 288–290.

Roches, F., "Rodin et l'architecture". In: *Architecture française* (Paris), III, January 1941, pp. 35–40.

Rodin, Auguste, "Äußerungen über die kambodschanischen Tänzerinnen". In: *Kunst und Künstler* (Berlin), IV, 1906, pp. 531–532.

Rodin, Auguste, *Les Cathédrales de France*. With an introduction by Charles Morice, 1st ed., Paris 1914.

Rodin, Auguste, *Die Kathedralen Frankreichs*. With drawings by Rodin. Leipzig, n.d. (1917).

Roger-Marx, Claude, "Dessins de sculpture". In: *La Renaissance de l'art français* (Paris), 1927, pp. 74–78.

Roger-Marx, Claude, "Rodin. Dessinateur et Graveur". In: *Arts et Métiers Graphiques* (Paris), September 25, 1931, pp. 349–355.

Roger-Marx, Claude, "Dessins de sculpteurs et sculptures de peintres". In: *Le Point* (Paris), VI, 1937, pp. 253–257.

Roger-Marx, Claude, "Le couple". In: *Formes et Couleurs* (Paris), 1946, pp. 29–38.

Roger-Marx, Claude, *Histoire de l'aquarelle*, vol. IX, Paris 1950.

H. R. [Hans Rosenhagen], "Von Ausstellungen und Sammlungen. Berlin". In: *Die Kunst – Kunst für Alle* (Munich), vol. 19, 1904, pp. 165–166.

Rostrup, Haavard, "Fra Lautrec til Segonzac. Moderne franske grafik i Kobberstik Samlingen". In: *Tilskueren* (Copenhagen), 1, 1936, pp. 379–388.

Rostrup, Haavard, "Dessins de Rodin". In: *From the Collection of the Ny Carlsberg Glyptothek*, vol. 2, Copenhagen 1938, pp. 211–226.

Sabile, Jacques, "Essai sur l'évolution de la représentation graphique du corps humain". In: *Courrier Graphique* (Paris), vol. 20, 1938, pp. 5–27.

Sailer, Anton, "Lob des Aktzeichnens". In: *Das Kunstwerk* (Stuttgart), I, 1946/47, no. 4, pp. 9–16.

Scheffler, Karl, "Adolf Hildebrand". In: *Kunst und Künstler* (Berlin), IV, 1906, pp. 325–327, 332, 334.

Scheffler, Karl, "Ruth St. Denis". In: *Kunst und Künstler* (Berlin), V, 1907, pp. 160–162.

Schwabe, Randolph, "Six Drawings by Rodin. Notes". In: *The Burlington Magazine* (London), no. 38, November 1918, pp. 172–179.

Symons, Arthur, "Les dessins de Rodin". In: *La Plume* (Paris), XII, 1900 (*Rodin et son œuvre*, special number devoted to Rodin), pp. 47–48.

Symons, Arthur, "On Rodin's Drawings". In: *Camera Work* (New York), no. 12, October 1905. Reprinted in: *Camera Work* (New York), no. 34/35, April/July 1911, pp. 63–64.

Symons, Arthur, *Studies in Seven Arts*. London 1906, pp. 18–19.

Thorson, Victoria, "Symbolism and Conservatism in Rodin's Late Drawings". In: Elsen and Varnedoe, New York 1971, pp. 121–139.

Thorson, Victoria, *The Late Drawings of Auguste Rodin*. Ph. D. dissertation, University of Michigan, Ann Arbor 1973.

"Uffiziengalerie erwirbt zehn Zeichnungen Rodins". In: *Bollettino di Vita d'Arte* (Milan), January 1913.

Vaillant, Roger, "Esquisses sur un Portrait du vrai libertin". In: *Formes et Couleurs* (Paris), 1946, pp. 41–48.

Varnedoe, J. Kirk T., *The Drawings of Rodin*. See Elsen, New York 1971.

Varnedoe, J. Kirk T., "Rodin as a Draftsman—A Chronological Perspective". In: Elsen and Varnedoe, New York 1971, pp. 25–120.

Varnedoe, J. Kirk T., "Rodin's drawings, true and false". In: *Art News* (New York), LXX, no. 8, 1971–72, pp. 30–33, 65–66.

Varnedoe, J. Kirk T., *Chronology and Authenticity in the Drawings of Auguste Rodin*. Ph. D. dissertation, Stanford University, 1972.

Varnedoe, J. Kirk T., "Early drawings by Auguste Rodin". In: *The Burlington Magazine* (London), no. 116, April 1974, pp. 197–202.

Varnedoe, J. Kirk T., "Rodin's Drawings". In: Elsen, Washington 1981, pp. 153–189.

Vauxcelles, Louis, "Preface". In: exhibition catalogue *Dessins d'Auguste Rodin*. Paris, Devambez, October 19 – November 5, n. p. [Paris] 1908.

Yverdon: exhibition catalogue *Auguste Rodin. 150 sculptures, aquarelles et dessins*. Hôtel de Ville, August 8 – September 24, 1953, Yverdon 1953.

Photo Credits

The Musée Rodin kindly provided us with photographs of works in their collection, which are designated with Musée Rodin inventory numbers. These photographs were taken by Bruno Jarret, Paris. We also received from the Musée Rodin a number of documentary photographs whose authors, if not listed below, are unknown.

The authors of the essays provided their own illustrative material in cases where photographs were not available from the Musée Rodin. The architectural photographs on pages 134–145 were made by Arnold and Elisabeth Chase Geissbuhler.

Alinari, Rome 23 (right center)
Anderson, Rome 22 (lower left)
Charles Aubry 12, 294
Bergerac 62
Bibliothèque Nationale, Paris 16 (top right)
Braun 296 (bottom)
J.E. Bulloz, Paris 297, 298 (bottom), 301 (bottom), 305
Cesar 303
René Dazy, Paris 311 (bottom)
Eugène Druet 301 (top), 362 (bottom), 307, 313 (top)
Duchêne 292
Cesare Faraglia 310
Giraudon, Paris 16 (lower center, right)
Harlingue 132
C. Hourloff 315
Georg-Kolbe-Museum, Berlin 242, 290
Kunsthalle Bremen 75, 76, 240
John Marshall 314 (top)
The Metropolitan Museum of Modern Art, New York 15 (bottom right)
Museum der bildenden Künste, Leipzig 100, 258
Philadelphia Museum of Modern Art, The Rodin Museum 18 (bottom), 19, 137
Frederick A. Praeger, New York 15 (bottom left)
Rheinisches Bildarchiv, Cologne 238, 253, 276
Rilke-Archiv 309
Staatliche Graphische Sammlung, Munich 274
Staatsgalerie Stuttgart, Graphische Sammlung 244
Städelsches Kunstinstitut und Städtische Galerie, Frankfurt 255
Städtische Kunsthalle, Mannheim 254

Edward Steichen 312
Thiebault 295 (bottom)
Victoria and Albert Museum, London 26 (top right)
A.J. Wyatt 18 (bottom), 137

Source of Texts

Page 9: Camille Mauclaire, *Auguste Rodin*, Prague, 1907.
Pages 271–272: *Kunst und Künstler* (Berlin), IV, 1906, pp.531–532.
Page 273: *Kunst und Künstler* (Berlin), VII, 1908/ 1909, pp.223–224 (A letter by Rilke on an exhibition of Rodin drawings in Paris, written to the editors of the magazine).

Pages 358–359:
Auguste Rodin at the Hôtel Biron, about 1915 ▷

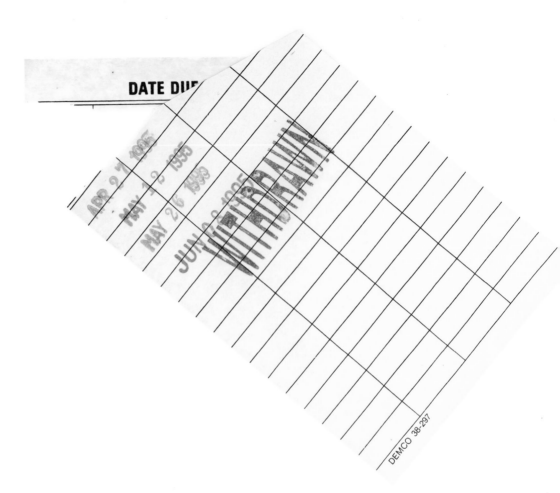